Straight from the
CEO

Straight from the CEO

THE WORLD'S TOP BUSINESS LEADERS

REVEAL IDEAS

THAT EVERY MANAGER CAN USE

G. WILLIAM DAUPHINAIS
and COLIN PRICE, EDITORS

Price Waterhouse

NICHOLAS BREALEY
PUBLISHING

LONDON

First published by
Nicholas Brealey Publishing Limited 1998

36 John Street
London
WC1A 2AT, UK
Tel: +44 (0) 171 430 0224
Fax: +44 (0) 171 404 8311

17470 Sonoma Highway
Sonoma
California 95476, USA
Tel: (707) 939 7570
Fax: (707) 938 3515

http://www.nbrealey-books.com

ISBN 1-85788-195-8

British Library Cataloguing in Publication Data
A catalogue record for this book is available from the British Library.

Printed in Finland by WSOY

CONTENTS

Part II
RADICAL CHANGE: TURNING UP THE VOLUME 79

Part III
LEADERSHIP: GIANTS OF VALUE CREATION 129

BOARD OF CONTRIBUTORS

The following Price Waterhouse contributors were responsible for providing insights, ideas, expertise, and strategic guidance to the following CEO authors. It is through their efforts and through their leadership that this book was possible:

PRICE WATERHOUSE CONTRIBUTOR	CHIEF EXECUTIVE OFFICER	COMPANY
G. William Dauphinais	SOUTHWOOD MORCOTT	DANA CORPORATION
	MELVIN R. GOODES	WARNER-LAMBERT
	JAMES J. SCHIRO	PRICE WATERHOUSE
Colin Price	PERCY BARNEVIK	ABB ASEA BROWN BOVERI LTD.
	SIR RICHARD EVANS	BRITISH AEROSPACE
	COR HERKSTRÖTER	ROYAL DUTCH/SHELL
	MICHAEL Z. KAY	LSG/SKY CHEFS
Henrik Andersen	FLEMMING LINDELØV	CARLSBERG GROUP
Kevin Bacon	KENNETH W. KIZER	U.S. VETERANS' HEALTH ADMINISTRATION
Ian Beesley	SADAKO OGATA	THE OFFICE OF THE UNITED NATIONS HIGH COMMISSIONER FOR REFUGEES
Jermyn Brooks	HEINRICH VON PIERER	SIEMENS A.G.
Kevin Carton	PETER GEORGESCU	YOUNG & RUBICAM
Grace Chopard	JUSTUS VEENEKLAAS	PHILIPS AUSTRALIA
Deborah Cohen	MICHAEL CRITELLI	PITNEY BOWES, INC.
James G. Crump	KENNETH L. LAY	ENRON CORP.
Richard Davey	SIR COLIN MARSHALL	BRITISH AIRWAYS
Bill Eichhorn	DOUGLAS HYDE	OSHKOSH B'GOSH, INC.

Price Waterhouse Contributor	Chief Executive Officer	Company
Andy Embury	Patrick Haren	Northern Ireland Electricity
Matt English	Don Argus	National Australia Bank Group
Frances Engoron	David M. Kelley	IDEO Product Development
Joel Garlot	Serge Tchuruk	Alcatel
John Jordan	Robert B. Shapiro	Monsanto Company
Charles Keeling	Michael Z. Kay	LSG/SKY Chefs
Hideki Kurashige	Minoru Murofushi	Itochu Corporation
Sergio Loginsky	Dirk Blaesing	Fairway Filamentos
Jeff Margolies	Eckhard Pfeiffer	Compaq Computer Corporation
Sunil Misser	Glen L. Urban	MIT Sloan School of Management
Carlos Mota	Mário Pais de Sousa	Vulcano-Termodomésticos
Don Nicolaisen	Walter Shipley	Chase Manhattan Bank
Juan Carlos Palomo	Javier Herrero	Iberdrola
Bill Reeves	Douglas Sims	CoBank
James J. Schiro	Rahul Bajaj	Bajaj Auto Ltd.
Kemal Stamboel	Tanri Abeng	Bakrie & Bros.
Peter Wilkinson	Felix Rosenberg	Swisscom

FOREWORD
What We Can Learn from CEOs

MORE AND MORE, THE people of the world have a need to know to know what is going on in the minds of the corporate leadership. This is a new development. A generation ago, presidents and chairmen of companies seemed to be faceless men—yes, men—whose policies and strategies were shaped and carried out in private. Nowadays, by contrast, the corporate leadership seems eager to win acceptance of their ideas and approval for their deeds, while the public has became rightly concerned about the effects of those deeds on the distribution of capital, technology, and jobs. Management is no longer just the specialty of managers; it is now everybody's business: governments, citizens, shareholders, customers, workers.

Straight from the CEO makes a valuable contribution to our understanding of today's corporate leadership across the globe—from big companies and small, from the countries in the Organization for Economic Development (OECD), from Latin America and the Pacific Rim. The book offers readers an opportunity to hear chief executives express their approaches to critical management problems in their own words and to describe the kinds of remedies they've applied to those problems. Alongside the CEO—acting the role of Virgil to his Dante—there is a Price Waterhouse partner adding valuable insight and perspective.

Collectively, these chapters convey a strong intellectual richness and express the urgent determination of these CEOs to create radical improvement in the functions and processes of business. The heightened pace of change and of global competitiveness is here vividly reflected in the thoughts and responses of these CEOs. Through them, the reader can see the transmission of the central ideas of our times: the search by managers for better knowledge and techniques, the quest for institutional vitality, the will to raise their organizations to new heights of sensitivity and responsiveness to the needs of markets.

Many of these CEOs have not, like their predecessors, waited for circumstances to force them to action. Instead they have undertaken radical (and sometimes painful) change programs and launched dramatic corporate makeovers to maximize preparedness for the megacompetitive environment. And this environment with which they wrestle daily is complex, volatile, and fraught with unintended consequence. We cannot know all the ramifications that arise from technological progress's compressions of time and space. Ten years ago, for instance, it would have been difficult to foresee the speed with which advanced technology could be thoroughly assimilated in the less developed parts of the world. Yet in about the length of time it takes to bring a large mineral deposit into production, that has become fact: High technology, high productivity, and high quality plus low wages are commonplace in many countries. Countries that only ten years ago were confined to low-tech, labor-intensive economic activity are now able to produce at low cost goods and services that were previously monopolies of the advanced industrial nations.

Equally we cannot know the multiple impacts from the tripolar world, with East Asia catching up to and surpassing Western Europe and North America by the turn of the century, or how Europe and North America will cope with the likely demise of a continuously rising standard of living. The possibility of a political backlash against the multinationals, chief agents of the delocalization of production, cannot be ruled out. And the same uncertainty hangs over some countries' toughening of stances on international trade issues, which could lead to greater international tensions and conflicts.

Furthermore, conflict could arise from the decline of the corporate "stakeholder" ethic in the United States and Europe and its replacement with what one observer called "share value fetishism." The dominant role that transnational corporations play today in international trade and in the competition between nations for fresh direct capital investment create the perception that there is today a definite shift of power in favor of the capital markets and financial capitalism.

Let us make a clear distinction here between those corporate measures dictated by mega-competition (such as the relocation of production to low-wage areas) and the allegation that the pursuit of shareholder value tempts managers to shortchange the future (for example, by cutting research and development) for an immediate gratification in equity stock price. How much of the latter occurs is difficult to determine. But most multinationals (and most of those in *Straight from the CEO*) are not myopic and they have shown sensitivity in managing the shareholder-stakeholder equation.

Business leaders are the key players in the great challenges of our times—more so, perhaps, as the moral authority of governments has declined. Business is a stakeholder in globalization and bears a heavy responsibility to contribute to the stability of the global system. And one of the ways it can meet that responsibility is to do what business does best: innovate, invest, and grow—grow knowledge, build infrastructure, and create jobs. For a rare snapshot of how these goals are being met by typical CEOs, I'd recommend that you read on.

KLAUS M. SCHWAB, *President*
World Economic Forum
Geneva, Switzerland

INTRODUCTION
CEOs Demand the ABCs—Awareness, Belief, and Conduct

THIS BOOK PRESENTS SOME of the dominant ideas of today's CEO elite in their own words and shows how those ideas animate and enhance corporate performance. A team of Price Waterhouse management consultants has combed the world looking for CEOs who have excelled as agents of change. The result of their collaboration is this wide-ranging response from the executive trenches. Cumulatively, they present a broad and heterogeneous picture of the key strategic and operational insights that are driving corporate change from Bangkok to Oshkosh, from Düsseldorf to Dallas.

This book is rare in one respect. CEOs don't usually write about management. The literature is mostly dominated by consultants and educators. Result: The world seldom hears from the great contemporary practitioners—the chief doers and shapers of management. To be sure, they make brief appearances in company financial reports, and now and again in the media spotlight. But the public is rarely treated to deep insights into their management and governance thinking, to clues on how they distinguish valuable ideas from the conventional wisdom. One reason, of course, is that they're usually too busy getting things done. After all, it wasn't Napoleon, Marlborough, or Robert E. Lee who wrote books on military strategy. Clausewitz did.

Yet the minds of CEOs are, in aggregate, a tremendous center of power in society. Upon these minds—how they tick, how they prioritize, how they view the vectors of change—depends the transmission of know-how, technology, capital, and jobs. And as globalization waxes, the socioeconomic impact of their thought becomes all the greater. Which is why the partners at Price Waterhouse sat down with a broad cross-sample of the global CEO population, seeking their most candid ideas on how to react to today's fast pace of change, and their ideas on human motivation, on innovation and creativity, on corporate revitalization, on globalization.

Behind their diversity of focus, however, a unity does emerge. And that is a determination to seek new ways of thinking, to push the envelope, and to experiment with new ideas that can be swiftly implemented and achieve greater efficiency. These are not, however, far-out ideas. Nor are they trendy. The CEOs in our sample have little to say about the "digital revolution." By reason of their position and responsibilities, CEOs are the least likely to be swayed by fashion and fads in management. Their ideas are pragmatic.

We live in an age of great intellectual fertility in management compared to a few years ago, and clearly, today's CEOs recognize that ideas—their generation, refinement, and application to real-world circumstances—can make a huge impact on bottom-line results. It might be that in a technological and increasingly service-based economy, brainpower is much more effective against brawn than it used to be. A decade ago, the great giants like General Motors, IBM, and AT&T looked unassailable. Since then, dozens of dominant firms have been toppled by initially weaker rivals, which suggests that the marginal importance of brains has increased as a competitive weapon. This book contains lessons from both the brawny companies that have been forced to reinvent themselves, and some of the brainy upstarts that needed to be rather unconventional to gain access to the global playing field.

The more than thirty authors of *Straight from the CEO* are chiefs of small and large companies, some celebrated for being on the cutting edge in management thought, others relatively unknown. Although the views they express are certainly full of variety and reflect their own personalities, the result is not a smorgasbord. Despite the different circumstances of these CEOs' companies, the chapters they have contributed to this book contain unities, parallels, and narratives that are all related to a common theme. This has made it easy to group them into the following six dominant categories: globalization, radical change, leadership, culture, innovation, and customer interface issues.

These are not, obviously, watertight categories. How can a CEO achieve innovation without leadership, or respond to globalization without knowing a great deal about corporate culture? There is, then, a certain amount of overlap and convergence in the themes of these chapters. The mind is by nature holistic, and the CEO mind is perhaps more so because of the range of its concerns. We will have much more to say about these themes further on, in the main body of the book.

Straight from the CEO does have one overriding theme that we have distilled from most of the chapters—one we did not anticipate at the outset of this project. Today's CEOs have, sometimes consciously and sometimes not, invaded the field of human relations and imposed their own stamp on it. Repeatedly their contributions to this book demonstrate an urgent focus on people: their motivation and actions. Twenty and thirty years ago, CEOs safely compartmentalized and delegated people issues to personnel chiefs, while they concerned themselves with strategy, portfolio diversification, foreign expansion, and the like. Today, such issues have not lost their importance, but they've had to make room for a new cluster of CEO concerns. We call them the ABCs: the Awareness, Belief, and Conduct of leaders and followers, of executives and the rank and file, of suppliers and customer-relations people—in short, everyone who influences the creation or perception of value.

"People are our most important asset" is a commonplace expression that goes back a long way. The interest of CEOs in human behavior is a constant. What is new, however, is their enthusiasm and passion for taking charge and pumping up results through changes in behavior. Meanwhile, what has happened to the human resources departments? After many decades of telling CEOs not to interfere, that the motivation and loyalty of workers were delicate matters and they shouldn't have demands made upon them, they've had to embrace the ideas of results-oriented behavioral change. The corporate leaders in *Straight from the CEO* have remarkably little doubt that their interventionist approach to behavior can lead to sweeping performance improvements.

In former, less competitive times, the view used to be that if workers were given suitable incentives through remuneration and advancement, then their conduct with suppliers, colleagues, and customers would be just fine. However, the emphasis on quality in the eighties exposed the weaknesses of this belief. Thereafter, many top managers vowed that they would intervene much more vigorously than in the past into work structures, processes, and behavior on the front lines.

It is worth recalling that little more than a decade ago in the business world such concepts as behavior, values, and culture were considered "soft," and often greeted with derision as topics of interest and amusement, but not the source of wealth creation. And even today some executives feel uncomfortable with such "soft" concepts and long for palpable ideas that let them go out and kick the tires. Well, they'd better get with it—clearly, behavior is a key factor in competitive advantage. The "soft" stuff is the lodestone of value.

The views expressed in this book dramatically capture the core focus on behavior in CEOs' consciousness. These men and women are not adherents of the behaviorist school of psychology. They are no less respectful of workers' rights and individuality than their predecessors. However, their current interest in behavior proceeds from the belief that workers want to be liberated from inefficient systems and work structures; that they don't like being dazed and confused about the purposes of the organization; that they're tired of having their yearnings to be effective at work frustrated.

The remedy: first awareness, then belief, then conduct.

Awareness. Sometime after the mid-eighties, many CEOs began to see that perceptions of the causes of profit and loss were not as deep-seated in society as they needed to be. From the perspective of the boardroom, the corporation was clearly an organism of many interdependencies. But detached and uninvolved employees didn't see it that way. Problems, obstacles, bottlenecks, lateness, cost overruns were management's headaches—certainly not the workers'. However, the explosive increase in competitive pressure made it imperative that CEOs try to make a dent in this alienation. They resolved to make workers aware of the mutual interdependency of management and labor; that neither could afford to take the other for granted. Another term for this awareness is, of course "economic literacy."

Belief. Developing an awareness of the dynamics of competition and the consequences of failure is only the first requirement. The next imperative is to take this awareness and internalize it into people's beliefs and convictions, to ensure that it does not remain passive. Belief also involves an understanding of the role played by individuals; how the seemingly small and inconsequential details of their jobs have ramifications—positive and negative—on suppliers, customers, shareholders, joint venture partners, and so on.

Conduct. The last decade has been marked by an increasing recognition of the limits of organization. There is just so much that the most brilliant thinkers on organization can achieve. The same is true for the common replacement of organizational silos with cross-functional matrices. The only way to transcend those limits is with individual conduct that spontaneously furthers the goals and visions of the organization. Up and down the value chain, performance depends on the right conduct of individuals, along with their personal determination to enrich their own competencies, skills, and personal growth. That's why people are so often urged by CEOs to "live the values."

"By far the greatest difficulties we faced," Sir Richard Evans, CEO of British Aerospace, has said of his ambitious change program, "are people difficulties. Because the program is behavioral, and the biggest problem in the whole process is to get people to behave differently and then—having got that—to recognize that it [behavioral change] applies to everyone. It isn't somebody else who needs to change their behavior." That statement shows that nobody can stand back and be disengaged. The new focus on behavior falls squarely on the CEO's shoulders. Both his or her capabilities and inhibitions as a change maker are subject to minute analysis, and sometimes criticism, within the company. Nowadays, newly appointed CEOs are given a relatively short window of opportunity to convince stakeholders that they've got the right stuff. Those whose leadership fails to reflect a capability to effect change and renewal are soon removed.

The CEO focus on behavior can be interpreted as a reaction to the sharp cutbacks in middle management over the past decade. Faced with fewer organizational layers between the production line and the boardroom, CEOs have had to take a personal hand in changing culture in ways that are attuned to corporate strategy and goals. The behavioral changes they're looking for fall into four categories:

- Behavior changes demanded by the pressure and/or shock of new external conditions
- Behavior alteration by means of better-crafted rewards and incentives
- Behavioral enrichment through the dissemination of new competencies and skills, including knowledge of corporate strategies and culture
- Behavior that unleashes the power of the individual and adds to the group's internal coherence

Many of the companies represented in this book, like British Airways, have adopted behavioral change with customers definitely in mind. Others, like Monsanto, want to link behavior to the promotion of shareholder value. Companies like LSG/SKY Chefs imposed new and seemingly impossible demands on workers in order to effect a dramatic recovery of profitability. Still others, like Siemens, have a more operational goal in mind, such as relating rich internal technological capabilities to shifting external markets. Whatever the goal, what stands out in these essays is a precise and clear vision of the kind of behavior that these CEOs demand in order to achieve it. They've come a long way from that vague feel-good philosophy of "our people are the greatest," and from the time when they considered the ability to call their workers by name great personnel practice.

Much of the corporate paternalism of the past was in fact myopic. An earlier generation of CEOs failed to confront the issue of undermotivated and alienated workers—a problem that goes back to the dawn of industrialization. If the whole man or woman is not present mentally and emotionally on the job, then how is he or she to find work meaningful and fulfilling? When men and women bring only a stripped-down robotic version of themselves to the workplace, they're unlikely to experience satisfaction and pride in the work they do. In fact, they're quite likely to disengage their mental and creative energies. And in old age they will find that work, which consumed most of their waking hours, has not made their lives richer except perhaps in a financial sense.

In the ABB Asea Brown Boveri chapter, Percy Barnevik, chairman of ABB, eloquently speaks to this issue. "I would say that we in the Western industrialized countries still are 'prisoners of Taylorism.' [Frederick Taylor is best known as the inventor of time-and-motion studies.] Workers are regarded as a commodity, still seen as sort of machine specialized in certain functions—maybe using 10 percent of their brain capacity. The way they are rewarded is through collective bargaining. But when these people go home after work they build a summer house, raise a family, and manage a family budget. It is a disgrace that much of this competence is not used in our factories."

Barnevik is one of many CEOs in this book who exemplify a willingness to structure and animate work so that this "disgrace" is at least minimized, and the gulf between toil and toilers is shrunk by greater commitment and involvement. For companies headquartered in North America and Europe, much depends on the success of this behavior initiative: Engagement may be the one factor of production in which they can outcompete low-wage countries. How far these CEOs can go toward curing worker alienation remains to be seen. What is historically significant is that they have made some beginning steps down this road.

Why has this great opportunity emerged only now? Why not ten, twenty, thirty years ago? In the decades following World War II, much of the world was locked in an ideological war with communism, and in response created the corporate liberal state, which accepted worker alienation as a given. In addition, the prevalent "stakeholder" view of corporate responsibilities made profit-seeking a coequal value with community, labor interests, and national interests. Because of the rhetoric of class war in the air, it was not the time for management to make demands of its workforce for commitment and a greater share of mental energy.

Today's zeitgeist is different: Many of the old constraints on profit-seeking have fallen away. Management has a new freedom to demand that workers intimately identify with their corporations and commit themselves completely to their goals, thus freely producing and creating to the maximum. By implication, the CEOs in our book are saying that workers will be happiest jettisoning the dialectics of labor-management conflict and making the fitness and health of their corporations their primary mission. These same CEOs are also affirming another truth: All workers are in a global struggle for job retention and standard of living enhancements. And that competition is reflected in all six thematic categories around which we have structured *Straight from the CEO*.

- *Globalization*. New behaviors in all facets of management are demanded by the uncoupling of the corporation from the nation-state. Rapid free flows of technology, capital, and employment contribute to this "global village" effect. Many CEOs realize that they have to begin to break out of their old Euro- and U.S.-centered values and approaches.
- *Radical Change*. There continues to be a tremendous convergence of best practices and skills around the world. The advantages of any superior management know-how and technique are short-lived. Superior awareness, beliefs, and behavior, however, can be a lasting competitive force, hence the spread of such ideas as "transformational change" and "perpetual renewal."
- *Leadership*. Perhaps the question most frequently asked of consultants by CEOs is not "How do I get my cost structure under control?" or "Where can I make best use of information technology?" or "What's the best practice in merger management?" Rather, it's "How do I personally need to change to become a better leader?" Exceptional leaders like General Electric's CEO Jack Welch or British Airways' Sir Colin Marshall have had a demonstrable effect on all CEOs' sense of the possibility of change.
- *Culture*. The concept of corporate culture has been floating around for several decades. But it wasn't until the Japanese demonstrated supremacy in automobile and electronic production that Western managers began to take this dimension seriously. Culture fitness is no longer an option. It's a baseline competitive necessity—dramatically so for the global enterprise.
- *Innovation*. Innovation and creativity used to be regarded as the province of R&D and marketing people. Nowadays, setting the ground and the climate for total organizational creativity is the goal of many organizations that feel they've not done enough in the past

to unlock the creative potential of workers, suppliers, and customers.

- *Customer service.* Peter Drucker has written that "there is only one valid definition of business purpose: to create a customer." Overcapacity of many global products makes this an especially difficult challenge these days. The balance of power has shifted from producers to consumers, who are high on demands, low on brand loyalties, and skeptical about image manipulations. Consequently, CEOs are urging production and marketing behaviors that "live the brand."

By entering the territory of human behavior and seeking results in this radically new way, the CEO is opening Pandora's box. Some of these initiatives will succeed, some will not. From a historical perspective, this may only be the early stages of the learning curve. Further experiments and initiatives lie ahead. But make no mistake: The behavioral curve is one that every management has to jump on and ride to the top.

G. WILLIAM DAUPHINAIS, *New York*
COLIN PRICE, *London*

PART I
Globalization

"GLOBALIZATION" IS A TERM that triggers strong emotions. Depending on one's point of view, it is dreaded or admired, perceived as a great leap forward or a stumble backward. It contains many references wrapped in a single word, including: the recent and projected expansion of world trade; the greater flows of direct investment to the formerly less-developed countries of Asia and Latin America; the lightning speed of technological transmission; the giant sucking sound of European and North American jobs lost to the emerging economies; the global dominance of such power brands as Toyota and Coca-Cola, CNN and Nescafé; and the wholesale deregulation of telecommunications, air transport, and energy utilities—to name but a few of its many ingredients.

Not surprisingly, experts are divided on the importance of globalization. Certainly the majority agree with British economist Martin Wolf that it is "the great economic event of our era," while a dissident minority, including MIT economist Paul Krugman, believes that its impact has been overhyped. "What explains this propensity to overstate the importance of global markets?" he mused in the *New York Times* of February 13, 1997. "In part, it sounds sophisticated. Pontificating about globalization is an easy way to get attention at events like the World Economic Forum in Davos, Switzerland, and Renaissance Weekends in Hilton Head, S.C."

From present-day facts, Klugman is less than half right. As he pointed out in the *Times*, there are no Asian airlines offering local service in the U.S. But contrary to his views, there is a lot of cross-border activity in telecommunications. However, belief in the power of globalization lies not in its present reality, but in the perceived strength of its potential.

The great power of globalization can be seen in the strength of its lifeline. As a report of the International Monetary Fund dryly stated, globalization reflects "the growing economic interdependence of countries worldwide through the increasing volume and variety of cross-border transactions in goods and services and of international capital flows, and also through the more rapid and widespread diffusion of technology." This hydra-headed growth is more than another macroeconomic trend. It is shaping a new epoch where the tempo and breadth of change in the international economy both alters the character of the multinational corporation and makes porous the economic frontiers of the state. Result: a different paradigm of opportunities and interdependencies, as well as new terms and conditions for competitive success.

Just as water changes to a solid when the temperature drops one degree at the 32° mark, so there is a threshold (if humankind hasn't crossed it yet, we will soon) where the addition of one more degree of globalization will create a totally different reality in which corporations as the agents of capital and technology must adjust. This is why the subject of globalization resonates at the World Economic Forum at Davos and similar conferences and seminars, and why it has the air of historical inevitability despite the continuing vigor of trade protectionism and the spread of regional trading blocks. No corporation can run the risk of ignoring its opportunities and dangers. A company's failure of anticipatory intellect, or a lack of vigilance and preparedness, could have terrible consequences.

Big corporations in advanced countries haven't been slouches at foreign expansion in this century. However, they have been constrained by local protectionism and by a conservative approach to geopolitical risk— a reasonable stratagem while the Cold War was in progress and domestic growth was sufficient to keep shareholders happy. While those geopolitical risks are still real, the abundant capital, technology, and overcapacity in home-base countries have made those risks more palatable than they were a decade ago.

The old multinational corporations were quasi-colonial institutions that used the less-developed world as a dumping ground for secondhand technology, and often for second-rate executives. They can't profitably do that today because of the democratization of technology, capital, and management know-how. The new factories going up in Asia and Latin America have the benefit of low wages *and* state-of-the-art technology. Five years ago a prediction that Bangalore, India, would become a world-class software center would have been absurd. Not anymore. In the future, we can expect centers of excellence in other technologies to crop up in many formerly unlikely places.

The properties of the truly global corporation are still in the early stages of evolution. Most CEOs are just breaking out of the old Euro- and U.S.-centered values and mind-sets. They're groping for ways to make their companies more flexible and responsive to differing local environments, while preserving the advantages of global reach and scale. It's as if they're hoping to invent an amphibious octopus with another brain at the end of each tentacle.

Big oil companies are old hands at globalization in terms of geographic reach and in the ethnic diversity of their leadership. But the way even they approach the world is changing in response to a more competitive market in developed countries. Faced with a forecast of demand growth of a mere 1 or 2 percent in OECD nations, the petroleum giants are hoping to benefit from recent and prospective deregulations of state-run monopolies in other parts of the world. As a result, they're vigorously making new downstream investments in emerging economies. But for them, globalization has yet another dimension—the quest for true enterprise integration via big investments in new communications and information systems. By reengineering their back offices, and integrating the information and business process functions of hitherto independent subsidiaries, they expect to capture economies of scale that have eluded them in the past.

Here is another important facet of the globalization phenomena: the way companies are reshaping their cultures, organizations, and systems in a quest for "seamlessness"—melding the characteristics of centralization and decentralization in a new global synthesis. In 1996, Price Waterhouse began a bold initiative of this type. In chapter seven, on the new phase of globalization, chairman James Schiro details how this premier accounting and professional services firm has reorganized itself. While retaining the valuable attributes of the decentralized partnership form, Price Waterhouse has evolved a new global structure with superior responsiveness to client needs, and a more finely tuned service delivery of its knowledge resources. As Schiro points out, "It is no longer a compelling point of pride to declare: 'Our company has offices—or factories—in X countries worldwide.' All the best competitors meet that mark, and so much more is expected. Genuine points of pride have to do with global coordination coupled with well-accepted local identities."

"Think global but act local" has become the mantra of globalization discussions. Unfortunately, its frequent repetition tends to make it sound easy, when in reality it is fraught with contradiction. Complex and subtle paradoxes confront those who apply it rigorously. Just how local should "local" be in product features, image, and service delivery? Where and how does the global approach add to or detract from the local?

These are not new conundrums; as Flemming Lindeløv, Carlsberg's CEO, observes in chapter one, Carlsberg has been international for over a hundred years, because it had to leap over little Denmark's borders in search of growth. For Carlsberg, globalism comes down to projecting the image of a foreign-born premium product into local markets where taste preferences are distinctly different from Denmark's. The trick is to produce and market a local formula that nevertheless has the "feel" of a foreign product. The power of the Carlsberg brand has to be maximized in both dimensions. And its organization must move adroitly between these separate realities, each with its different needs and claims.

What makes the global economy different from the merely international is not simply the greater intensity of trade, technology, and capital flows, but the levels of complexity and the number of variables that managers must deal with. Whether it's deciding where in Asia to build a new plant or whom to team up with for Latin American distribution of a packaged goods product, the number of options are many times greater than a decade ago. So too are the interdependencies across technologies, markets, organizations. To think globally these days is to take a quantum leap in complexity. And for the time being, anyway, some facets of a company may not quite fit into a seamless whole.

So far we've talked about the good news—the promising developments and plans and intellectual chartings. But there are areas where progress has been frustratingly slow. A requisite skill for globalization, and one in which most multinational corporations are deficient, is the need to be politically integrated into the fabric of local society, which includes countries with very different political histories and institutions than those of OECD nations.

Imagine you're the CEO of a Japanese company that four years ago built four offshore factories in South Korea. Now you want to shut two of them down and shift their output to a new factory in Kuala Lumpur. How are you going to justify your acts in Seoul? And what's the likelihood that the two remaining factories will be allowed to chug along as if nothing had happened? Yes, the global economy is more open, but it has many areas that are mined with uncertainty and danger.

The dynamics of globalization are like those of oceanic tides: There is an overall direction, but embedded within them are separate streams moving at different speeds and at different angles to the main thrust. According to an OECD study, by the year 2020 a third of world output could be accounted for by China (with the biggest economy), Russia, India, Indonesia, and Brazil. Over the intervening years, all developing nations could raise their Gross Domestic Products (GDPs) by an average of 270 percent, compared to 80 percent for OECD nations. Translating these large change forecasts into corporate strategy is no easy task. However, it's equally dangerous to get too far ahead of the present into the unrealities of futurism as it is to get too caught up in day-to-day battles that obliterate the future from corporate consciousness.

Managers don't need a perfect crystal ball to forecast the timing of globalization. But what they do urgently need is vigilance and preparedness in developing capabilities and aptitudes for globalism. A global business requires global systems for the transmission of information and knowledge, yet most global systems in existence today are still very rudimentary. Corporate information systems remain predominantly domestic in origin, orientation, and functionality. Similarly, it could be argued that few in the upper echelons of most multinational corporations have adequate international exposure via travel or attendance at seminars and conferences offshore. Their boards of directors almost never include a nonnational—although it should be noted that the logistics of getting directors from around the world to a monthly board meeting are insuperable.

The fundamental management challenge posed by the new global environment is this: Corporations must seek out value-enhancing interdependencies that were simply not technologically or geopolitically possible in the past. Many are responding with a ferment of experimentation in new types of linkage and nonhierarchical relationships, forming transient ad hoc organizations that can interact, perform a "handshake" (for example, a knowledge exchange), and then break off.

ABB CEO Percy Barnevik perceived these needs nearly a decade ago when he pioneered such now-accepted practices as centers of excellence and internal benchmarking. In chapter two, Barnevik tackles a number of globalization issues facing a $36 billion firm operating through more than a thousand legal entities in federations that span 140 countries. According to him, since new products have only a short life span before being imitated or surpassed by the competition, the path to global supremacy is via "a lasting competitive edge through the excellence of your organizational structure. ABB is far from fully exploiting the advantages of its organizational structure. But I believe this is the winning recipe in the long run."

The hectic pace of globalization is occasionally accelerated by explosive events—such as several Big Bangs we've seen in some financial markets (with a few, like Japan's, still to come) and the quantum change resulting from the overnight deregulation on January 1, 1998, of European telecommunications. In chapter three, Swisscom's CEO Felix Rosenberg describes how his company spent two years working on radical change programs to prepare for the crossover to free markets. Even before that, he'd established the company as a player in global mobile communications, with more "roaming agreements" on service delivery than any other telecom company. Consequently, Swisscom's customers can use their digital cellular phones in no less than fifty countries.

An equally intriguing instance of global technological transmigration originates in Swisscom's local habitat. Train travelers trying to use telecommunications technology through the beautiful but heavily tunneled Swiss Alps may have wondered, "What good are these mountains?" Well, for one thing they forced Swisscom to develop exceptional skills in designing and engineering mobile networks over difficult terrain. "The company leads the world in radio propagation in tunnels and mountainous regions. And it has leveraged this expertise," Rosenberg says, "to its own advantage in Malaysia, as well as in Delhi, India, and in three adjacent states, via partnerships with local telecom operators."

The idea of "comparative advantage" is the classic justification for free trade—for example, that there's an economic "logic" in world trade concerning the geographical distribution of sources of production, such as movies in Hollywood, luxury automobiles in Bavaria, ceramics in Italy, toys in Hong Kong. But today, global economic competence can emerge in unexpected places. Take the case of Portugal's Vulcano-Termodomésticos, which a decade ago began production of water heaters under license from Germany's Bosch Group. Its factory was so inefficient that Vulcano was unable to break into the export market and thus exploit the advantages of the lowest wage structure in Europe.

But CEO Mário Pais de Sousa, who appears in chapter four, understood and corrected the causes of his company's initial defeat through unstinting application of Japanese factory productivity-improvement techniques. Today, Vulcano is a profitable subsidiary of the Bosch Group. But more importantly, it is now the company's international competence center for gas-powered water heaters, and has provided advice and technical support for new Bosch facilities in many countries. Some 80 percent of the manufacturing equipment for a new Chinese facility was designed and made in Portugal.

Try to imagine the Swisscom and Vulcano stories repeating themselves thousands of times a day across the globe. The conclusion is inescapable: The benefits of globalization's dissemination of knowledge, and consequently control over the natural world and wealth creation, are undeniable. Key global players in this dissemination process are the Japanese trading conglomerates, or *sogo-shosha*. One of them, Itochu, has taken major positions in a diverse portfolio of strategic and technological assets, ranging from more than a score of industrial and distribution system start-ups in China, to stakes in the United States in Time Warner and a Silicon Valley Java software venture. In chapter five, Itochu CEO Minoru Murofushi explains the logic and strategy of, in the words of *The Economist*, "taking on risks and management challenges that might disturb even the most expansive of Western conglomerates."

An amazing range of international know-how across a score of primary industries is reflected in Itochu's kaleidoscopic portfolio. And if by Western standards its conglomerate organization looks weird and archaic, let's not forget that the *sogo-shoshas* have been wide-ranging global institutions for several generations. Their honed deal-making skills, plus their hands-on knowledge of hundreds of industries and countries, may well be exactly the right credentials for superior exploitation of the forces of globalization.

Which brings us to the question of likely corporate winners and losers from globalization. In Europe and North America it is possible to hear commentary on globalization that carries a faintly patronizing ring: As if beneath its skin, globalization is simply a continuation of the old North-South dialogue and consequently the attributes of less-developed countries continue to be denigrated. In chapter six, Rahul Bajaj, CEO of Bajaj Auto, kingpin of the Indian scooter market, points out that too many Western managers think of globalization as a one-way street. "Western and Japanese businessmen are burdened with the legacies of their ancestors' early forays into the emerging markets," he writes. And again later he complains that "foreign business executives rarely take the time needed to understand the rhythms and flows of social and business interaction, preferring instead to fly in and fly out again, demanding signatures on contracts in the shortest possible time. This kamikaze style creates an immediate clash with local customs."

Bajaj is signaling an important truth. The futuristic glitter of globalization should not blind managers to the implications of ethnic and economic differences, or dull sensitivity to different customs and mores around the world. Globalization is, after all, an economic and structural tendency, not (or not for a long time yet) one that leads to cultural and national homogeneity. And considering the importance of cultural, political, *and* management shrewdness, who is to say that the likes of Bajaj or Itochu won't be the winners in the long run?

1

THE BEST INTERNATIONAL BRANDS ARE "GLOCAL"

Flemming Lindeløv, Carlsberg Group

In a country where long service to a single employer is the custom, Flemming Lindeløv stands out for the number and variety of the positions he held before becoming Carlsberg's CEO. A Ph.D. in chemistry, in his mid-twenties he headed research and quality control for Denmark's large co-op retail chain. At thirty-two he was promoted to the operation's fresh food unit, with sales of $1.5 billion and six thousand employees, where he radically changed the distribution logistics.

Lindeløv's first experience in consumer product branding was as CEO of Tulip International, an $800-million-a-year meat processor and canner. Tulip had one leg in Denmark, while in the rest of the world it focused on being "local with the locals" in its production and marketing. Lindeløv swiftly became a prominent advocate of the benefits of consolidation for the Danish meat-processing business, and he pushed for the creation of a single selling company for bacon and other processed meat products in support of a powerful national brand.

Accepting Carlsberg's offer in 1996 was not a difficult decision for the forty-eight-year-old Lindeløv, for here was a company with the quality image and highly evolved branding skills that he'd tried to create in meat products. What's more, Carlsberg brands have been gaining strength despite sluggish growth in many of the more mature markets in the developed countries—volume has surged by 50 percent in the last five years.

IN RECENT YEARS a number of management thinkers have urged multinationals to structure their operations with characteristics that are both global and local—sometimes compressed into the buzzword "glocal."

The surfacing of this term in the management literature, and the advo-
cacy of "thinking globally but acting locally" by prominent CEOs like
ABB's Percy Barnevik, testifies to the prospect of a big change in the
perceptions and organizational approaches of multinationals. However,
the truth is that while the phrasing may be new, going "glocal" isn't a new
concept. Its fundamental ideas have been practiced by a handful of companies for several generations. One of these is Carlsberg, which not only
has a glocal organization but, more importantly, a long-standing glocal
culture.

Glocal companies possess the skills to be international in range and
scope, while maintaining local relatedness to markets. Most reached this
point after a long evolutionary process of experimentation and adaptation. As a result, they now have a significant competitive advantage at a
time when some of their rivals are just starting down this pathway.

The old organizational model among transnational corporations reflected the view that customers and markets around the world are pretty
homogeneous, or at least homogeneous enough. Any lack of adaptation
to local conditions, they imagined, could be offset by the economies of
scale gained through centralized global production and marketing. Aside
from the arrogance of this point of view, it is shortsighted. Lost opportunities, stalled momentum, local managers frozen in the harsh headlamps
of headquarters' directives—all have high costs.

Over the long term, failing to adapt to local conditions leads cumulatively to low market shares, if not total defeat. The purely global transnational is likely to be myopic and arthritic when faced with the often
profound differences between one local market and another. They're
powerless to respond with flexibility and sophistication to a multiplicity
of local challenges. By contrast, the glocal company operates simultaneously in two dimensions. Being rooted in local circumstances yet tran-
scending them, such a company has the capacity to capture the true
advantages of globalism—it sees the big perspective and deploys resources with maximum global advantage, without compromising its roots
in local communities.

Many global brands carry a strong symbolic image of their country of
origin: Coca-Cola is American, a BMW is German, and Armani is the
apotheosis of Italian style. In consequence, these marketers have to decide whether to stress this identity of origin or downplay it. German car-
makers used to flaunt it, but nowadays they seem to use a more global
selling approach. These brands have a dual, hybridized identity—as does
Carlsberg. On the one hand, it is Danish, reflecting the Danish values of
wholesomeness, dependability, quality, and a good civic society. On the

other hand, it is not-Danish, in the sense that it is an integral part of the consumers' array of choices of beer in global markets. In some markets the company adds to this range of choice by featuring both its flagship Carlsberg label and its Tuborg brand, which are targeted to different types of consumers. In other markets, only one brand will be the contender—often together with local brands.

The genesis of Carlsberg's glocal culture lies in the combination of a limited domestic market in its home country, where the company has been making beer for a century and a half, coupled with a strong profit-maximizing drive that sent it first into exports, and then into export substitution. In the process of this expansion, the company has acquired deep know-how in international branding at the high-quality and high-price-point end of its market.

Carlsberg beers are currently sold in 120 countries, a high number considering that the top six global brands (Colgate, Lipton, Lux, Maggi, Nescafé, and Palmolive) are sold in no more than 67 countries. And if you look at such prominent global firms as Colgate, Kraft, Nestlé, P&G, Quaker, and Unilever, less than 4 percent of their combined brands have been described as global in an academic study. However, in the last fiscal year, 84.2 percent of Carlsberg beer sales were abroad.

The global link between Carlsberg beers brewed in various markets is that they are perceived as having the same taste everywhere—a taste associated with high quality and premium price. Maintaining local quality is almost an obsession with the company, which both supports and monitors quality performance from headquarters. Similarly, the core of the powerful marketing infrastructure is located centrally. This is where the overall brand's characteristics are maintained and promulgated, and where benchmarks for regional promotion and advertising are determined and monitored. Other core marketing skills, such as sports promotions, are distributed from headquarters on an as-needed basis.

If that seems to indicate a highly authoritarian central command, let's take a look at the other side—Carlsberg's intense focus on the local dimension. While headquarters imposes the uniformity, consistency, and continuity necessary to give the brands their lasting identity and power, local operators are given considerable latitude to respond to local market conditions. People everywhere differ in their preferences for salt, sweetness, gumminess, crunchiness, and so on. There can be pronounced variations even between neighboring regions. Within little Denmark, for example, people in the western region have a significantly stronger sweet tooth for carbonated drinks than do Danes in other parts of the country. Similar fluctuations exist all over the globe. With beer, the big variable is bitterness. Accordingly, the product formulations of a global beer have to adapt to preferences on the bitterness scale at the local level. But it must do this without impinging on the brand's identity or the perception of its properties. It is critical that the brand's "fingerprint" be maintained.

The glocal model demands a flexible and adaptive organization of dispersed autonomous country assets and people, backed up by the instruments of centralized brand control. The result: a strong yet subtle responsiveness to market particulars, together with the global distribution of best practices in all skill areas. Particularly in the case of beer, this means production know-how. One should not go glocal without recognizing that local entities' freedom must exist within a framework of centralized policy. There is also the regional dimension to consider—there, marketing promotions sometimes overlap national boundaries. At Carlsberg, there is considerable uniformity of approaches between regional levels around the world, but variations are permitted and even encouraged at times.

Without a highly evolved glocal outlook, a company will probably fail to respond adequately to the fact that its products are perceived and used differently in different parts of the world. According to a report from McCann-Erickson Worldwide:

"To Brazilians, beer is not an alcoholic beverage—it's a soft drink. Germans firmly believe their beer must be locally brewed to be any good. [Which is why there are over twelve hundred breweries there.] The English have only recently adopted lager beers. Americans see it as a boy-meets-girl drink. And Australians see it strictly as a man's drink. Beer is still different, culture to culture."

Thus, a glocal corporation's marketing approach must project a unified image of quality, style, and character, while eschewing cookie-cutter-type global advertising. While the company should convey the same point of view about its brands, that view must be expressed in many different ways to take into account religious and cultural sensitivities from region to region. To do this successfully, a glocal company has to be able to deconstruct brand images into which elements are global and which are local.

As we see it, here are some of the characteristics that go into a world-scale quality brand:

- *Religious dedication to quality.* In all functions, quality must be a primary and consistent force. From production to distribution to marketing, there must be dedication to the highest standards. Any deviations from these standards must be detected early and corrected promptly.

- *Long-term vision.* Quality brands must be backed up with a consistent, long-term strategy of enrichment—regardless of the ups and downs of business cycles. A faith in the value and durability of the brand demands that it be strengthened in good times and bad.
- *Mystique and style.* Quality brands must cultivate symbols that suggest contentment and satisfaction. They should convey pleasure in consumption and a stylish enjoyment of the good life. The surge in world tourism contributes to the perception of superiority of high-end global brands.
- *Global reach.* Quality brands have an air of success and capability. They display market dominance and thus the power to attract millions of consumers. However, this means they need an ever-widening geographical spread. Which is why many multinationals have been aggressively exploiting the geopolitical openings presented by the fall of the Iron Curtain and the growth of China's economy.
- *Tradition and generational renewal.* Established quality products are being challenged by the MTV generation, who need to assert themselves with consumption choices different from their parents'. Accordingly, brand managers in these categories should invest in youth-oriented promotions to establish a platform of long-term use and loyalty.

These points are a good template for many industries. But they are particularly relevant to the beer industry today, where the number of new and potential global players has grown dramatically. Many one-time domestic brewers in developed markets have now accumulated big war chests and are ready for foreign expansion via export and direct investment.

At the same time, the expertise required to make quality beers in large volume is no longer the proprietary technology of a few, mostly European, players. It has now been widely dispersed around the world. In short, high-end beers have moved from the craft mode to mass production. And finally, the economics of brand-building—the staggering investments required—suggest that there are a number of mergers and buyouts waiting in the wings. Ten years hence it is very likely that there will be fewer than ten brewers with possibly a global share of over 50 percent.

Needless to say, there is intense competition to win this struggle for dominance. Many of the players are implementing "lean and mean" operational efficiencies in order to sink the resulting economies into higher brand investments. Carlsberg, for instance, is changing its distribution logistics in the home market: eliminating captive family-owned distributors and building a direct-to-retailer network. One result of this change has been a much better assessment of distribution costs between different classes of retail outlets in volume and location.

Beer is experiencing an intense struggle for dominance between international rivals at a time when the public in many markets is displaying an appetite for variety and innovation—a time, too, when marketing gurus talk of an epidemic of diminishing consumer loyalty as brands become commodities. Thus, producers of branded traditional products are faced with the challenge of diversifying into new taste areas with new products or brand extensions. This is why Carlsberg has pushed hard at new products at home in the increasingly popular dark beer sector.

In all likelihood this process of commoditization will not diminish. The trend is being fueled in part by the greater economic power being wielded by retailers. Accordingly, there has been a polarization of brands between high-end and low-end/private-label products. Many manufacturers have decided that the best strategy is to defend existing high-end brands than to create new ones.

The recent slowing down of growth rates for many consumer products in the developed world has been steadily enhancing the value of strong brands over weak ones. But these positions have to be supported with cash outlays and a vigor not required in the past. In addition, larger outlays for promotion are needed as a defense against retailers who have the capacity to destroy the accumulated value of a brand, built up by a manufacturer over many years, by selling the item below cost.

Glocal players have the resources and the infrastructure to fight either defensively or offensively. Non-glocals don't have the combination of deep pockets, functional skills, and roots in the distinctive soil of different countries and regions. Therefore, in all foreseeable scenarios, the glocals are far more likely to win and maintain competitive terrain against the merely local, or the merely global.

2
CREATING A FEDERATION OF NATIONAL CULTURES

Percy Barnevik,
ABB Asea Brown Boveri Ltd.

Percy Barnevik is a titanic manager—a category that also applies to General Electric's CEO, Jack Welch. And what is titanic about them is their ability to electrify massive corporations in a way that overcomes the inertia of scale.

Barnevik first came to prominence as one of the masterminds of the 1988 merger between two giants in electrical engineering and equipment, Switzerland's BBC Brown Boveri and the Swedish ASEA AB, when he was appointed CEO. The company's main products include power generation, transmission, and distribution; industrial and building systems; and rail transportation. Organizationally, ABB is divided into some one thousand companies, managed via a corporate matrix system, in 140 different nations. More importantly, the organization is both structured and animated with a dominant goal: both to respond to the forces of globalization and to be sensitive to the differing needs of local markets. During Barnevik's tenure, ABB's revenues have grown, thanks in part to over one hundred acquisitions, from $18 billion to $36 billion in 1996, while returns on employed capital soared from 13 percent to 23 percent.

Barnevik, who stepped down as president and CEO but remained chairman of the ABB board at the beginning of 1997, has been justly hailed as a radical decentralist, a man of great personal energy who relentlessly pushes responsibility away from a minimalist corporate center with less than two hundred people. He has pioneered such now-fashionable practices as internal benchmarking and corporate "centers of excellence" where core global skills reside. "If Europe has a management superstar it is Percy Barnevik," wrote The Economist *on January 6, 1996.*

"In the end, however, a lot of ABB's corporate glue comes from Mr. Barnevik's own relentlessness. ABBers around the world speak reverently about his ability to get by on four hours of sleep a night and his familiarity with every nook and cranny of the organization. He reckons that he speaks personally to 5,000 of his employees every year."

The message he often communicates is one of liberation and empowerment, as many managers of acquired companies testify. One spectacular illustration of his method and philosophy occurred in the United States upon the 1989 sale by Westinghouse of its troubled power transmission and distribution business. The operation was just marginally profitable. Three years later under ABB, it had the performance profile of a hot growth company, accomplished without any significant management changes. Operating profits doubled, while export sales surged. The secret of success: a synthesis of the power of globalization (particularly technological know-how and management insights from other units of ABB) and the power of local autonomy, where local managers were freed from the old structures of hierarchy and second guesses by superiors remote from day-to-day involvement in markets.

Christopher Bartlett of Harvard Business School and Sumantra Goshal of the London Business School have declared in the July 1996 issue of Strategy & Leadership, *based on close observation of ABB, that "Percy Barnevik has emerged as one of the decade's most visible corporate revolutionaries."*

In the following interview, Barnevik is, as usual, at the barricades, showing us how to wage the fight against inertia, bureaucracy, and myopia toward local market conditions.

Price Waterhouse (PW): ABB is a $36 billion firm operating in 140 countries. This is large by any standard—yet you describe ABB as "multidomestic." What important message does that word communicate?

Percy Barnevik (PB): ABB was built almost ten years ago by merging and acquiring companies in many countries—many of them more than one hundred years old with proud national histories. We have preserved and promoted these national cultures, and our organization today can be regarded as a federation of national companies. We are not homeless; we have many home countries. We are not a Swiss or Swedish company; we are Italian in Italy, American in the United States, Polish in Poland, Indian in India. We consist of more than a thousand legal entities, and each lives close to the customers in each country. The entities are managed by nationals who develop products and export and import like any other local company. That they belong to a global group does not change the strong national identity, it just adds advantages.

PW: *How do you create a cohesive culture and cross-border sharing in such a decentralized company?*

PB: While we respect and promote the national cultures, we have also developed a global ABB culture—you might say an "umbrella" culture. This is what holds us together and makes us stronger than we would be going our separate ways. That global culture ensures that we do not split up into national islands.

Take, for example, transformers. We have annual sales of about $2 billion from some sixty factories in thirty-five countries—we are by far the biggest manufacturer in the world. The average factory size is not so big, on the order of $30 million to $40 million and one hundred fifty to two hundred people, and each one lives close to its customers as part of a national group. At the same time, all of our transformer plants also belong to the global group, within which they share technology and best practices. For example, to achieve economies of scale each plant specializes in specific transformer products for development and manufacturing, and each has its allocation of export markets. But in purchasing we have the huge advantage of ordering large quantities from a few global suppliers. So while each plant operates like a local, medium-sized family company, each also derives benefits from its membership in the global group. When our managers experience the major advantages of working together, it really helps build global cooperation.

We have summarized our visions, values, and policies in a sort of "ABB bible." It is not a glossy corporate brochure with generalities like "being a good citizen." It is a practical handbook on what we stand for, how we should behave toward customers and other external interests, and how we should behave internally. Because we have many profit centers, people can tend to suboptimize and become narrow-minded. For this reason, we have emphasized shared priorities: the customer first, then the group—and only then the individual profit center.

Cross-border cooperation is enhanced by striving for mixed-nationality teams, and working in preestablished multinational consortia that serve the different types of plants. In this regard, it is important to set the tone from the top and reward people who promote the global group and support other people.

PW: *Has it been difficult to rally people in the West for expansion in the East? Are people in Western Europe and the United States afraid of competition from low-wage countries?*

PB: To succeed in penetrating Eastern Europe and Asia we need good people there, and the full commitment of our people in Western Europe, North America, Japan, and Australia to support these investments by transferring technology, capital, and expatriates, and bringing people from developing regions to their countries for training. There have certainly been worries and some resistance in the industrialized countries, but today I believe we have largely overcome that. It is a matter of trust and communication—and of course a matter of developing a track record supporting what you say. For example, when we invested heavily in Poland in the late eighties, our German employees worried that low-wage Poles would eventually eliminate jobs in Germany. Now, seven years later, we can see that German exports to Poland have increased fourfold thanks to the presence we have built in that country. Asia is another example. In 1988, we sold $2 billion in the region, of which West European and American exports amounted to $1.5 billion. In 1995, we sold $8 billion in Asia, four times more than 1988, with the share of exports up threefold to $4.5 billion. In recession-struck Europe, our people are really happy to have that export business now. The pattern illustrates how investments and transfers of technology go hand in hand with more exports.

PW: *How do you get your managers to think globally?*

PB: Global managers are not born—they must be developed. Among our twenty-five thousand managers we need some five hundred truly global managers with global business responsibilities. One key route toward creating this group is to transfer promising young managers to other countries. Another is trainee programs where part of the training is assignment to another country. While we have many people from emerging markets and Eastern Europe training in the West, we also have many Western Europeans and Americans spending two to four years on foreign assignments. They pick up another language and increase their understanding of other cultures before they return to Muncie, Indiana; Mannheim, Germany; or Barcelona, Spain. This is how we develop a population of global managers to choose for major global assignments.

PW: *How can you control a decentralized and geographically widespread organization with some one thousand companies and five thousand profit centers?*

PB: Decentralization goes hand in hand with central monitoring—and decentralization must not be confused with abdication. While we apply a far-reaching decentralization of authority and responsibility, senior management has the right and the responsibility to intervene, to coach or correct when things go wrong. Therefore, we have an extensive financial reporting system serving the different layers of supervision. On the tenth of every month, for example, I look at the total picture of the group's performance, including all the individual companies with regard to orders, margins, results, employment levels, et cetera.

When it comes to communication, I personally meet four thousand to five thousand people every year, and my colleagues in the Executive Committee do the same. When I stop in India, Brazil, or Finland, I do not want to talk to five managers but to one hundred or two hundred. We also bring people together regularly along global business area lines, in the regions and in functional areas. Once every eighteen to twenty-four months, we gather four hundred to five hundred managers for a week and some one hundred key managers come together twice a year.

We pay a certain price in the form of higher communication costs than other companies that are more homogeneous and concentrated in one country. However, the communication investment is a relatively small price to pay for the speed, flexibility, and many synergies we gain through decentralization.

PW: *You have often referred to the benefits of smallness. Your highly decentralized structure is an attempt to mirror this. Why not just spin off companies from ABB?*

PB: I used to say, "Small is beautiful." Frankly, I am obsessed by the idea of creating a small-company and entrepreneurial climate as far as possible within our big group. We are willing to suffer some extra costs, some difficulties from fragmentation, if we can create small-company speed and flexibility, with employees living close to customers, understanding the importance of their own individual efforts for the success of their profit center, instead of feeling hidden away in a big bureaucratic organization. I grew up in a small family company environment, a printing shop with fifteen employees. If one of the workers stayed home Monday morning or caused a quality problem, he knew the direct consequences for the company and its customers. I have seen so much waste, inefficiency, slowness, and bureaucracy in big organizations. I have seen "corridor people" who survive by floating around and never sticking out their necks. In ABB's transparent organization you cannot hide. You are visible and accountable. That is not a threat but an opportunity. In ABB you are allowed to make mistakes. What is not allowed is not to correct them or to be passive.

PW: ABB has been very successful in financial terms. Since the merger in 1988, your sales have doubled and profit has increased four times. Your Swiss shareholders have seen the stock value increase on average by 25 percent annually for almost nine years, and since 1980, the Swedish shareholders of ABB have seen an average annual return of 30 percent. The stock value has increased fifty-four-fold over this seventeen-year period, dramatically more than the general stock index. With this background of success, how do you motivate your people for even more improvement and continuous change?

PB: You can never rest on your laurels, you have to improve your position every year, every month, and every day. Just two or three years of complacency can destroy a strong and successful company. So you must constantly strive for improved performance, toward higher targets. You must create a corporate culture of continuous change, where people see change not as a threat and disturbance but as something positive, something necessary and even fun.

Apart from the internal improvement targets, change is also required by a changing environment. The demand for infrastructure investments has moved from West to East. The market for new power plants in the United States has dropped 90 percent, and 60 percent of total global demand is now in Asia. These are unprecedented changes. You have factories where you don't need them, and where you do need them, you don't have them. These changes in the environment require major internal changes.

PW: Your Customer Focus program emphasizes speed. How much opportunity exists for cycle-time reduction?

PB: To be a truly customer-driven organization, you must first achieve operational excellence. It doesn't help to love your customer—he won't love you if you don't perform. It was natural for ABB to address operational excellence first by reducing cycle times and raising overall quality. Then you build customer relations and eventually create partnerships with your key customers.

When it comes to targets for reduced cycle times, there is no end to the improvements you can achieve. You reduce 50 percent, then you aim for another 50 percent reduction. In 1988, the time required to build a medium-sized combined-cycle plant was three years. Then it fell to two years—and now we quote ten months. Delivery of large machines in Finland used to take eighty days; now it's down to ten. These are improvements you could not dream of ten years ago and we must continue on the route toward ever-decreasing cycle times while aiming for zero defects.

PW: How do you ensure that innovation and creativity are exercised—and encouraged—throughout the group?

PB: A key to entrepreneurship and innovation is decentralization and the creation of the "small company" inside the big group. It is particularly important to create an innovative climate in R&D, where we spend $2.7 billion per year. While we work systematically with payback calculations, et cetera, it is important that we also have enough resources for speculative and risky R&D, where meaningful payback calculations are impossible. Recently we started what we call a High Impact Program to mobilize the creative forces in the company.

PW: Many people point out the high failure rate of mergers and acquisitions, yet ABB has acquired many companies over the last few years. Why? And how have you ensured successful integration?

PB: Let me first state that we have had our fair share of problems and disappointments. In Eastern Europe we have had to withdraw from some ventures because we could not work with the partners. In some parts of Asia some acquisitions have taken much longer to show profit than expected. In America we have done very well in making internal performance improvements, but the unexpected collapse of the deregulated power market was a negative experience after we bought the transmission divisions of Westinghouse and the whole of Combustion Engineering.

Yet, overall, we have been successful with most of our more than a hundred acquisitions. We have learned the technique of integrating them quickly into ABB. We go for local people rather than expatriates in management positions everywhere. I would rather have problems communicating with a Polish, Russian, or Chinese manager than he or she having a problem communicating with people down the line. We have also developed mentorships through which Western and Northern companies "adopt" Eastern and Southern ones.

A recent experience in the integration of new companies is to build on competence within the "new ABB home markets." In the sixties, seventies, and eighties, it was a question of using expatriates from Western Europe and North America in the emerging markets or Eastern Europe. Now we use Poles and Czechs to build the presence in Russia, Belarus, Ukraine, and Central Asia. They speak Russian, they understand Slavic culture, and they have lived under communist regimes. Once they are converted to the Western management style and the ABB culture, they are much more effective in building new business than Americans, Germans, Scandinavians, or other Westerners. Similarly, we use Brazil with seven thousand employees as a base for supporting expansion in Latin America. South Africa has responsibility for Sub-Sahara Africa, and we use Chinese-speaking people from Thailand, Singapore, Hong Kong, and Taiwan for the penetration of China.

PW: We hear a lot about management process at ABB. But what about the workers? How do you communicate with them, and motivate and develop them?

PB: I would say that we in the Western industrialized countries still are "prisoners of Taylorism." Workers are regarded as a commodity, still seen as some sort of machine specialized in certain functions—maybe using 10 percent of their brain capacity. The way they are rewarded is through collective bargaining. When these people go home after work they build a summer house, raise a family, and manage a family budget. It is a disgrace that much of this competence is not used in our factories.

Within ABB we have gained good experience with so-called "high-performance teams," particularly in Sweden. The idea is that teams of production workers take over new tasks from the white-collar people. They handle supply, customer complaints, quality supervision, et cetera. Individual workers get a chance to advance. They are trained in handling a PC, basic statistics, et cetera. We have had an extremely positive result from this far-reaching delegation of responsibility to the shop floor. Continuous training is not just a catchword, it has become an integral part of our organization with real substance. We have increased worker training by a factor of three or four in recent years.

PW: *What is your personal role? What drives you?*

PB: What drives me is to achieve something of lasting value. That was the case when I had the challenge twenty years ago to lead Sandvik's entry into the U.S. cutting tools market. The market orientation, decentralization, and internationalization of Asea in the early eighties was another phase of major change. Then, of course, the world's biggest cross-border merger in 1988, the creation of ABB and the building of its particular culture.

In the nineties it has been rewarding to pioneer the buildup in newly opened Eastern Europe, to lead the enormous effort to expand in Asia, and to transform the company's environmental thinking to include life cycle analysis and the like. In these latter cases I have also felt great satisfaction from contributing in a wider sense to a better world. I had, for example, strong personal feelings about the plight of Eastern Europeans under communism and was privileged to be able to contribute to bringing some light into their darkness there and to help their integration with the West.

It is, however, important that you do not get carried away with your own feelings or personal interests but remember that at the end of the day you must provide a return to the people you work for: the shareholders.

PW: *Were you to summarize what ABB stands for and the paradoxes it includes, how would you put it?*

PB: The three paradoxes are decentralization—but central monitoring and control; global—and local; big—and small.

PW: *And what do you consider to be your major competitive advantages?*

PB: I believe you can build a lasting competitive edge through the excellence of your organizational structure. In regard to product development, today you have only a short time of advantage against your competitors. Within one to two years they will have copied you or come up with an even better solution—new developments spread fast around the world. When it comes to process development, you tend to get a more lasting competitive advantage. See how the Japanese in the automotive industry, headed by Toyota, built their competitive advantage over some fifteen years. Now the Americans and Europeans are catching up—but it took a while.

The most difficult competitive advantage to copy is the organizational advantage. After nine years ABB is far from fully exploiting the advantages of its organizational structure. But I believe this is the winning recipe in the long run.

3

POISED FOR THE "BIG BANG": WINNING IN THE DEREGULATION GAME

Felix Rosenberg, Swisscom

Swisscom is the national telecommunications operator of Switzerland. With annual sales in excess of $10 billion and a workforce of more than twenty thousand people, it is a leader in its field. It has the world's highest international traffic per capita as well as one of the world's highest telephone densities. It was also one of the first operators in Europe to completely digitize its network, offering customers a range of advanced digital voice and data communication solutions well ahead of the competition.

Yet, despite its successes, the company found itself hurtling into the unknown in the late nineties. Industry deregulation in Europe—popularly known as the "Big Bang"—meant massive upheaval and an uncertain future. Literally overnight, on January 1, 1998, incumbent national operators such as Swisscom had their once-secure markets thrown open to international competition.

To meet this challenge, two years before deregulation was scheduled to take effect, Swisscom launched a transformation initiative of its own. Called "Change Telecom," the initiative was designed to shake Swisscom, then known as Swiss Telecom PTT, free of its heritage as a traditional, government-owned corporation, and reposition it for a future as an international commercial carrier with a commitment to superior customer service. A mandate went out from CEO Felix Rosenberg: Nothing except the customer is sacred. Nothing—no business practices, assumptions, or individuals—will be immune to change.

Rosenberg, formerly governor of Thurgau Canton, one of Switzerland's twenty-six regional governments, was appointed head of Swiss Telecom in 1989. His earlier government experience, coupled with his training as a lawyer, has served Swisscom well over the years. Among other things, it helped him win support for the company's plan to transform itself from a government entity to free-market operator.

SWITZERLAND IS FAMOUS FOR many things, from chocolate to superior private banking services. It is also home to successful companies such as Nestlé, ABB, and Novartis, all of which have transformed themselves from local successes into internationally respected multinational companies with worldwide customer bases.

Less well known perhaps is Switzerland's cultural diversity. The country's rich blend of German, French, Italian, and Reto-Romantsch languages and cultures is a source of considerable national pride. It is also the wellspring of our country's fierce independence—as well as its abiding resistance to change. Witness, for example, the country's decision to stay out of the European Union. While this diversity has given Swisscom a unique multicultural experience, it has also posed a significant challenge to a company looking for national support for an ambitious plan to grow beyond its borders.

Well aware of the devastation that followed hard on the heels of deregulation in other markets, we understood that Swisscom had little choice but to press ahead with its plans. If we did not change, the company would die, since in earlier rounds of European deregulation, incumbent telecommunications operators lost up to 25 percent of their market share, while watching prices decline by some 30 percent. For telecommunications companies, deregulation meant the sort of restructuring witnessed in the U.S. airline industry and the British financial services sector.

For incumbent telecom operators, surviving deregulation depended directly on our ability to effect and harness massive change. No simple task. At a minimum, single-shareholder monopolies had to transform themselves into free-market competitors responsive to thousands of shareholders. Companies that were once technology-driven bureaucracies had to evolve into market-led, customer-responsive enterprises offering a broad menu of services. And once-national operators had to move well beyond their borders, leveraging economies of scope and scale to match competitors and to reach customers wherever they might be in the world.

When you add the need to deploy the latest technology, systems, and business processes to gain competitive advantage, it's easy to see why transforming Swisscom was a daunting management challenge.

In 1996, Swisscom set to work on many fronts: In the legal and parliamentary arenas, we lobbied to split the telecom business from the postal system and to create a joint stock company. Finding early support for our new vision, we began preparing for partial privatization, unleashing a torrent of change initiatives. For example, we:

- Negotiated with regulators of future competitive market and pricing conditions
- Underwent a major organizational restructuring
- Appointed a new management team
- Introduced a total quality management (TQM) program
- Initiated business-process reengineering across the organization
- Launched major financial and billing systems initiatives
- Made significant capital investments at home and abroad
- Launched a massive culture-change program for employees

All of these initiatives flowed from a two-pronged strategy that I championed. I knew I had to be unrelenting in my commitment to change. First, we had to internationalize: look beyond domestic boundaries and become a business capable of serving customers anywhere in the world. Second, we needed to look inward and reinvent the company: create an environment that encouraged risk takers to do the deals that secured international reach, lead the transformation at home, and build the business of the future. I believe that the success of a change program depends on management's ability to remain focused on outcomes by fine-tuning initiatives to the company's specific ways of doing business.

We knew it was critical to leverage Swisscom's diversity, since transformation is best fueled by drawing upon the many different strengths, cultures, and ideas of managers, staff, and trading partners. We have used our global business alliances to benefit our customers and to help drive our change program.

We motivated our managers and staff to work with alliance partners, encouraging them to apply domestically what they learned abroad. Employees were empowered to achieve real results, and we focused time and energy on helping them achieve change. We also treated cultural diversity and language skills as key competencies, carefully nurturing and exploiting them.

For CEOs facing similar upheaval in their own industries, I would like to offer some of the most valuable lessons Swisscom learned:

INTERNATIONALIZE

Think "Outside the Box" to Define Home Markets

It's all too easy to accept the status quo. Historically, national borders have defined domestic markets, and the rules of international commerce have reinforced those barriers. Deregulation challenged European telecom operators to justify why customers should pay substantially more for international calls than they do for calls within their own country—especially when the international call is being made to a nearby area.

This challenge led Swisscom to redefine its domestic reach. Early in the transformation process, we began to think of eastern France, the south of Germany, and the northern parts of Italy—areas where the company had strong language, cultural, and trading links—as part of our home market. With the help of local business partners, we are extending our network into these areas, roughly doubling the size of the market we are able to serve with our existing infrastructure and staff. Given our high penetration in Switzerland, this strategy gives Swisscom needed headroom for traffic-volume growth.

Form Alliances to Enhance Global Reach

When customers go global, companies must follow. For telecoms, however, this simple business axiom poses complex challenges. For example: Should a telecom operator build its own global network, or should it lease capacity from other operators? The problem is that the first solution is prohibitively expensive, and the second weakens the company's control over service. So Swisscom opted for a third alternative—using a global alliance to provide complementary services in any world market.

This decision flowed from our membership in the AT&T–Unisource alliance. Alliance members, drawn from the worldwide telecom-operator community, deliver each other's customer traffic to its final destination. The alliance also offers global solutions—for example, international intranets and Virtual Private Networks—that no one company would be able to offer on its own. The alliance also provides a single contract, and a single point of contact, for sales and customer service for multinational businesses.

For alliance members, competitive advantage comes from global reach, economies of scope and scale, common service offerings, single brand promotion, joint procurement, network standardization, and research and development collaboration.

Exploit Core Competencies in Growth Markets

As one of the world's highest international telephone traffic carriers per capita, one of Swisscom's core competencies is its ability to negotiate bilateral communication agreements and pricing arrangements with other countries. This know-how has enabled the company to branch out aggressively into the mobile communications market. We have more roaming agreements in place than any other telecom operator, and our customers can use their digital cellular phones in more than fifty countries worldwide.

Swisscom has also developed considerable skill in designing and engineering mobile networks over difficult terrain. We lead the world in radio propagation in tunnels and mountainous regions. And we have leveraged this expertise to our own advantage in Malaysia, as well as in Delhi and three surrounding states in India, via partnerships with local telecom operators there.

One of Swisscom's core competencies is the efficient design, procurement, installation, and operation of modern digital networks. We are actively exploiting these rapid-response capabilities in emerging countries, most recently in the Czech Republic and Hungary. Establishing a foothold in an emerging market has other benefits as well. For example, in Malaysia, in addition to assisting the local operator in building and operating its mobile network, Swisscom is lending a hand in the development of long-distance and international network licenses. This operation as well as the one in India will become regional hubs for Swisscom's international traffic.

REINVENT THE COMPANY

Prepare for Massive Change Inside the Organization

Deregulation, and the entry of new competitors into home markets, forced us to make further changes in how we serve national business and residential customers. The "Change Telecom" initiative led to a fundamental restructuring of Swisscom's organization, management team, business processes, corporate culture, and thus employee behavior, technology, and systems. To succeed, we had to draw deeply on the diverse skills and backgrounds of each of our employees.

Engage Key Stakeholders in Change Initiatives

Much has been said about the need to engage participants at all levels of an organization to create a successful change program. One of the toughest challenges is getting middle managers fully engaged in a process that could lead to the elimination of their positions.

We met this issue head-on by asking our regional managers to design and fully implement the change program. Reporting back to the executive board at key checkpoints in the process, the seventeen regional managers took leadership roles in Swisscom's transformation. In the months leading up to deregulation, they redesigned the entire regional structure—eliminating all but four regions—and worked to engage subordinates in the change initiatives.

Under their leadership, some three hundred people worked full-time on change programs, and many more were involved on a part-time basis. The result: high acceptance among employees of the need for change. The sense of urgency in finding new solutions was kindled by our front-line managers, who could feel the heat from intensifying competition.

Build a Learning Alliance to Move Forward

While many of the alliances discussed so far are aimed at achieving quantifiable results such as gains in market share or revenues, there are substantial intangible benefits to be gained as well.

The members of the Unisource alliance—all of whom are responding to the same driving forces of privatization, market liberalization, and transformation—share a strong commitment to learning by doing. While some are at more advanced stages of the process, each has found it has much to learn from the others, and this is encouraging multilevel contacts throughout Unisource.

The learning-by-doing ethos applies to formal as well as informal learning. Swisscom provides management training and exchange programs for our own employees as well as for those of current and prospective partners. In collaboration with the Université de Fribourg, we have founded the International Institute of Management for Telecommunications, which offers postgraduate courses leading to a unique MBA in telecommunications management.

Focus on Outcomes

Too many change initiatives focus on the methods used to carry out a program rather than on the desired outcome. For example, focusing on reengineering product development processes can distract employees from focusing on the all-important outcome, such as getting a new product to market faster than the competition. It's easy to get so bogged down in the how of doing something that you forget about why it needs to be done.

At Swisscom, we broke our change program into specific offensives. Each was designed to address a particular business issue and produce a specific outcome. But all focused on the key attributes of urgency, speed, and action.

Swisscom launched a "Customer Offensive," for example, to find ways to retain customers and minimize market share losses. The tasks included matching the company's service portfolio to market-segment needs; redesigning the sales, marketing, and customer service organizations; improving business processes that dealt directly with customers; and deploying new customer-care and billing systems.

The starting point for these initiatives was an assessment of key interaction points between Swisscom's customers and its employees. Understanding that a telecom company can have up to eighty customer-interaction points scattered across its organization, we studied our own operation and designed or redesigned processes to meet customer needs efficiently and to ensure customer satisfaction.

Similarly, we introduced a "Production Offensive" to improve network efficiency and gain cost reductions. We are now consolidating our regional structure; reducing the number of work centers; improving service initiation and repair cycle times; and making network planning, operations, installation, maintenance, and repair processes more efficient and cost-effective.

We put other offensives in place to improve responsiveness and support-service efficiency; to develop new management policies, processes, and instruments for the decentralized business units; and to make the current business culture more customer oriented and competitively commercial. We also began an initiative to coordinate communications throughout the change program.

Understand the CEO's Role

One of the CEO's primary responsibilities is keeping the change program—and the management team—moving forward. It's a given that in any major change program, some things will not go according to plan. This is why the CEO must never lose sight of the company's long-term goals.

It's the CEO's task to rank issues in order of importance and to steer a path through today's crises to reach tomorrow's goals. However, given all that a CEO has to do on a daily basis, it's difficult to maintain that long-term focus. At Swisscom, we addressed this issue by appointing one group of senior managers to run the current business, and another to breathe life into the new organization. This arrangement freed me to become the coach and to communicate the new vision throughout the company.

We also took the major step of decentralizing our operations, creating business units or value centers. Internal and external candidates competed avidly for the top eighty management positions created by this move. Initially, the success of the individual units will be measured by their contributions to Swisscom's corporate value. After privatization, success will be measured by contributions to stakeholder value. Clearly, having the right people in place is the key to future performance.

Let me sum up my experience in one last piece of advice: Treat time as the most precious of resources—and use it wisely.

4

SMART SHOPPING IN THE WORLD SUPERMARKET OF MANAGEMENT IDEAS

Mário Pais de Sousa, Vulcano-Termodomésticos

Mário Pais de Sousa, board member of Bosch Thermotechnik (Wernau-Stuttgart) and chief executive director of Vulcano-Termodomésticos, based in rural Portugal, was a twenty-six-year-old electrical engineer with little business experience when the company was started in 1979. After taking a year-long course in industrial management, his philosophy evolved into the belief that economic victory goes to the focused, obsessive, low-cost producer.

It was an outlook that suited a company, and a country, with little financial or managerial resources. Vulcano could not then afford the latest in sophisticated capital equipment, or a German organizational model like the Bosch Group's, which supplied the technology and the component parts for Vulcano's instantaneous gas-powered water heaters. But the very austerity the company faced made it think creatively about factory organization. By sheer intellectual effort it pulled itself up by its bootstraps, and by the nineties it had become a major factor in the European market for its product, gaining significant share in a mature market.

MORE THAN IS USUALLY recognized in New York, Tokyo, London, or Frankfurt, there has been a tremendous dispersal of management know-how around the world. The captains of industry in the most developed nations send their legions to faraway places, thinking that they're bound to conquer because the natives lack anything resembling evolved management skills. However, the truth is that today, good business ideas fly around the globe as fast as hit pop songs. Anyone can seize them, adapt and implement them—even improve them. The global village is a free market in best practices. Every day, in almost every country, rich or poor, real-world managers—often less than fully literate in any foreign language—are wheeling their shopping carts around this global supermarket in management thought. They buy and apply those intellectual packages that fit their problems.

To support my thesis, I offer the story of Vulcano-Termodomésticos. My firm began as a small Portuguese start-up, but we honed our production skills so swiftly that in less than a decade we ranked as a global player in our chosen field. Our specialty is residential gas-powered water heaters. But although the name on the door is Portuguese, when you open it and look inside at our ideas and skills— which are far in advance of our local peers'—you will see that they clearly come from all over the world, especially Japan and Germany. Of course, these ideas have undergone some mutations and adaptations to our company's particular circumstances, but their contribution in giving Vulcano a significant share of the total European market has been profound.

Vulcano's genesis was hardly propitious. Studies commissioned by Portugal's Directorate-General of Industry pointed toward slim opportunities for the production of any kind of domestic appliances in our country. Because of a bitter revolution in the seventies, following a long and isolating dictatorship, the general level of the country's managerial infrastructure was poor. Nonetheless, in 1979, Vulcano became a licensee of Junkers, a division of the Bosch Group, and so acquired a kernel of technology. Looked at from a global perspective, the early Vulcano was a pretty primitive operation: Junkers supplied the components, and Vulcano assembled them. Two years later, we undertook some local parts manufacturing, but the value added was nothing to brag about.

There are striking parallels between the early days of Vulcano and the way Japanese managers in automobiles and consumer electronics started from a base of almost nothing at the end of World War II. In both cases, we had terrible scarcities of technology and capital, but nevertheless primed our companies for success with a combination of sheer managerial acumen and a relentless focus on factory efficiency. At Vulcano, as with the Japanese, production skills and productivity enhancement became an all-consuming religion.

There is one other important parallel: As in postwar Japan, Portugal's labor costs were dramatically lower than many other European countries—half those of Spain, a quarter those in Germany. It was reasonable for us to assume that this massive wage differential gave us a strong competitive advantage. In theory, yes. But in practice, capturing this advantage was nearly impossible at first, principally because of the burden of bad methods and procedures on the factory floor.

Initially, we were a little myopic about how far down the learning curve Vulcano actually stood. Then came the turning point, a blinding insight that was to determine Vulcano's strategic emphasis and character. It began with a lesson in humility. In 1982, we made a bid on a contract to supply the Bosch Group with finished heaters, confident that the bid would be accepted thanks to the buffer of the wage gap between Portugal and Germany.

Imagine our astonishment when the puzzled Germans wrote back saying they did not understand the ingredients of the bid, which had come out 40 percent higher than Bosch's costs of assembling the same items! Why this dramatic difference? the Germans asked. The explanation was simple. The Germans figured on fifty-seven minutes for assembly time, whereas Vulcano's workers took four times longer! Because of our inadequacy at the factory level, we had (for the moment) squandered our opportunity.

I immediately embarked on a productivity improvement project based on traditional manufacturing functional solutions, which led to a wide-ranging global hunt for best practices in production know-how. The search led to Masaaki Imai's book *Kaizen*, published in English in the mid-eighties. Imai describes continuous improvement concepts that are arguably the most influential set of management ideas to come out of Japan. *Kaizen*-consciousness is based on a group of values rooted in Japanese culture, such as self-realization, recognition of diverse abilities, and trust. These are values that lead to a strong belief that individual workers know better than anyone else how to interpret and improve their work, because they're the experts.

From this it follows that workers are encouraged to propose suggestions for improvements—no matter how small—that management then considers with great seriousness and implements wherever possible. Whereas many management ideas in the West have a magic-bullet quality and are based on hopes of a great leap forward, *kaizen* is just the opposite. It literally means "gradualist progress," which translates into "incremental innovation."

I held no less than thirty discussion and debating sessions on *kaizen* processes with my top managers. As they were increasingly exposed to these ideas, it became clear to them that *kaizen* had transcendent importance in manufacturing settings anywhere in the world. One of the appeals of this approach is that it is a powerful analytic tool for exposing inefficiency.

As practiced by Toyota, the five "whys" of *kaizen* were especially relevant to Vulcano's situation. When a problem arises, the first "why" is asked and a cause established. A second "why" questions the reasons behind the emergence of this first cause, and so on down through five deeper levels of "why." By peeling layers off the onion, the investigation proceeds from identifying the initial trouble to finding the ultimate source of the difficulty.

Another major Japanese insight that reverberated with Vulcano's top team was *muda*, or "waste." There are seven classes of *muda*: (1) overproduction, (2) waiting time at the machine, (3) waste in transport, (4) processing waste, (5) waste from excess inventory, (6) waste in motion, and (7) rejects.

This isn't the place to go into all the many facets of *kaizen* and *muda*. Suffice it to say that the whole Japanese approach was an eye-opener. It was an intellectual package that released a whole world of possibilities. I knew that if we applied those technologies intelligently, they'd be an "open sesame" to a leap forward in factory efficiency—perhaps giving us a platform that would one day support export sales.

Once Vulcano began to enjoy huge yields from *kaizen* and *muda*, a second important source of know-how also emerged from Japan: the Kawasaki Production System (KPS), a just-in-time (JIT) philosophy that had originated in the Kawasaki Heavy Industries group. These insights opened the floodgates of creativity and internal adaptation for our management team.

By 1983, we were in a position to bid successfully to supply the Bosch Group with heaters. By 1988, many years after the fifty-seven-minute bogey had been beaten, the Germans were sufficiently impressed with Vulcano's capabilities to buy equity control. And in 1994, Bosch made Vulcano its International Competence Center for this product. A score of Vulcano people have provided technical support and supervision for various Bosch Group projects in emerging markets in Turkey, North Africa, Latin America, and China. In fact, some 80 percent of the manufacturing equipment for the Chinese facility was designed and made in Portugal.

It is difficult to tell our story of continuous improvements and refinements to factory methods over more than a decade at the level of detail that it deserves. So let's zero in on a moment some three years ago when we completed a major surge forward in productivity. By this time, the old inadequate Vulcano was a thing of the past. We had become a world-class operation with productivity in high gear and significant export sales.

Yet there were recognized shortcomings in the final assembly area of the factory, which has five lines that integrate internally generated components with those from outside suppliers. During the final assembly the cover is assembled and the unit is tested and packaged. Several elements were unnecessarily adding to its costs. There was the rework required by defective components; slow response to the need for unscheduled components, which led to stoppages; and issues in various subassembly manufacturing operations—for instance, overinventory of pressed metal covers and other in-house components because of long setup times required by equipment or die changes. Then too the batch machining of the heater's combustion unit suffered from uneven workload distribution, large distances between workstations, and excessive waiting times between operations.

Enter the KPS method, which addressed each of these issues by introducing the maximum amount of flexibility and the elimination of heavy reliance on batch processing. Analysis showed that our past investments in automated production were inefficient because of the secondary costs they entailed. We scrapped them along with an automated subassembly line and warehouse.

Under the new method, we now test for defects in manufactured components immediately after they're completed, and we make them in much smaller batches. Result: Untested parts are no longer stored until final assembly when the discovery of defects would slow the line. The results have been a 50 percent reduction in setup times in the metal press and work-in-progress areas; and waste elimination and flow improvements in the final assembly area, which are yielding productivity increases in the 20 to 30 percent range. In addition, work in progress has been cut from nine to four hours between sub- and final assembly.

What's next? More of the same relentless drive to be a model of excellence. More of the same focus on basic building blocks of factory work. If we can keep this up, Vulcano will continue to grow and evolve, and we will also be able to pass on our knowledge to local managers in other companies. Who knows? Maybe one day a Portuguese manager will give the world supermarket of management ideas an item as powerful as *kaizen* and *muda* have proved to be.

5

An Agile Giant

Minoru Murofushi,
Itochu Corporation

In the last two years it has become fashionable to describe Japan's big trading conglomerates as organizationally obsolete and poorly adapted to the new global competitive climate. "To Western eyes, the sogo-shosha, *as they are known, seem prehistoric creatures. . . ." said* The Economist *on February 17, 1995. "They are the world's biggest jacks-of-all-trades, with, arguably, a corresponding inability to master any of them." Asian Business has observed that the* sogo-shosha *are often called lumbering dinosaurs destined for extinction.*

These uniquely Japanese institutions may be somewhat inscrutable to outsiders, but enough is visible to suggest a quite different picture. In fact, the sogo-shosha *often demonstrate a highly effective mixture of caution and entrepreneurial daring, of extreme diversification and yet very targeted strategies. If these are dinosaurs, then they are dinosaurs that can dance, and that are flexible and adaptive—as Itochu, one of the largest of the breed, amply demonstrates.*

One of Itochu's most striking characteristics is its size and multiple sources of revenues. Annual sales are over $120 billion, and come from over a thousand distinct subsidiaries employing more than ten thousand people who handle a cornucopia of different industrial and consumer products. Some of its major groups include textiles and foodstuffs, basic industries like iron and steel, forest products, machinery, aerospace, electronics, and construction. Its interests range from textile mills in Italy to steel mills in Australia, and from satellite broadcasting in Asia to investments in the Silicon Valley. Few other companies can boast such skills in the management of gigantic diversity around the globe.

But while a significant portion of Itochu's revenues stems from the traditional sogo-shosha role of being a low-margined trading intermediary,

Itochu is increasingly, in the words of The Economist, *"taking on risks and management challenges that might disturb even the most expansive of Western conglomerates." Itochu's bold willingness to make significant long-term investments in new pastures is dramatically manifest in three initiatives: (1) a massive and early commitment in the sixties to expansion in China that has created several hundred joint ventures there in glass, cardboard, clothing, trucks, beer, retail, and other areas; (2) leading-edge technology in the United States and Asia; (3) multimedia investments that will reach some $1 billion in fresh investment by the end of this decade. Itochu's portfolio in this area is already bulging with promise due to significant investments in Time Warner, communications satellites, cable TV, a rock-music channel, an Internet infrastructure for Southeast Asia, and mobile communications for controlling trucks, to name but a few.*

The chief architect of the restructured and redirected Itochu is President and CEO Minoru Murofushi. He has trimmed the ranks of middle management and undertaken a divestiture program for underperforming subsidiaries. He also initiated the drive for higher operating margins and rates of return. In the following interview he explains his strategy and his vision.

Price Waterhouse (PW): What is your vision and strategy for Itochu and the sogo-shosha in general, in the twenty-first century? As a result of the globalization of many of our industries, it is said that the value added by the traditional intermediate trading organization is deteriorating. Do you agree?

Minoru Murofushi (MM): The answer is yes, if you mean a business conducting traditional intermediate trading, complete with its own foreign language difficulties, cultural differences, and trading barriers. We have already begun steps to transform ourselves from that intermediate trader to a globally integrated business developer. However, as you know, since the beginning of the economic growth in Japan around 1960, and even today, Itochu and the *sogo-shosha* have been more than just intermediaries. We have carried out the role of business developers and organizers of the general flow of value across the business system.

For example, instead of simply intermediating steel material from the steel mill to the auto assembly maker, we have started to invest in iron ore and coal mining. And at the other end of the logistics chain we have invested in auto sales distributors' networks. So we have established positions along the entire business flow, from iron ore and coal mining, to steel mills, to auto assemblers, through auto sales distribution. Other areas where Itochu has developed global "value chain" integration include natural resources development, social infrastructure construction, and consumer products distribution.

In the next century, the paradigm of our global society will expand drastically—it exceeds our capacity to imagine what its shape will be. In this environment, "value exchange" will be a fundamental activity of human society. We at Itochu and the other *sogo-shosha* will add further value by organizing, integrating, and globalizing various new and dynamic business functions in the future. We will be able to contribute a great deal to this process thanks to our role as a facilitator, integrator, and organizer of capital and technology flows. The sum of this contribution will exceed the considerable social benefits that the *sogo-shosha* have yielded in the latter half of the twentieth century.

PW: *In your first year as the CEO at Itochu, you initiated what you have termed a "Corporate Identity" program: What was its purpose?*

MM: The Corporate Identity program had two goals. One was to transform our highly matured corporate culture into one that was much more challenging internally. Another purpose was to use the program to recall, learn from, and reaffirm Itochu's original highly entrepreneurial culture and mind-set. The overall goal of the Corporate Identity program is to help us push toward being a stronger and more capable developer of globally integrated businesses.

At the time the program was put into effect, our culture suffered from what I call "Big Organization Disease." In effect, it had a too-conservative, bureaucratic mind-set. As a result, some of our people tended to operate in an environment of intellectual comfort, to compete only in proven and mature markets rather than forging ahead into risky, unknown frontiers. Although traditionally Itochu has been one of the more aggressive *sogo-shosha*, we had to recognize that our initial corporate culture of risk taking, positive thinking, and self-motivation had been diluted. The culture needed to be revitalized and reinvigorated.

The heart of the identity program was a corporatewide envisioning of our environment and our business in the next century. This futurist perspective was designed to develop a globally integrated entrepreneurial network that was then shared among all employees. Discussions on how to specifically implement the vision in their daily activities were held around the corporation throughout a twelve-month period.

PW: *What were the results of this effort?*

MM: We developed new "action principles" that now guide and inspire individuals toward global entrepreneurship. Many employee workshops were conducted at all levels. Our challenge was to upset and reinvigorate the mind-set of every employee—from top to bottom.

These action principles include the ideals of YES, WE CAN—which is designed to challenge complacency; FIGHT FAIR—because we believe business integrity is an absolute; and BE OPEN-MINDED—so that we foster interactive creativity.

Our new credo was expressed by Itochu as: "Committed to the global good." And this provides direction to our people.

PW: *Do you evaluate the results of this cultural reengineering? And if so, how?*

MM: Although the goal of the Corporate Identity program was not oriented toward achieving short-term gains, it already seems to have influenced the spirit and actions of the firm. For instance, look at our recent business-development efforts in China, Southeast Asia, and in the multimedia industry. We've established more than two hundred subsidiaries in China alone since 1990. And our investments in the information technology industries have been further accelerated. Since October 1996 we have introduced PerfecTV, one hundred channels of JCSAT-3 Satellite TV broadcasting. So you see, we are beginning to harvest the reward from the effort we put into the Corporate Identity program.

PW: *Of all the ingredients of that program, which one is the most important?*

MM: Without question, the most critical part of the program is the effective development of our human resources. This is the key to realizing our vision. The difficulty, of course, is that nowhere is there an established "best practices" model to guide our management processes, our practices, and systems safely toward this new world. If I were to describe our new human resources model, it would picture an individual armed not only with a Western-style MBA but also with an Eastern-style networking mind-set combining the attitudes and behaviors that the Chinese call *Lao Pengyou.*

PW: *Would you describe* **Lao Pengyou** *a bit more?*

MM: When you visit China—a country that is sure to be an economic global giant in the twenty-first century—you are often asked, "Have you come for business or a long-term relationship?" A long-term friend is *Lao Pengyou.* It describes a partnership for life. *Lao Pengyou* is, of course, not unknown in the Western business culture. We understand that we must develop the human resources that succeed in both the Westernized business paradigm and in this *Lao Pengyou* network.

We have made internal progress toward building the resources to do so—including three hundred Mandarin-speaking Japanese staff in addition to our Chinese staff. One of the current leaders of our business in China has carried out his responsibilities for more than thirty-five years—even though through much of that period the Japanese government had frozen official relationships with China.

PW: *Having set these goals, what do you see as the next steps the company must take?*

MM: We will begin by developing a new human resources evaluation system. Then too there is a need for new training programs that are more in accordance with our vision for the future. So we will gather the best practices of global management and leadership models from both the West and the East.

We will simplify and segment our personnel into three categories: (1) entrepreneurs, (2) organizational management, and (3) specialists. We are also planning a two-dimensional system for personnel evaluation. It will segment competency and performance, values that have been mixed up and combined for a long time in Japanese society. We may also add a third dimension that reflects the strategic importance of the management target. The framework for our new human resources system is already in place, and our system reengineering has strong momentum.

6

BAJAJ: THE NEW FACE OF EMERGING MARKET COMPETITION

Rahul Bajaj,
Bajaj Auto Ltd.

Companies are going east and south and farther east in search of lower costs of production and new markets for their products. However, they are encountering strong domestic competition from local companies that know how to grow businesses in these countries. The CEOs of these domestic companies, such as Rahul Bajaj, chairman of India's Bajaj Auto Ltd., are laying the foundation for the new business leaders of the twenty-first century.

When Rahul Bajaj took charge of the company in 1968, it was a relatively small manufacturing concern employing five hundred people, with an annual production capacity of approximately twenty thousand two-wheeled vehicles. By the mid-eighties, that production figure had exploded to four hundred thousand units. Bajaj credits the quantum growth of his company to the ability of his team to focus; others cite his single-minded determination.

Educated at Harvard, Bajaj brought a different perspective to Indian industry. In the sixties, a time of substantial uncertainty in India, Bajaj saw beyond the constraints. He imagined a world-class company in his homeland because he had seen them in action in Europe and the United States. He understood the meaning of consumer needs and successfully adapted a European product—the scooter—for India, while also modernizing the traditional rickshaw into the three-wheeled vehicle that now populates the streets of not only India, but Thailand, Indonesia, and other countries.

One can debate the proportional mix of control, focus, and vision in Bajaj's corporate strategy, but the results are undeniable. In 1996, Bajaj Auto *employed twenty-two thousand people and produced over 1.3 million ve-hicles—forty-four and sixty-five times more, respectively, than when he began.*

Under Rahul Bajaj's firm control, Bajaj Auto has enjoyed market lead-ership in the two- and three-wheeled vehicle market for more than two decades. He squeezed out every ounce of opportunity his homeland of-fered in order to build this company, not only in the good times since the liberalization of India's economy in 1985, but also during the difficult years of government intervention in business. His legendary vision makes him look to the horizon, where he sees new challenges arising from foreign competition, and he is not content to rest on his current competitive ad-vantages. Neither are many of his peers.

THROUGHOUT HISTORY, EVERY COUNTRY that has enjoyed a period of economic growth and prosperity may look back thankfully to industrious individuals who pioneered new industries. They accumulated significant personal wealth as their reward for envisioning and pioneering future core industries. They were simultaneously revered, respected, and re-viled depending on whether one shared their vision or not. They left be-hind such things as affordable transportation, financing, and, more recently, computing. Their names are Ford, Toyota, Getty, Hughes, Morgan, and Gates.

No matter what one thinks of robber barons past or present, they cre-ated conditions that spawned competition and ultimately benefited the population. They saw a need and filled it, wringing every ounce of op-portunity from the marketplace. They took risks where others did not or could not.

However, as the United States, Europe, and Japan developed their economies, the risk takers gave way to caretakers more concerned with protection than creation. This has enabled the Asian tigers and other newly industrialized countries to rise, and has created a new handful of industrious individuals—emerging-markets CEOs—who see the future more clearly than most in the developed countries. The future they en-vision is a borderless economy made possible by advanced communica-tions reaching the farthest corners of the globe. They understand the needs of their markets because they have managed to create viable busi-nesses despite the bureaucratic stranglehold imposed for decades by their socialist governments.

These emerging-markets CEOs are more global in their outlook be-cause they are well traveled, and many have been educated abroad. Not many of the Western CEOs were educated in China, India, or the Soviet Union, but many emerging-markets CEOs earned degrees from top universities in Europe or the United States. This breadth of experience has gained them knowledge that their peers, both at home and abroad, lack. They understand the need to balance costs and growth, and their experiences have enabled them to find imaginative solutions to problems their colleagues in other industrial houses have not yet even identified.

As a result, companies like my own Bajaj Auto, which have become household names in their home countries and have enjoyed some export success, are well positioned to move abroad. To support this internationalization, more members of the next generation of emerging-markets executives are currently being educated in the top international business schools and world-class training organizations.

Most of my fellow CEOs from the emerging markets have a strong sense of national loyalty, reflected in their decisions to return to their home countries. Many of them go straight into family businesses, taking them from cottage industries to major industrial concerns. This marks them with an outward nationalism that many foreign investors mistake for stubborn pride at best, or stupidity at worst. However, their success gives them leadership standing in their communities. In return, they become patriarchal, bound by both nationalism and local tradition, which conflicts directly with their global outlooks. In short, the emerging-markets CEOs of today are caught between two worlds and are looking for ways to reconcile them.

Above all, these CEOs are realists and survivors. One capability that separates the leading-edge domestic CEOs from others is the ability to realistically assess and address critical business issues such as competition. Bajaj Auto is currently the leading low-cost producer, but that position is potentially threatened by a new crop of low-cost producers likely to emerge from China and Vietnam over the next five years. It would be folly to address these competitors in the same way as competitors from the United States, Japan, or Europe, so new strategies will be implemented long before the emerging competition can grab market share. Few international executives expect these CEOs to put theory into practice, but the CEOs are fully aware that the survival of their companies may depend on implementing such change, so they must be ready to make it happen.

Unfortunately, Western and Japanese businessmen are burdened with the legacies of their ancestors' early forays into the emerging markets. Revolutions in India at the beginning of this century, and in South Africa more recently, were reactions against annexation and the foreigner's attempt to replace the system with his own. The Americans have brought their own version of annexation in the form of corporate buyouts, demonstrating that they don't trust management if they don't own and control it. But in doing so, they lose the obvious benefits derived from local knowledge.

Successful joint ventures involving companies of different cultures provide an important model for managing relationships with emerging-markets CEOs. Centuries of experience have proven that lasting partnerships can only be built on collaboration and compromise for the mutual benefit of all the participants. An important facet of this collaboration is that no one culture dominates, and in fact the mutual activity fosters an entirely new culture within the organization. This requires a significant up-front investment in management time, but it can pay substantial dividends over many years into the future.

Yet, more often than not, this up-front investment is not made. In the emerging markets, unfortunately, many foreign incursions have resulted in the erosion of the personal relationships upon which the local business environments have been built. Local CEOs are fierce, smart competitors, and they have the advantage of local knowledge and personal networks.

Foreign business executives, however, rarely take the time needed to understand the rhythms and flows of social and business interaction, preferring instead to fly in and fly out again, demanding signatures on contracts in the shortest possible time. This kamikaze style creates an immediate clash with local customs. But rather than recognizing the root of the problem, these managers blame the local market and its lack of transparency when business relations break down.

While this lack of market transparency is a problem in varying degrees, merely blaming bureaucratic nontransparency is no solution. Failure to understand the difference between lack of communications and lack of transparency adversely affects relations between potential business allies, creating an environment of unmet expectations, distrust, and disrespect.

Naturally, this business style has created resistance from top-level emerging-markets CEOs who are unwilling to subject their companies to the intrusion and humiliation brought by foreigners—no matter how much they need the foreign investors' capital and technology. These CEOs respect the economic power of foreign multinationals, but they are no longer intimidated by it. They have often built their companies with their own skills and imagination, and they believe that on their own they can solve the problems of liquidity and technology. Thus, they will survive—and prosper—without paying the high price of involving foreigners.

These CEOs seek skills, technology, and market access. A foreign partner could help them attain the technological upgrades needed to improve quality, but local CEOs find that imported technology comes at the price of their independence. They believe that, ultimately, foreign partners are interested only in majority control, and any stake below 50 percent is equivalent to portfolio investment or being an employee.

Solutions lie in two areas: strategic alliances and the development of indigenous technology. Underlying both of these solutions is a new assertiveness not seen in the international business community since Japan made its move to world-class status in the seventies.

Strategic Alliances

Local CEOs are increasingly inclined to form strategic alliances. In Malaysia, for instance, the government investment agency, Khazanah Nasional, has built an entire industrial strategy around the strategic alliance. Through Khazanah, the Malaysian government hopes to form strategic links with foreign technology companies. The agency has already identified nearly twenty companies in Asia, Europe, and the United States able to supply important technologies, know-how, or strategic positions in key regional markets.

The emphasis on strategic alliances signals an interesting and important trend in the major emerging markets. No longer content to take a passive role in the development of their economic interests, companies are aggressively looking for opportunities outside their national borders, such as the recent acquisition of Lotus, the U.K. car manufacturer, by Proton, Malaysia's national automaker. Proton was less interested in adding a high-performance sports car to its product line than it was in importing the engineering talent Malaysia could not hope to produce for many years.

Developing Indigenous Technologies

As the pace of change in the international marketplace accelerates, local CEOs continue to study the big picture while they focus on their core businesses. They know that the major foreign companies that have invested in the emerging markets over the past decade have had difficulty competing locally because the cost of foreign inputs—particularly labor costs—are often more than twice what local producers pay. The local producers, however, are beginning to lose ground to foreign manufacturers at the top end of their markets; and as the growing middle classes of these countries acquire more discretionary income, this is a trend local manufacturers are anxious to reverse.

Currently, the foreign competitors' ability to meet customer needs is much faster, and their product range is much larger. At Bajaj Auto, it used to take about six years to develop and introduce a new product. We have reduced this to three and a half to four years. Nevertheless, at present, Suzuki or Honda can do it in approximately two years. Lack of technology and quality are the things that keep Bajaj Auto from becoming a Honda, or any other domestic manufacturer from becoming a world-class producer. Every employee in an emerging-markets company, from the CEO to the shop-floor workers, is at a disadvantage without modern know-how.

The development of indigenous technology has, therefore, become a high priority for maintaining market leadership. In their travels, the local CEOs have found small companies in the technology-rich environments of Japan, the United States, and Europe willing to explore alliances. This would enable the CEOs to import R&D talent to augment in-house capabilities. By combining in-house R&D abilities with international expertise, these companies can maintain their low-cost production advantage while upgrading their product. Right now, "Made in India" is a handicap, but thirty years ago, so was "Made in Japan."

With all of the domestic activity in emerging-markets countries, it may seem surprising that many of the CEOs actively plan to increase exports. But there are a number of reasons. Increased revenue is certainly one incentive. Another is to secure a middle-market-product brand based on quality and innovation to prepare for a future scenario in which these successful CEOs might lose their exceptional competitive advantage to the next generation of low-cost producers, such as China, Vietnam, and Taiwan.

Most importantly, foreign consumers provide useful information for product development, so exporting actually helps local producers improve their product's quality. In the emerging markets of India, Poland, or Mexico, local customers may ask manufacturers one question about their product; in Singapore, Britain, or Canada, customers ask ten questions. Every question gives the emerging-markets CEO another view of what needs to be done.

Executives from developed markets may still find short-term advantages in their kamikaze techniques—but not for long. The CEOs of emerging markets have built their companies profitably, and learning from the multinationals, they will take their competitive advantages into the global marketplace themselves, and soon. Their ability to create and maintain market share against world-class competition needs to be recognized. Their new, aggressive strategies signal a determination to take their place at the table. Failure to recognize the potential of these CEOs and to work with them as equals dramatically increases the chance that today's multinationals will become the new set of takeover opportunities in the next century.

RELATIONSHIP-BASED BUSINESS AND THE TRUST FACTOR

If, as we predict, Asians become front-rank business leaders of the future, CEOs in mature markets will find themselves doing business in a different style. Even the Japanese, who already rely heavily on personal relationships in their domestic business dealings, have been slow to improve their approach to their foreign collaborations. What is needed is the recognition of the actual role of personal relationships between businesspeople, in contrast to the current emphasis on the contractual correctness of an agreement. This is not to say that lawyers will lose their jobs, but legal issues may become secondary to the success of negotiations.

A great deal of learning must take place first. Emerging-market CEOs are generally comfortable in international settings, and they know what they have to do to drive their businesses globally. Therefore, international agreements are not difficult to achieve. However, these same executives already know how to drive their businesses locally, and these different modus operandi often confuse foreign business colleagues, leading them to the conclusion that the local executives are duplicitous. Local executives contend that this confusion does not occur among people who have taken the time to get to know one another.

Questions of "ethical behavior" must continue to be addressed in an open and collaborative forum. Each country subscribes to its own ethical standards as set out in its values and laws. Difficulties arise when one country tries to impose its ethical standards on another. But, increasingly, global CEOs are choosing to walk away from businesses that compromise their ethical standards. CEOs of successful multinational companies agree that there exists a set of values that cannot be compromised in a global sense, and that as more international collaboration takes place, people will naturally hold each other to this higher moral standard.

To become members of the global business community, emerging-markets CEOs must also subscribe to these standards, and this could have an interesting effect on their domestic markets. As reformist governments break down the bureaucracies that underpin corruption in many emerging markets, the importance of these CEOs as role models in their business communities will only grow.

7

THE NEW PHASE OF GLOBALIZATION

James J. Schiro,
Price Waterhouse

A funny thing happened to a number of large-scale professional service firms in the last decade: They went from being popularly thought of as old dowagers, out of touch with the times, to being perceived as models of organizational excellence. And why? Because of a simple concept: partnership. This old lady is the hottest thing in management structures these days. Just about every large corporation is seeking to demolish hierarchy and replace it with internal partnership organizations, nonhierarchic pools of talent that are speedy, responsive, flexible. Meanwhile, James Schiro, who became the eleventh chairman of the U.S. arm of the century-old Price Waterhouse partnership in 1994, is busy looking for ways to expand and enrich his firm's responses to the increasingly sophisticated demands of its blue chip customers. Outgoing and intensely competitive, the fifty-one-year-old Schiro passionately believes that partnering is the management paradigm for the next century. In this chapter he explains the basic advantages of partnership and demonstrates how the dynamics of partner power at Price Waterhouse will yield greater quality in service delivery and a richer intellectual product—all within a global framework. To further the development and delivery of integrated skills and services, in late 1997 Price Waterhouse announced its intention to merge with Coopers & Lybrand. Jim Schiro will serve as CEO of the new organization and Nicholas G. Moore of Coopers & Lybrand will serve as chairman.

MANY PARTICIPANTS IN THE global economy sense that its development has crossed an invisible threshold. There is a striking difference in the "feel" of business today, and in the organizational strategies that promise the greatest success, whether you are managing a worldwide company from headquarters in New York, Tokyo, or Rio. Lately, I have been asking myself what that difference is. At the same time, my colleagues and I have been reshaping our own organization to better serve our clients around the world in professional services. And I am well aware that our reading of the global environment and its demands must influence—and is influencing—our own change process. In this chapter, I will use the experience of Price Waterhouse and that of the professional services industry as a whole to explore the novel features of global business today and the strategies that seem to me best suited to this new environment.

Some people used to fear—and others eagerly anticipated—that globalization would lead to uniformity in consumer markets from Patagonia to Poland. This forecast turned out to be wrong. While some products have been successes around the world for decades and new waves of products have achieved this status, globalization has been accompanied by rising consumer expectations, proliferation in the number of product niches, and the creation of entirely new categories. We expected uniformity. What we are actually getting is more like the design of a complex city, with broad boulevards (global brands), and a multitude of distinctive neighborhoods, side streets, and suburbs (new niches, new categories).

This much is clear: In nearly every business, territorial representation (be it in 20 or 120 countries) is now merely a minimum qualification for becoming a global player. The real qualifications lie far beyond that. They include a new level of coordination among the units of an enterprise, embracing strategy, technology infrastructure, R&D, sourcing, manufacture, distribution, pricing, after-sales services, and cultivation of the customer. They also include the opposite virtue: better adaptation to local conditions than in the past, with all that this implies in terms of flexibility.

It is no longer a compelling point of pride to declare: "Our company has offices—or factories—in X countries worldwide." All the best competitors meet that mark, and so much more is expected. Genuine points of pride have to do with global coordination coupled with well-accepted local identities—the achievement of a global brand with satisfied and enthusiastic local buyers. This is hard enough for companies that manufacture and distribute products. It is harder still for companies that rely primarily on intellectual capital to produce valued solutions for clients.

It is also clear that the corporate provider of goods or services must bring to bear its full competitive muscle everywhere it operates in order to generate scale. A dominant position in just a handful of world markets is unlikely to last in today's environment. It must be supported by broad geographical representation and high market shares or it will quickly lose ground. Nor is a dominant position in the developed economies enough to guarantee long-term success.

A global player must span both the developed and less developed worlds, and manage the resulting complexities in such a way that the best technology, the best products, and the best management support are available in both. This is new, different, and unfamiliar. It means that the export of hand-me-down technology is as obsolete as the traditional view of overseas management assignments being out of the main career stream. Global companies that fail to attack any significant regional market with world-class skills and resources will soon find that competitors are stealing the march on them.

Just a few years ago our Price Waterhouse supply-chain consultants were concentrated in our largest regions. A robust practice could be built by helping clients focus on little more than the U.S. and European markets. Today, such a geographically limited deployment is inconceivable. We have to maintain a dynamic network of supply-chain experts from Zimbabwe to Singapore. We need seasoned professionals in Moscow who are completely aware of what the largest global retailers are asking of their suppliers. We need top people in Sydney who understand how the biggest consumer goods companies are facing off against their customers worldwide. In the global arena, nothing can buy insurance from competitive vulnerability except success that is continually reinvested in the struggle for more success.

In the face of this challenge, multinationals are exerting greater pressure every day on their suppliers—including service providers—to support their efforts with impressive expertise, equal scale, and coordination, dedication, and passion. In the list that follows, I offer an inventory of the most strategic capabilities that a professional services firm must have to be a strong player in this new environment:

1. *Delivering multiple disciplines locally.* Corporations once turned to professional service firms for very specific functions. In the past, multinationals might ask our firm to help craft strategies to minimize their effective global tax rate. To respond effectively to that need, we fielded creative, meticulous, international tax professionals. Today, the requests are altogether different. Clients want creativity, yes. They want ideas, yes. But, more important still, they want us to help them integrate and implement those ideas and

share in the resulting creation of value. Global companies now closely evaluate a supplier's depth and breadth of service capabilities—whether that "supplier" is a consulting firm like Price Waterhouse, an international bank, or a custom software designer. Clearly, multiple capabilities are winning out over stand-alone capabilities.

2. *Identifying and deploying winning project teams quickly.* Suppliers to global companies need to be sure of their speed of coordination. The ability to quickly assemble the right resources wherever required worldwide is a given in today's environment. Those resources typically include masters of distinct business disciplines; plus individuals who know how to get things done in a specific territory; plus the communications capabilities and other technological support needed to accomplish the mission. In all likelihood, the resulting team will be multinational and multiethnic in its composition because no other approach works as well. Global business today is dissolving harmful and unnecessary barriers between people.

3. *Building "integrative" skills in your people.* Too little attention is paid to the ultimate lever of knowledge in today's global organizations—the individuals who must integrate the analysis and information generated by the organization's knowledge networks. It is these integrators who must craft real-time solutions to today's most complex business problems.

However, too many professionals have a natural reluctance to share knowledge or to make the effort to "work" solutions with others who hold different views. Many such experts also lack tolerance for the kind of ambiguity our white-water business environment throws at those solving messy problems. Problems today demand deep technical and functional expertise—no question about that. But few major problems are solved without masterful, real-time integration of these skills.

Be wary of professionals who push the technique and theory of their disciplines to unworkable extremes, when what is needed is an effective synthesis of facts and ideas, a creative and resourceful resolution of seemingly conflicting concepts, a careful balance of theory and pragmatism, a blend of the rational and the political. And this often has to be achieved at great speed in today's frenetic world of work. The objective is the integration of the best ideas. The result is high performance in a chaotic environment.

4. *Providing one-stop shopping for global services.* Service providers increasingly face the imperative of offering one-stop global shop-

ping. They must be able to sell at a global level and present a single face to the customer even when offering services to be delivered worldwide. And they must have the capacity to execute those services market by market—with highly coordinated delivery.

Our consumer products manufacturing clients are being challenged by their largest customers to make goods available regardless of where they are inventoried. This necessitates making inventories around the world instantly visible to the managers serving those customers. And, just as important, the managers must be able to commit those inventories. At Price Waterhouse, we are no different. Our clients want their account executives to know, in real time, the full complement of Price Waterhouse resources, no matter where they are officed. And they want rapid access to those resources when needed. A tall order. But one we must address.

5. *Building—and periodically upgrading—communication and systems networks.* Internal management networks have become a primary determinant of success in global service businesses. The necessary balance between global coherence and local client service relies to a remarkable extent on networks. What earth and plow were to the farmer in olden times, the network and its software have become today—the basis of wealth creation. Global service firms with literally scores of specialties and many thousands of distributed experts compete to get there fastest with the most value for clients. And it is the network, in effect, that gets them there. Increasingly, as business expands, network capabilities must expand with it, despite the daunting price tag. Your success can outgrow your network: That is not a formula for sustained competitiveness. To develop business and serve clients, an E-mail address is now more important than a corner office.

6. *Cultivating powerful individuals within the organization.* The most important ingredient of a global business network cannot be expressed with diagrams and organizational charts. Just as a chain is as strong as its weakest link, so too is a network. Conversely, a network populated by individuals who have drive, imagination, experience, and insight will prevail over a better-designed network of less able, less aggressive practitioners. In the end, it is individuals who think, act, decide, produce, and serve customers. At a recent meeting of the World Economic Forum at Davos, Switzerland, Percy Barnevik, the chief executive of ABB, said, "Our people are allowed to make mistakes. What is not allowed is to be passive."

ABB operates one of the most evolved management networks on earth.

The greatest leaders in the decade ahead will set a vision for the whole that engages the many. They will understand the organization by knowing its people. And they will optimize performance in the aggregate by maximizing the potential of each.

The importance of the individual becomes evident when you examine organizations and teams that are effective and those that are not. You will find, for the most part, that ineffective organizations and impotent teams are brimming with dysfunctional individuals. The reverse is true as well—good people make good teams. Individuals in ineffective organizations often lack the peripheral vision required in today's globe-spanning "horizontal" organizations. They're simply unprepared for the level of social interaction required by the very different world in which we are all operating today.

THE NETWORKED PROFESSIONAL

Recognizing and rewarding effective entrepreneurial individuals requires nothing short of a culture change in many large service providers. Many years ago, Price Waterhouse would go to universities and recruit the best and the brightest, the most imaginative and creative people. Once they came to work, they were encouraged to become the world's best and most experienced technical accountants or tax advisors—but not necessarily encouraged to become thought leaders in their fields, or resourceful advisors to the companies they served in technical capacities.

Today, we support creativity and out-of-the-box thinking. We expect the technical skills. But we also regard that level of professional attainment as just the threshold to something far more valuable: men and women who are fully at home in global industries and are enormously effective in adding value to their clients' businesses above and beyond applications of their technical excellence. Price Waterhouse has adopted a massive culture-change program to cultivate this new professional profile as deeply and as swiftly as possible.

The networked professional in today's global professional services firm has more scope for achievement than at any time in the past. And the same is true of the networked executive in a manufacturing firm or financial services institution with worldwide operations.

THEN AND NOW

The need to achieve scale and effectiveness on a global basis presents an unending challenge. Never before in human history have the GDPs of emerging markets soared so high and for so long. Seeking a greater share of this wealth, large multinationals and their service providers must be prepared to grow at unprecedented rates. The failure of a global services firm to adapt to the growth imperative will swiftly lead to loss of credibility, owing to the hectic pace of change and loss of client "share of mind." The global prospects are great. The cost of failure is high.

At the beginning of this chapter I was reflecting on the difference between then and now. Then, we had a Cold War. We had great continental markets and nearly off-limits markets. We had political ideologies that shut down the natural entrepreneurial spirit of whole peoples. We had worldwide communications that seemed marvelous at the time, but now seem almost primitive in comparison to the intensive network of E-mail, fax, Internet and intranets, and cellular communications technologies that power today's global business.

Now we have a sense of open frontier. The world is finally almost whole, for the first time in history. Many of the formerly closed markets are open and needy. Multinational companies are evolving into global companies. And small- to mid-sized entrepreneurial companies are finding that outstanding services, products, pricing, and customer relations can command profitable niches without necessarily bringing them into mortal combat with daunting global competitors.

This is a much more attractive world that we find ourselves in today. But it is a hundred times more demanding, and it requires more skills, talents, and resources from all businesses, including my own, than ever before.

PART II
Radical Change

TURNING UP THE VOLUME

LEAF THROUGH SOME OLD *Fortune* magazines from the seventies and eighties and you'll probably come across many CEOs who are quoted on the "challenge of change." It might make you wonder if this change stuff isn't a needle stuck in a very old record. Actually, no. The fact is that current usage has a compound meaning. On the one hand, change in the old sense continues to apply to economic, political, technological, and demographic change—the view-from-the-bridge type of change. On the other hand, change has recently come to imply the kind of far-reaching organizational adaptation usually demanded and orchestrated by the CEO.

Although change-management initiatives are often disappointing—and the field gets its share of disenchanted criticism—competitive exigencies compel CEOs to try again and again to get it right. And even if the art or science of change management is still in its infancy, this won't stop the emergence of many more radical change programs in the coming years. Why? Because from where they sit, CEOs constantly feel frustrated by their organizations' missing out on too many opportunities as a result of rigid procedures and unimaginative decisions. They know too well the limits of power. The French novelist Honoré de Balzac once said that a bureaucracy "has the body of a giant but the brain of a pigmy." Change management in effect tries to increase the size of the corporate brain.

So ubiquitous have change-management programs become that "change fatigue" is now a common organizational complaint. The spread of change-management programs supports the thesis elaborated in this book's introduction that human behavior is increasingly the focus of CEO priorities. This observation is endorsed by Sumantra Goshal, professor of strategic leadership at the London Business School, who coauthored with Christopher Bartlett the influential *Harvard Business Review* article "From Strategy to Purpose" (November/December 1994). According to Goshal, there has been a decided shift in how top management sees its primary mission—moving away from structuring tasks to shaping behavior. And as CEOs have traveled this experience curve, they've gotten smarter and bolder. The bravest of them have pumped up the volume, advancing from the more modest goals of continuous change and renewal to the hazards and big payoffs of radical change.

So what is radical change, and how is it different? In our opinion, it has four defining characteristics:

1. *A CEO recognizes that his company's failures are systemic.* He then applies the levers of change on many fronts simultaneously

because the dysfunctions cannot be viewed and corrected in isolation. For example, the problem isn't just high manufacturing costs, or poor customer retention, or an arthritic internal bureaucracy—it's all of the above.

2. *Radical change demands deep top management involvement and exposure.* While single-dimensional change may be pursued in a relatively hands-off manner, this isn't true of radical change.

3. *Radical change efforts are bet-the-company deals.* They're also likely to bring to a head internal policy and strategy disputes, which may even result in the dismissal of senior executives who refuse to sign on—an event that can sometimes punish market capitalization in the short term.

4. *Radical change efforts cause most CEOs to undergo an initial period of self-doubt and heightened anxiety.* Understandably, the CEO doesn't want to be the one to unleash all the disruption that will ensue, and at the same time put his credibility on the line should the program fail to meet expectations. However much radical change programs strive to put on a gentle face, most contain an element of attack on all the fine people who've given so much of themselves for the good of the firm for so many years. Thus the CEO is under pressure to hit the ball out of the park. And if he doesn't, then maybe it's best to take early retirement and leave someone else to clean up the mess.

At all big organizations there's lots of noise and static in the air. Thousands of issues, problems, and situations clamor for attention—from product launches to organizational politics, from new information-technology systems to office relocation. There's never enough time, never enough data. A radical change program needs to find a way to lower the noise and get its share of the spotlight.

The Royal Dutch/Shell story in chapter eight is a good illustration of this point. It is an exemplary company, regarded by many as an outstanding practitioner of the best in modern management. Shell generates some of the best profits in its industry and demonstrates technical competence second to none. So how do you get Shell to change? Complacency was the number one enemy of Cor Herkströter, Shell's chairman. He identified three areas of focus and concentrated on them relentlessly. His targets were financial returns, the contribution of the corporate center, and the role and rights of management. He wasn't distracted by the plethora of possible alternative targets.

He succeeded by keeping well away from operating unit structure. He didn't meddle with manufacturing performance. He kept clear of R&D effectiveness. And he got attention for his agenda by keeping it short. By contrast, most change programs that fail are unfocused and overly ambitious.

Symbols are a big part of the radical change weaponry—new symbols versus old ones. They should be used judiciously. Programs that depend on T-shirts, mugs, and cartoon wall posters to keep the momentum and enthusiasm going may only convey superficiality. Apt symbolic communication, however, can be a great reinforcer. For instance, the goal of the Siemens change program discussed in chapter nine is designed to help its technologists relate to markets; to convey the idea that the company is not in existence to be a job provider for the German nation; and to convey the idea that productivity and profits must match the levels of its chief international rivals. As a symbolic gesture, Siemens has installed a stock market ticker at its Munich headquarters that continually flashes the up-to-the-minute price of its stock. A small thing, to be sure, but along with other symbols described in the chapter by CEO Dr. Heinrich von Pierer, it does underscore the company's identity as a capitalist institution—not a research foundation or an arm of the state.

The five narratives that follow offer the reader a rich and varied menu of insights into radical change. In chapter ten, speaking with the air of a veteran, Patrick Haren, CEO of Northern Ireland Electricity, offers a sophisticated assessment of the dos and don'ts of change efforts. Haren points to an area where change programs are the only option—industries that have lately been deregulated, or companies that have been privatized. Without change programs that drill deep down into the fabric of hidebound processes and operations, such firms will be unlikely to withstand the rigors of the marketplace.

Considering the overhang of state or quasi-state enterprises still in existence around the world and much in need of privatization, radical change management programs have a bright future. Furthermore, they have made big inroads into the noncorporate sector. In chapter twelve, you'll read how the Veterans' Health Administration executed one of the biggest change programs ever seen in Washington, D.C.

A no less daunting challenge was faced by Serge Tchuruk, CEO of one of the biggest and messiest conglomerates in Europe—scandal-tainted Alcatel Alsthom. Its turnover of more than 160 billion French francs was spread over nine hundred different legal entities—including telephone switching gear, high-speed trains, and transoceanic cables—plus a raft of minority interests, including automobiles and publishing. In just two years on the job he has rationalized many of the businesses, shed most of the minority interests, gotten rid of thousands of jobs, and turned a massive loss into profits. Of Tchuruk's regime, one Paris security analyst has said: "The engine is getting under steam again, and the performance is getting better and better." In chapter eleven, Tchuruk unveils the ideas that drove the first phase of his radical makeover of Alcatel.

External crises or hemorrhaging red ink make it easy to justify radical change initiatives. But what of the case of a CEO who sees the need for a preemptive strike, who demands change when there are few compelling externalities? Shell CEO Herkströter is one of the exponents of this increasingly prevalent tactic—the anticipatory initiative. Such efforts look beyond the comfort zones of present success and radically improve an organization's fitness for future battle. This approach is the product of today's relentlessly competitive environment, which has become the breeding ground of radical change projects. A further source is the dilution of the strong national character of many firms, and the compulsion to measure up to world-class benchmarks.

There is yet another important aspect of change efforts. There should be closure—perhaps a farewell party with champagne. Radical change is extremely stressful, and if it is prolonged, it will sap people's energy and detract from their day-to-day responsibilities. If the company subsequently runs a few plain-vanilla change efforts in some department or subsidiary, that's fine. But another full-court press could be the last straw.

Skeptics of radical change programs might want to consider the outcome of the main phases of the change programs described in this section. British Aerospace's stock price more than tripled; Shell's also soared; and Siemens remained profitable despite massive sales price declines on hundreds of key products. Northern Ireland Electricity has also had a huge upswing in market capitalization, and Alcatel too. And lastly, the Veterans' Health Administration registered a big improvement in cost-benefit measures, as well as in quality and depth of service.

FIVE MYTHS OF CHANGE MANAGEMENT

With tens of thousands of managers, academics, and consultants around the world engaged in change programs of one kind or another, a number of ideas about the field have gained wide circulation. However, many of them are simply myths.

Myth One: Change management is about envisaging the future of the organization in some detail and then working out how to get there. That's fine if the environment is stable and predictable. But most highly competitive environments are mined with discontinuities and surprises. So it simply isn't helpful for a CEO to adopt the "climb a mountain, see into the distance, and come down with the tablets of stone" approach. In the real world, the volatilities are just too high. There is no stable vantage point. More often, what is needed is a platform of capabilities that can be deployed with flexibility as opportunities emerge.

The British Aerospace story in chapter thirteen is an outstanding example of radical change focused on the creation of "platform-based competitive strategies." Imagine you're in the shoes of Sir Richard Evans, CEO of British Aerospace. Your company has shrunk from close to a hundred thousand employees to under fifty thousand in three years—partly by downsizing, and partly through efficiency measures. The end of the Cold War has put a jinx on defense expenditures. U.S.-based competitors are merging at a frenzied pace, and the European governments are increasingly talking about consolidation of their defense industries. Your company already has many joint ventures and is actively pursuing still more.

In these circumstances would you attempt to identify a concrete goal that would define your business in ten or even five years' time? Not a chance! However, what you can do is focus on the capabilities that will enable you to compete in whatever market circumstances may arise—a platform for all seasons.

Myth Two: Good change management is built on good detailed analysis. Many experts in change management want to get all their ducks lined up in advance. But the dangers of "analysis paralysis" are real. We believe the 80/20 rule applies in most cases: That is to say, 80 percent of the benefits of a radical change program can be obtained from 20 percent of the analysis. Increasingly, change programs have to respond to the need for time compression. Strong momentum is a good defense against inertia.

Myth Three: First decide business strategy, then align the culture with radical change. Intellectually this may be a fine idea. Unfortunately, business strategies typically work on a one- to three-year cycle, but changing corporate values and culture may take between five and fifteen years. It can only be shortened with drastic measures—such as firing two-thirds of the top echelon—a course of action that would be too damaging in most cases.

Myth Four: People will resist change if there is nothing in it for them. But a change program that sticks its head in the sand over pain/gain issues is doomed to failure. In fact, many change managers have learned to respect workers' capacity to understand the case for change, even when they're not its beneficiaries. The legitimacy of a radical change program depends on everyone in the organization's being exposed to the facts, with candor, whether the news is bad or good.

Myth Five: To effect positive change, the CEO must win the hearts and minds of employees with broad-gauged communications programs, focus groups, videos, newsletters, and so on. Again, this may be a desirable goal, but its pursuit is both expensive and time-consuming. The accepted view is that radical change requires consensus, but this rarely occurs. In practice, the CEO needs to go the extra mile to win over the one-fifth of the people in the organization who are held in highest esteem—executives, union leaders, opinion leaders, and rainmakers who bring in a lot of revenue. These are the people who represent the organization's "will to act."

8

ROYAL DUTCH/SHELL: REWRITING THE CONTRACTS

Cor Herkströter, Royal Dutch/Shell Group of Companies

Royal Dutch/Shell (referred to here as Shell) long enjoyed the reputation of being one of the most admired corporations in the world, boasting a model federation of decentralized operating companies. There was only one thing wrong with this image: It was false. Inside the company many in the leadership complained of an introverted, bureaucratic culture. Under its matrix system an operating manager could have as many as three superiors—a country boss, a functional chief, and a business unit leader—which diluted accountability. Another critical perception was that at Shell the center didn't manage. Rather, it "coordinated"—at the cost of considerable delays in decision making.

There were, to be sure, defenders of the Shell organizational style who argued that the advantages outweighed the disadvantages. Besides, why fix what isn't broken? Shell had an excellent financial record. Total revenues were marginally below those of rival Exxon, but total profits were the highest of any oil company. Eventually, those who argued the case for change won out in the group's councils, and Dutch national Cor Herkströter, chairman of the Committee of Managing Directors at the Shell Group of Companies, was made standard-bearer of the streamlining—an awesome undertaking.

Shell is not the only one of the Seven Sisters to restructure of late. But the depth and sweep of Herkströter's changes far exceed those of its peers. For example, in one of Shell's businesses, seven or eight layers of management were cut to three, geographical reporting was abolished, and all units are now measured by business results. In addition, decision times have speeded up enormously. In some cases, decisions that previously took a month and a committee of twenty people to get through now need only one person and one day.

Seldom in the history of business has a huge corporate bureaucracy undergone this kind of redirection, reorganization, and shift of corporate culture and psychology on such a scale and at such speed.

EVERYONE KNOWS THE HANS Christian Andersen tale about the "Emperor's New Clothes." If you'll remember, none of the emperor's court or subjects was willing to tell him the truth about his nakedness. The story we're about to tell begins in a similar fashion, but it has a very different ending. For in the case of Shell, the emperor himself (and a few of his cleverer subjects) actually did see the embarrassing truth and corrected the mistake.

In the case of this big, complex corporation, the "mistakes" were deeply embedded in the organization and not easy to identify or repair with quick fixes. One way of describing the change process at Shell is to start with top management's role in the group's key relationships, or "contracts." Three of these contracts were the source of Shell's difficulties. It was by deconstructing and revising them that the sought-for transformation was achieved.

The behavior of companies is influenced by a number of informal understandings, or company "culture," that govern the relationships of people within the organization and between the organization and the outside world. Changing employee behavior at Shell first meant changing the company's culture. This also meant changing our contract so a combination of external events, as well as an internally generated need for new approaches and practices, spotlighted the three contracts where Shell's performance was unsatisfactory:

- *The contract with investors* suffered from the perception among oil analysts that management performance was lagging, particularly in the key measure of return on net assets.
- *The corporate center's contract* with the operating units was flawed. The center felt it wasn't effectively driving and inspiring the operating companies to make badly needed improvements, from production costs to increased customer satisfaction.
- *The contract with managers* sent the wrong signals. It was freighted with old assumptions about lifelong job guarantees and expected routes of promotion and compensation.

Any one of these challenges would be monumental in a group of companies with more than a hundred thousand employees, operations in over 120 countries, and an average daily cash flow of more than 25 million British pounds. Yet, in essence, our challenge was no different than those faced by managers in much smaller companies—discarding what is no longer relevant and carefully crafting new modes of thought and action.

THE *OLD* INVESTOR CONTRACT

As might be expected with such an economic powerhouse, Shell has been an old favorite of institutional investors. However, in the early nineties, oil analysts began complaining that while our profits were growing year by year, the group's investment base was growing even faster. Result: Shareholder returns on net assets were well below those of our competitors. Analysts insisted that we present them with a plan to reverse this trend. They also insisted on a new plan for replacing dwindling oil reserves. While Shell's replacement ratio was effective, it was not the best in the industry. However, although these same issues had been raised and keenly debated by our Committee of Managing Directors, the main body of the organization had refused to see that a crisis was imminent.

THE *NEW* INVESTOR CONTRACT

The Committee of Managing Directors realized that if Shell was going to meet the demands of the investment community, we were going to have to change our ways—and fast. We decided to spell out an entirely new set of performance targets: Overall the Shell Group would aim for an aggregated figure of 12 percent return on average capital employed (a fifth higher than the average of the last five years). In addition, since some business lines were mature, they had to hit the 15 percent return on average capital employed.

To reach these goals, divisional managers were told to forget past return standards—simply downsizing to lower costs wasn't enough. It was now imperative to improve cycle times as well as speed-to-market and productivity gains. However, the overriding imperative for all Shell units was growing the business through gains in market share.

Even in mature businesses, the managerial tactic of milking a profitable asset for a few years and then moving on was no longer acceptable. It was now clear that our overall profitability targets could only be achieved through a growth in unit volumes—either through market share gains or through increased production profitability. This sent a shock wave throughout the entire system. Never before had Shell managers been told that they had to improve profits *and* go for growth at the same time!

The *Old* Contract with the Operating Units

For at least three decades Shell had functioned through a matrix organization. The goal of this form is to capture the dynamics of knowledge and cooperation within the firm. In our case, it was a tripartite matrix, reflecting cross-relationships and linkages between functions, business locations, and lines of business around the globe. But while the matrix did indeed capture important facets of how our business was conducted, it came with a huge price tag in administration and coordination. These, in turn, slowed the decision-making process to a crawl and made Shell less than nimble in the marketplace.

One of the drawbacks of our matrix was that central services lacked credibility, while the central authority lacked authenticity. On top of this, the cost of maintaining these functions fell on the shoulders of the business units, which had no say about the effectiveness of those services. Along with its fiats, the central office blithely continued to present operating managers with a higher bill every year to cover mounting costs.

There were clear signs that the organization was drifting apart. It became painfully apparent when our top fifty managers met as a group for the first time to thrash out organizational issues. Many sharply questioned the value of maintaining the central office. Meanwhile, the Committee of Managing Directors was making things worse by bearing down on the performance of the business units. The situation was ripe for discord.

The continued existence of the center was no peripheral issue. It employed over three thousand people, many of them among the highest paid in the group. And its costs had become increasingly disproportionate—particularly in view of the business units' opinion of its value. But the real heart of the matter lay in the center's effectiveness, not its cost. It was seen as difficult, slow, and cumbersome by the operating units. Many believed that if a real problem arose in your operating company, the last place you'd go for help was the central office. It would only tie you up in interminable red tape and bring action to a halt.

THE *NEW* CONTRACT WITH THE OPERATING UNITS

What is truly interesting about our company is that no discord erupted. Instead, those of us at the center as well as at the unit level recognized that both areas required serious transformation. After all, the central office and the companies shared the same needs: less bureaucracy, less duplication of effort, and more individual responsibility, including a clearer reward structure for individual contributions.

I realized, as did the other managing directors, that we had to change our contract with the entire organization if the reforms were to succeed. The central office could no longer remain an ivory tower, aloof from the fray. To improve accountability, our first move was to abolish the old functions/area/operations matrix. Instead, the key responsibility for lines of business was placed in the hands of senior operating managers, working together in "business committees." Departments and regions became history. The chairman of each business committee is now in direct touch with me and the Committee of Managing Directors, and we are now close to the action.

Next, we developed a brand-new structure for the center. The fact that it had always worn two hats was now formally reflected in its charter for the first time. Its primary role was defined as corporate governance, control, and standards—the glue that holds any dynamic organization together. To fulfill this role, a new "Corporate Center" was created. Limited to no more than 150 people, this unit assists the Committee of Managing Directors in guiding and directing the operating units. It is made up of small teams of experts from Treasury, Human Resources, Legal, Planning, Environmental and External Affairs, Financial, and Business Strategy.

The second hat the center wears is quite different. This one is concerned with securing economies of scale in the provision of cross-business-unit services. Since it is clearly uneconomical for each business unit to provide its own full range of information-technology services, transaction accounting, training and management development, and the like, these functions and others were reborn as "Professional Services Units." Each function is now a distinct unit that charges for its services, and regularly benchmarks its effectiveness against external providers.

Defining these roles served two purposes. First it allowed us to take a cold, hard look at the areas where costs outstripped their value to the business. Even more importantly, it clarified power relationships. It now became obvious to everyone that while a small part of the center played a critical role in guiding the various businesses, by far the largest part worked for—not above—the operating units.

THE *OLD* CONTRACT WITH MANAGERS

The old Shell contract with managers was fairly benign. Performance expectations imposed on individuals were far from demanding. Only rank incompetence was punished, while mediocrity was shunted aside and tolerated. There were few formal job covenants, but there was an informal understanding that almost everyone could climb the career ladder through automatic advances.

In short, the old Shell had fostered a culture of security—one in which corporate objectives and individual rewards were unrelated to each other. At the same time, guidance and communication came down like the Ten Commandments from Mount Sinai.

THE *NEW* CONTRACT WITH MANAGERS

We faced the challenge of creating and stimulating change that would add value. In our new contract we proposed:

- Shocking changes in the old system of security
- New objectives tied to new rewards
- Structural changes linked to new purposes
- Communication as an instrument of change
- Positive leadership from the top

By far the most difficult thing for Shell people to absorb was the abrupt loss of the guarantee of employment for life. At Shell today no one, no matter how senior, has a job contract that runs to retirement. This created an uproar that is still echoing throughout the organization.

As lifetime employment vanished, so did the key elements of job security. Appropriately, this transformation began at the top, where the hundred leading jobs were reconfigured. No one in the central organization will remain in his or her present job for more than three or four years. Senior people must then rotate to similar positions elsewhere in the organization—perhaps in the operating companies. The enforcement principle is clear: Either people adopt these new behaviors or their future with the organization is threatened.

New objectives tied to new rewards go hand in hand with the very clear accountabilities and responsibilities managers are now carrying. They also dovetail with the changed performance indicators for each business. Under the old contract, excellence (or the reverse) barely affected remuneration. Under the new one, managers have a powerful incentive to get fully involved in continuous improvement. This is due to another innovation for Shell—variable pay. Managers must now focus on achieving higher performance targets, with return on capital as their overarching goal.

Our most dramatic reform was the abolition of the role of coordinator, along with its functions of oversight and liaison. Under the new contract, managers have to accept these increased responsibilities themselves. With the abolition of so many administrative layers, there's less scope for vertical promotion. But people can still grow with Shell in the future as in the past; it's simply more likely to occur within a particular discipline or at different locations. The rotating membership of the senior business committees is also playing a powerful role in spurring the evolution of Shell's culture.

Since clear communication is an essential instrument of change, we have invested heavily in proclaiming the new order and making certain that it is understood in all quarters. The communication process began from Day One.

At least once a month, I personally lunch with younger managers, who are free to raise any topic. At first, there was a lot of confrontation as managers came face-to-face with the new cultural approach. It directly challenged our time-honored contractual principles—including the old unwritten law that "in Shell, you never hear about mistakes."

Another key part of the communication program was designed to deal with the necessary downsizing, since the new reformed Shell would need 30 percent fewer employees at Corporate Center. The managing directors and I expected negative reactions. But our announcement was seen as honest and forthcoming, and this helped produce a constructive outcome.

All of Shell's senior executives feel it is imperative for us to act as positive role models in the group's culture change. I took an unprecedented step in demonstrating commitment to the change process by personally telling people about the new reforms and the effect these moves would have on their lives. My gamble paid off. The new openness and candor spread like wildfire throughout the organization. Since then I have spent at least half a day a week making an unannounced visit to a company facility to personally check on how the change program is faring, and to communicate directly with Shell's people.

THE WAY AHEAD

The process of change at Shell is far from complete. It has only been operational for two years, and parts of the program are still new in some segments. It will take a few more years before we reach the return on average capital employed that our contract with investors promises. Nevertheless, that community now views Shell as a company that has banished complacence and is running hard.

The second and third contracts dealing with power sharing, responsibility, and the careful management of human resources are now firmly established within Shell's new corporate culture. And the best news of all is that, as culture shock abates, anxiety is being replaced with a high level of enthusiasm, drive, and commitment.

9

CHANGING SUPERTANKERS INTO SPEEDBOATS

Dr. Heinrich von Pierer, Siemens A.G.

For sheer technological muscle there are few companies in the same league as Siemens. In electronics and electrical equipment, its sales just trail the three behemoths of the industry, Hitachi, Matsushita, and General Electric. But in terms of R&D, its outlays are greater than all global corporations except General Motors and IBM. A global innovation survey by CHI Research has placed Siemens in the top twenty-five of two hundred companies measured on three critical counts: (1) the number of U.S. patents awarded, (2) the relative frequency with which patents get cited in the literature, and (3) the median age of patents.

However, it cannot be said that Siemens has recently been wonderful at translating research into profits. While its returns on sales and assets compare favorably with Japanese companies, they lag behind the likes of General Electric and Motorola. Reversing this state of affairs is the central preoccupation of CEO Dr. Heinrich von Pierer, a former lawyer who won his spurs in the power plant business. He is masterminding the makeover of a company whose past successes have made it rigid, overly bureaucratic, and excessively proud. This chapter describes his methods and the progress to date.

A BIG CORPORATION BEARS a strong resemblance to a supertanker or an aircraft carrier. In both cases the captain finds that shifting directions and changing strategic course is a slow and cumbersome process. Today's increasing competitive pressures are not forgiving to the superships of the corporate world, who must transform themselves into a flotilla of high-speed motorboats with all the maneuverability needed to react to the twists and turns of the market and shifts in customer preferences.

Our efforts to mutate in this direction at Siemens have meant modifying many of our old monolithic features—carryovers from a time when scale, plus a massive scientific infrastructure, were much more of a competitive advantage than they are today. At Siemens we are now attempting to combine the benefits of size with nimbleness, flexibility, and responsiveness to change. It is a transformation that must be viewed against the backdrop of the conservative German sociopolitical climate, which imposes more economic restraints and social obligations on large employers than is the case in most other countries. Within this context, the bold and radical changes we are making at Siemens are surging through a vast and diversified organization, and they're already beginning to yield productivity gains.

It all began eight years ago when we shifted to a more decentralized organization—moving from a functional "stovepipe" structure for R&D, production, sales and marketing, to a more vertical form, where each one of some 250 businesses incorporates those functions and performs them autonomously. The resulting release of energies has been sweeping. Cycle times, time-to-market, costs, productivity, and customer service all improved dramatically.

But I soon realized that these advances didn't go far enough. It became clear that Siemens' people had to be stimulated to think differently and behave differently than they had in the past. It was imperative that they develop a mind-set more focused on markets and profit-making. But for this to happen, we had to introduce more flexibility and personal initiative in the workplace. We had to find a way to release our vast, untapped reservoirs of human potential and creativity. And we had to encourage entrepreneurialism and suppress bureaucracy.

To be candid, in the past Siemens' people sometimes acted as if profit were a by-product of the company, not its central raison d'être. This was particularly true in the area of research and innovation where the emphasis was on discovery, with too little focus on whether these discoveries were exactly what the market required. To address these issues, three years ago the "*top* program" was born. *Top* is an acronym for "time-optimized process." This was not a culture-change program directed from the top with a lot of fanfare and big programmatic goals. Rather, it was a small seed, designed (if the experiment succeeded) to evolve as we felt our way and tested, validated, and refined it.

Top is unique because it springs out of the bedrock of Siemens' character. It seeks to generate new and more effective managerial behavior, reinforced by concrete, measurable results. It is aimed at breaking up old corporate mind-sets about "the way we do things here," and at stimulating personnel at all levels to seek out new processes, procedures, and pathways in their minds. It is also aimed at improving our collective sense of identity, and eliminating the rivalry—and sometimes arrogance—that led to poor cooperation between departments.

The *top* program is holistic and multidisciplinary, and it has been evolving one step at a time—slowly gaining legitimacy within the company. The term "time-optimized process" was initially chosen to underline the necessity for the speed-up of all processes and to optimize their efficiency. And the double meaning of *top* exactly expressed management's purpose—to make Siemens top, preeminent in all respects, not only in the number of its inventions.

The name of the program—like the little *top* lapel badges that all Siemens' people wear, from myself on down—provides something more; it's a rallying point for change, a goal to be aspired to. *Top* consists of three main elements: productivity, innovation, and growth. The basis and engine for all of them is culture change. Here Siemens seeks far-reaching reforms in four primary areas: (1) reducing hierarchy, (2) altering management style, (3) improving communications, and (4) demanding more interaction with and feedback from customers. However, we knew that a program this far-reaching couldn't fly without the full commitment of the powerful labor representatives at Siemens. It was after considerable discussion and debate that the Siemens' Works Council in Germany eventually endorsed the program.

Speedboats and big hierarchies don't mix. Thus the *top* program led to a shrinkage in the company's chain of command as the levels in the hierarchy were reduced dramatically. More importantly, *top* undercut the importance placed on rank and title, and the automatic esteem they generated. One of our boldest moves was to abolish titles in the German units—a signal that respect must be earned by peer recognition, not by the title on the door.

Big compensation changes, starting in the winter of 1996–97, further influenced changes in our style of management. The old policy of automatic annual pay raises has been scrapped. Instead, thirty thousand managers now work to fulfill the terms of their individual contracts, and they receive bonus payments depending on how effectively their predetermined goals have been met.

Performance and appropriate salaries will be assessed under a new appraisal system. Where subordinates were previously evaluated annually by their bosses, for the first time in company history the superiors will also be evaluated by those under them. They will be judged on the basis of goals, motivation, initiative, and other parameters. Upon receiving subordinates' assessments, a supervisor has to write up a plan of action and present a timetable for remedying the points of criticism.

This approach runs so counter to German culture that some managers found it a real challenge to be assessed by underlings. This was also true of the elimination of seniority-driven "career escalators," and the substitution of broad-banded pay arrangements. To obtain a significant promotion, an executive now has to make a strong value-added case for the move.

Although some of these measures might not seem radical in the United States, in Germany they are a revolutionary departure from the old norms. At Siemens we have gone farther down the road of pay-for-performance than any other large German employer, just as we have done by doing away with the culture of overorganization and relentless control. Siemens has also altered its criteria for manager selection and advancement. The importance of scientific and technical qualifications has been downgraded, and social skills, the ability to motivate people creatively, and international experience are being given much greater value than before.

Top has had an enormous impact on Siemens' internal and external candor and openness. For instance, the profit-and-loss data of a business unit used to be a closely guarded secret. It was feared that the information could become a competitive drawback in the hands of customers and competitors. But under *top*, this perception was stood on its head. It became clear that openness in this area would improve the linkage between worker behavior and economic results. This was especially true for a unit running in the red, since this information put urgent pressure on managers and workers to find remedies quickly.

As a result of this policy, Siemens now has greater earnings transparency, and more detailed lines-of-business reporting than any of its domestic or international rivals. The company's annual report provides information on all seventeen business units, complete with figures for new orders, sales, and income. This is very rare in any major company, let alone a German one. In a similar vein, the company's *Siemens World*, a publication that a year ago expressed only the management line, now also carries highly critical employee comments.

In order to obtain higher yields from its enormous technical and scientific prowess, we are placing new emphasis on links to the customer. In many cases this has meant involving the customer in development work. For example, the medical group's often brilliant inventions had been much too expensive for everyday diagnosis and had thus failed to generate enough sales. However, thanks to the new approach, the focus and effectiveness of the group's R&D has improved.

We are transforming the overall Siemens culture from that of an engineering-led company to a knowledge-based business in which accountability to customers is fundamental and pervasive. Operations follow a strict design-to-cost approach: The customer, not Siemens, defines the optimal time of market entry, the product features, and the price parameters.

In the last three years the reach of *top*'s objectives has been considerably expanded. *Top* now has four main branches, designed to create permanent profit improvements in four ways: increased productivity, speeded-up innovation, geographic and product expansion, and corporate culture change. At the same time there have also been some notable triumphs attributable to *top*: (1) a more than 20 percent gain in cost productivity, (2) a surge of innovation as inventions doubled to more than five thousand, and (3) major revenue gains in the Asia-Pacific Rim market. The latter are an important indication that our goal in transforming Siemens from a mostly German to a full-fledged international company is progressing. To further this success, English has been made the second official language of Siemens.

One of the ubiquitous changes wrought by *top* is the removal of the old buffers—some visible, some not—between individuals and the profit imperative. For instance, cross-subsidization was long practiced at Siemens, where funds from a rich division would be levied to support a less profitable one. Although there are clearly cases where this makes sense, it became a practice that diluted accountability and made rigorous scorekeeping impossible. What's more, it didn't always lead to appropriate resource allocation, since some of the subsidized units actually deserved to fail or be divested.

Top's transformations are far from over at Siemens. The process is open-ended in both content and timetables. Yet, at a moment when we are celebrating our 150th birthday, these recent changes need to be viewed in the context of its long history. One way or another, Siemens has always managed to stay attuned to our environment.

10

CONJECTURES ON CHANGE: A LETTER TO THE CEO

Patrick Haren, Northern Ireland Electricity

Northern Ireland Electricity (NIE) is the regional electricity supplier and operator of the transmission and distribution networks servicing 655,000 customers in Northern Ireland. It is Northern Ireland's second largest listed company and among the top ten employers.

Patrick Haren has been chief executive of NIE since April 1992, and was responsible for taking the company through privatization. Before joining NIE, he held various senior managerial posts with the Electricity Supply Board, Ireland, including board-level responsibility for engineering consultancy in the U.S. and U.K. markets, as well as for international financial services. Haren has a wide experience of the electric utility industry, and in his early career established an international profile through CIGRE, the international conference of large utilities based in Paris.

THERE IS AN APOCRYPHAL story of a newly appointed CEO who is handed three sealed letters containing advice from the previous incumbent. He is asked to open them in turn, but only when faced with a crisis. The first crisis comes, rather too quickly, and tearing open the first letter, the CEO finds the advice, "Blame your predecessor." This he does, and the crisis subsides. Some months later, a second crisis arises, and the contents of the second letter suggest that he "announce a strategic review." Disaster is again averted. Before too long a third crisis of epic proportions arises. The final note suggests that he "prepare three envelopes."

Today's CEOs are faced, if not with crisis, then with the challenge of transforming business performance—and often the business itself. The challenge arises in response to shifting expectations on the part of customers, the attentions of competitors, and the requirements of shareholders. Stewardship of the status quo, blame laying, or even a comfortable exit are no longer serious options for serious people. Rather, action and results are required, and these are often driven by a change program—a way of concentrating effort, communicating ideas, deepening impact, speeding progress, and sustaining positive outcomes. Corporations also appear to be using a greater proportion of organizational resources to support change.

So, in this context, what more positive advice might the envelopes contain for a latter-day CEO? I suggest looking at two important areas: first, the issues to consider at inception, when constructing a change program; and second, how the actions of the CEO can best support the endeavor.

AT INCEPTION

Initiating a change program is often a lonely task. It usually falls to the CEO and a few trusted colleagues and advisors. It is here that the shape of change, its form and style, are cast. Here are some thoughts and experiences in six key areas that might be valuable:

- *The case for change* is normally considered at inception, but too often it is articulated in terms of the tools we use to improve organizational performance. We aim to restructure, to empower, to delayer, to reorganize, to reengineer, to downsize, to become a learning organization, and so on. These tools can be important facilitating mechanisms on the pathway to performance improvement, but it is confusing to have means masquerading as ends. Tools for change should be measured in terms of their impact on business outcomes, not as ends in themselves. And without a clear definition of the desired performance outcomes, the many tools of change will merely be blunt instruments.
- *Setting the scope for change* and making it sufficiently operational—rather than remaining a prisoner of concepts—demands structure and precision sustained across the breadth of the organization. Where the scale of the chart is too small, more detail is required in order to navigate. Creating an operational blueprint of the vision is a prerequisite for action—a composite picture of the na-

ture of change required in all dimensions of the business. These dimensions should include products and services, customers and markets, business processes, structures and facilities, systems and technology, and people and culture. In many a change program the devil is in the details. These are questions of scope—and scope is usually set at inception.

Many organizations continue to effect structural change in, for instance, reporting structures, without defining the role design, work group design, performance measures, and integrating mechanisms (for example, cross-functional roles, communication, and decision-making forums) that are required to make structural change work. Structure in its narrow sense does not provide sufficient perspective and meaning.

Authentic change can be expressed in concrete terms, in a way that relates to individual behavior. The manager's plaintive cry, "You just don't understand marketing . . . or finance . . . or technology," usually means that the manager's idea is unsound at its core, or that the wrong people are leading it.

- *Methodology* is worth considering at inception, although the average CEO's eyes glaze over at the prospect. At worst, methodology can imply solutions in search of a problem, convergent thinking, even a lack of creativity. Yet, if used effectively, methodology can provide a starting point at a time of uncertainty. Methodology, however, should not be allowed to become a straitjacket. The issue is more about flow and sequence, building scenarios, and contingencies. And remaining flexible is essential.
- *Organizing for and resourcing change* should also be on the agenda at this time. Many managers are operating and thinking in programmatic terms more than ever before. But if deep change is the goal, then the manager needs to think about defining a specific program of work, about tracking progress, budgets, and benefits, often from information systems designed for another purpose. He should assess and plan to mitigate major risks. Skills in communicating and integrating change across all dimensions of the business—process skills to complement content skills—will prove useful at this stage. Handing the task to gifted amateurs may well be effective management development, but it comes with a price.

Marshaling resources for change can be emotionally charged because it is a turf issue. Do we organize a full-time task group and attack with overwhelming force? Or do we push autonomy down the line and trust segments of the business to do their own thing within broad parameters? It depends. Choosing how to organize for change will depend on the operating style of the corporation, and choices will be determined by the nature of the change being implemented. Great clarity and homogeneity in the sought for change, or immature local management, probably favor a more centrally driven approach. Diversity in goals and solutions, or maturity on the part of business unit leadership, are more likely to favor a decentralized approach.

The proposition that culture exerts a powerful influence on behavior, and thus on decisions and performance, has been well documented and widely accepted. Deep-set core values and beliefs are very difficult to change. Some authorities have argued that culture is transformed by using practical tools that influence and shape culture—performance measures, rewards, and structure—rather than obsessing about the values, beliefs, and behaviors that might be preferred.

The CEO might have to choose which set of problems to confront: breach the values and pick up the pieces, or influence values and culture over time by changing the levers that shape them. It is a perverse reality that, even if current values and beliefs are deemed appropriate, other noncultural changes in the business will change culture. This implies the need for diagnosis and tracking of culture and its impact on behavior and performance in all major change programs.

Inception usually ends with a plan. Sometimes a plan goes too far. A change plan is the end of the beginning. It is worth thinking about how far it represents a complementary or a contradictory statement of intent. Most organizations will have other business systems running parallel with a change plan—budgets, business plans, and functional plans, for example. The confluence of several independently constructed plans often leads to confusion rather than enlightenment. This represents a real challenge to the management process and demands considerable effort to resolve.

THE ACTIONS OF THE CEO

Successful CEO behavior is often full of contradictions. There are few pick lists that work, no credible standard recipes. Balancing competing priorities is often a matter of managing paradoxes. Here are some perspectives on the ambiguities that seem important to us:

- *Visionary realism.* The status quo in any organization exerts a powerful influence. Part of the CEO's job must be to challenge the prevailing paradigm of accepted norms of performance and behavior—to be a professional malcontent. On the other hand, understanding what is achievable within the existing culture is critical.
- *Relaxed high anxiety.* Behavioral change is often fundamental to lasting change. Edgar Schein, the venerable MIT professor, tells us that changes in behavior can occur where survival anxiety (the concern people have for their security and career prospects) is greater than learning/change anxiety (the natural anxiety people have about learning and doing new things). Clearly, a strategy to reduce learning anxiety (the key to the "learning organization") is a more positive long-term stance. But it may be necessary in the short term to heighten survival anxiety as a means of stimulating behavioral movement, especially where corporate survival is also at stake.
- *Rigid flexibility.* Relentlessness and the refusal to compromise must be combined with a pragmatic sense of what is achievable. CEOs can too easily compromise on the delivery of results—delivery later than planned, at greater cost, or less than planned. Thus, an uncompromising position is essential in securing results. On the other hand, as change is implemented, unforeseen obstacles will emerge. Flexibility is required in the "how" of change.
- *Stable acceleration.* Successful change often requires significant stability, in plans, in continuity of thinking, and in aspirations. Stability gives people at least some constants. But there is also a need for momentum, and sometimes for acceleration. As change is implemented, the corporate landscape also changes. Fresh opportunities come into view. CEOs should recalibrate their expectations in real time, even as they push for more.
- *Mandated empowerment.* The CEO is a powerful role model for others within the organization—for good or ill—and his actions are always a more potent influence than his words. But there are dangers in the CEO's taking a central role for all major changes. CEOs risk spreading themselves too thin, weakening accountability, and disempowering their people. They can become the bottleneck through which all ideas must pass, and as such will become part of the problem.

   Initially, a shift in direction and in performance can only be carried on the shoulders of a small band of managers. How to enlist the support of these people is an important issue for the CEO. Finding people who can develop an idea and engaging them in change is crucial. It can be helpful to "recontract" with this group, fixing new roles, new expectations, new goals, new ways of working together, and instituting a deeper and sharper frankness in communication.

POSTSCRIPT

Taking action to mitigate risk, to improve rate of return, and to exploit latent opportunity in today's (or tomorrow's) change program must be more worthy than conveying words of wisdom to a successor from twenty-twenty hindsight.

For example: NIE's vision is to be a premier Northern Ireland company; a first-rate performer in the eyes of its investors, its customers, and its staff; and a recognized contributor to the social and economic development of the community in which it operates.

This vision and the values that underpin this goal are used to provide an element of continuity against which major step-by-step changes in performance can occur.

In a business that has seen a 34 percent reduction in core manpower numbers in a three-year period, few other elements remain constant. As levers of change, organization, skills sets, benchmarks of performance, and demands on the individual are constantly changing and under review, so too are policies, structures, working practices, business processes, and technology applications.

NIE's vision and values provide a navigational beacon for the company and a reassurance to the individual who needs to look back to the shore.

NIE tries hard to place emphasis on management by relevant facts, just enough to demonstrate substance and to support the necessary rhetoric that converts the numbers into a vision of realizable performance. The same facts are used across a diverse audience—from trade unions, to staff, to the investment community. Facts lend consistency and simplify the story line.

Management has a healthy skepticism about off-the-shelf methodologies that offer a panacea for all ills. Much of the groundwork for NIE's change was put in place through comparisons with other companies on an activity-by-activity basis. Methodologies have been employed against the background of a relatively well-defined management consensus on the problem areas that need to be resolved.

Intercompany comparisons, learning from external experience, and direct knowledge of the business and its potential all form the basis of defining expected thresholds of performance in each program of change. As implementation progresses and as experience in implementation lays bare the true scale of the opportunities in prospect, final outcomes are consciously refined and recalibrated.

A number of change programs have been carried through in recent years. These have been top-down, bottom-up, driven from the center, or empowered locally, depending on the circumstances.

The process of change appropriate to the circumstances has been found to vary with the "life cycle" of change. Early-stage change can be driven very effectively on the basis of a top-down analysis of opportunity and macromeasures of performance. Later-stage performance improvements require greater effort and more sophisticated analysis of how cost, quality, and customer service drivers combine to produce results. These later-stage improvements are obtained at NIE through the active engagement of an informed and involved workforce that understands the need for change and the performance imperatives.

In looking for an accelerated improvement in performance to meet the demands of a new (regulatory) price review, NIE has recently focused responsibility for the implementation of major change on a new group of general managers. These new roles carry with them the need for a broader understanding of the business, a facility in straddling functional boundaries, a shared sense of urgency, and the capacity to shorten debate and decision times.

Recontracting with this group represents a reaffirmation of confidence in the people appointed, a new reward structure, and reinforced accountability. It also signals the next stage in the organization's capacity to develop and implement change consistent with the pressures imposed by its operating environment.

11

DRIVING FUNDAMENTAL CHANGE AT ALCATEL: A NEW PRISM ON CUSTOMER FOCUS

Serge Tchuruk,
Alcatel Alsthom

In the summer of 1995, Serge Tchuruk took the helm of conglomerate Al-catel Alsthom. A few months later the company announced that for the year it would post the largest single loss in French corporate history, 26.6 billion French francs, largely the result of the costs of twenty thousand re-dundancies.

As the company's stock took a shellacking, the Marseilles-born former oil company executive of Armenian descent began his turnaround with a root-and-branch reorganization to cut costs. His campaign included strenuous disposals of marginal assets; the creation of centralized pur-chasing; and the restructuring of Alcatel's telephone switching business (in which it is globally the biggest) from the old nation-by-nation structures to product lines more appropriate for the deregulated environment. He moved to catch up on missed opportunities in the fast-growing mobile phone business. And he announced plans to shrink Alcatel's nine hundred separate legal entities to a more manageable five hundred units, as well as predicting more redundancies.

Shortly after the coolheaded Tchuruk completed his first year, Financial Times *wrote, "While the pace of change may have been unsettling both for investors and the company's nearly 200,000 staff, it looks like the action plan presided over by Serge Tchuruk may be starting to pay dividends." Subsequent events have confirmed that prediction. In 1996 the company returned to profitability, helped by cash from asset disposals. It even be-gan to appear that Alcatel was capturing lost ground after its late entry into mobile telecom.*

Price Waterhouse (PW): *You made a lot of changes at Alcatel Alsthom. Could you tell us some of the highlights?*

Serge Tchuruk (ST): We decided to transform the enterprise into a truly global group and not just a sum of national, single-client compa-nies. We felt this would allow us to meet the demands coming from clients who were themselves international.

We started by breaking down the restructuring process into two ba-sic areas:

- Globalizing the organization's structure
- Adapting the culture to make it more market-oriented

PW: *Before discussing these two aspects in more detail, what were your initial thoughts on managing change in Alcatel?*

ST: I don't believe in any miracle recipe for managing change. When I first arrived at Alcatel, I focused on understanding the company, and on examining its identity and strengths as a way of building a plan for the future. You first have to talk to the people who work for the com-pany to see where the real capabilities lie, and this enables you to ini-tiate change. I wouldn't know how to manage a company without first understanding what skills will be needed. And while I may not be di-rectly involved in every aspect of the business, I have been involved in all those where I've helped set priorities.

PW: *What were the means by which you transformed the organi-zation?*

ST: To give the group a truly international dimension, I set up an orga-nizational structure within the first two to three months that put the transformation of the entire company in motion.

We broke down our activities into business units. And we replaced our former geographic structure, which operated on a countrywide basis, with eight regional divisions having overall responsibility for their operating results. Within the divisions, the heads of the business units define the strategy, choose the products, and are responsible for their own resources. They are evaluated on the basis of their business units' results worldwide.

Giving our business this kind of vertical product- and customer-oriented structure was carried out in full knowledge that it could create conflicts of interest within the national units in charge of geographic markets. And, indeed, managers who retained geographic responsibilities had to give up a meaningful degree of control over the results. This created "positive tension"—the potential for conflict between the regional directors and the business unit directors—which in turn created a healthy dialogue about how best to serve customers in a region.

What was different about the new organization was the fact that we gave the eight major country leaders extended responsibility for entire geographic regions. For example, the director who handled Germany now also plays a role in developing his regional market—which includes Eastern Europe. The directors of the geographic zones are responsible for both the people and the assets in their particular countries, as well as for the operating results in each of the countries their divisions cover.

PW: Were you at all concerned that this kind of organization could result in a disorganized approach toward clients?

ST: Yes. That's why we created the position of key account managers—to make sure there was overall consistency. The account managers have significant power over everything in their purview. They receive all information concerning the client, and coordinate client contacts. In essence, they are the voice of Alcatel vis-à-vis those clients. And they make major decisions concerning the clients in collaboration with the rest of the organization—the business unit and country managers.

The way to avoid the danger of conflict in this type of matrix organization is to get people used to turning problems over as soon as they arise. I made a rule for myself that all questions submitted to me would have an answer within three days maximum, and that my colleagues would do the same.

There are two things that make this system work. The first is to provide answers quickly and accurately. The second, which is aimed at making the organization function smoothly, is to do everything in your power to help the people you work with develop skills that are both proactive and flexible. This has been a necessary step in the company's evolution from an engineering culture to a business culture. If you take these two actions, the system becomes self-regulating.

PW: *How has the multicultural environment of Alcatel affected this change?*

ST: Nothing I've just mentioned can be efficient if the teams themselves are not truly international. The Alcatel Group was originally French. However, since France represents 22 percent of our market share worldwide, it's now absolutely key for us to have a mixture of nationalities on our teams, as well as in each country. Our working language is English, and among the five hundred managers and directors in the group, fewer than 30 percent are French. The executive committee, which is responsible for managing Alcatel Telecom, consists of six members, including a Belgian, an American, three Frenchmen, and one Frenchwoman.

We began to build the international management capabilities we have today in the 1980s. Our mix of people from different cultures is the result of Alcatel's expansion through successive acquisitions—especially with the purchase of ITT's CGCT, which brought with it a large share of American culture. This cultural mosaic gradually became the norm for Alcatel.

My entire professional career has taken place in an international environment. I don't differentiate between nationalities, and I don't believe there are basic cultural differences. The notion that individuals in a company will behave according to the stereotypes of their home countries' culture is an erroneous cliché. What is important in our group is the culture of Alcatel.

Our priority has been to create an overall identity within the group. I have encouraged our people to learn to speak fluent English, and I've been pleased with the great strides they've made. Fluency in communication is also facilitated by the use of electronic communications. Important meetings often take place via video conferences. The meetings are prepared by electronic mail and our intranet, which connects fifty thousand people.

PW: *The big changes in the organization of Alcatel must have created a lot of resistance. What actions have you taken to overcome it?*

ST: My main goal has been to introduce a customer-oriented mentality. To do this, I found it was important to be bold in putting the "right" bosses in place; to preach and keep preaching about marketing within the company, using customer testimonials; to create a positive image of salespeople within the group, and in particular the key account managers; and to implement a training program to support people during the change process.

PW: *Could you give us some specific examples of actions you took to handle the culture change process?*

ST: Our problem was to embed customer-oriented thinking in a business marked by a strong engineering culture. To do this, I focused on developing a business mentality within the company—particularly in the area of research and development, to which the group devotes 5 to 15 percent of its turnover. R&D has a natural tendency to feed on itself and to try to dominate the market rather than the other way around. To deal with this, we've forged stronger links between R&D and the business enterprises. And we have shifted our strategic development thrust to software and services rather than simply product-based projects.

To bring Alcatel around to this new marketing approach, we had to optimize the way we use resources. To illustrate, let me offer you a brief summary of the actions I took. Alcatel has gone through two phases in the past several years. In 1990, the group was going ahead full steam, and faith in our prospects seemed limitless. But in 1994, we were hit with abrupt market shock. Suddenly there were doubts about the company's future brought on by this brutal loss of profitability. This made my plans to orient the group toward the customer even more critical, since we had to meet the demands of a quickly changing market.

To induce such a radical change in outlook, you have to destabilize the organization. You have to set up the new reality by being frank about the difficulties that maintaining the status quo would create. We had to be clear and realistic about our goals in regard to the key elements that create the future. On the other hand, you should only promise what can definitely be gained—without exaggerating the difficulties.

PW: *How would you describe the culture you've been creating?*

ST: I'm convinced that you cannot restructure without providing a positive medium-term vision. Fortunately, Alcatel is now in a favorable market, with an 8 percent annual growth rate, and the means to move even faster than the market growth rate. That's why I've been making a great effort to create what I call the culture of "positive anxiety," as well as to instill an economic outlook in the group.

PW: *How did you go about building this culture?*

ST: Well, for example, I reversed the basic rules for project approval. Before, when a director came to present a project to me, he'd justify it first by the technique he was using. Now I demand a two-page preliminary summary of the economic forecast for all projects. The step I took wasn't theoretical. It wasn't about imposing a "ten commandment charter" for management. It was about setting practical guidelines. I have also tried to encourage people to take the initiative and to develop a collegial spirit—for example, by setting up task forces around a project.

PW: *Have you been successful in creating a greater level of initiative in your managers?*

ST: Yes, definitely. It was when we were pushing the idea of taking the initiative to its limit that we came up with the idea of making emerging projects concrete by creating virtual start-up companies. For example, one of our American managers created a virtual start-up company using our existing management standards and infrastructure. His goal was to simulate the results a project would have if it were being developed by an independent company.

To bring this virtual company into existence, we set up a multicultural team and multibusiness units as needed. At first, this is on an informal basis. Then, as we formalize the process step by step, we come to understand what is required in very clear terms. This "virtual company," which can exist for six months or longer, allows us to test emerging markets or new technologies very quickly. It also makes it possible for us to evolve rapidly.

PW: *How would you judge your progress to date?*

ST: The journey is not yet complete, of course. World-class research, yes. Engineering excellence, surely. But now Alcatel's managers are dealing with the market much differently than they did in the past. And since satisfying customer needs is a value that is rising quickly—so is our future potential.

12

HEALTH CARE, NOT HOSPITALS: TRANSFORMING THE VETERANS' HEALTH ADMINISTRATION

*Dr. Kenneth W. Kizer,
U.S. Department of Veterans' Affairs*

Undersecretary for Health since 1994, Dr. Kenneth W. Kizer, is the master builder of a top-to-bottom reorganization of the Veterans' Health Administration (VHA). As the main part of the second largest federal bureaucracy—the U.S. Department of Veterans' Affairs—the VA, as it is commonly known, is far and away the nation's largest integrated health care system. It has an annual budget of over $17 billion, two hundred thousand employees, 173 hospitals, and over 1,000 sites of care delivery. It is also the major provider of graduate medical and other health care professional training, and one of the largest research organizations in the United States.

Dr. Kizer learned the ropes of transformational change as director of California's Department of Health Services, which he brilliantly reorganized. He has also held senior academic positions at the University of California, Davis, and at USC. He has served on the boards of Health Systems International (renamed Foundation Health System, Inc.), one of the nation's largest managed health care companies, and as chairman of the board for the California Wellness Foundation. He has also been a health care consultant to several foreign governments. Dr. Kizer is board-certified in five medical specialties and has authored over three hundred articles, book chapters, and other items in the medical literature. A former Navy diver, Dr. Kizer is an active member of the Explorer's Club and a nationally recognized expert on aquatic sports and wilderness medicine, and the founder of the International Wilderness Medical Society. Though a Beltway novice when he became Undersecretary for Health, he quickly built political bridges to Congress, which supports his Herculean efforts to reinvent the VHA.

ONE OF THE MOST profound transformations of any organization in U.S. history has been happening at the Veterans' Health Administration for the last couple of years. Replacing an older, monolithic, military-style top-down organization, this turnaround has involved a 180-degree shift in management philosophy and execution, plus an intense application of integrated management network systems.

The VHA's ambitious networks are the kind of new organizational structures that are rapidly coming to dominate the health care field. They have piqued the interest of management academics and researchers because these novel organizational links and architectures point to the way many large-scale institutions, both public and private, will be managed in the next millennium. The seed of the VHA's transformation came not from within government, but rather was inspired by such outside organizations as Kaiser Permanente and private health care groups.

However, what is remarkable at the VHA is that no other organization has heretofore applied the integrated network management concept on such a large scale. And none have had to first break down and reconstruct such a huge existing organization and aggregate of physical structures, while at the same time continuing to maintain good service delivery to the client population. Few entities anywhere have been at the nexus of as many forces of change.

TRANSFORMATION THROUGH NEW ALLIANCES— INTERNAL AND EXTERNAL

What is an integrated service network? Conceptually, it is based on the simple idea that whoever controls and coordinates the supply, production, distribution, and marketing of service delivery will be a vastly more efficient producer than the nonintegrated operator. An integrated network is a superior form because it has a higher rate of asset and service utilization. It can also bring to bear at one point and at one time a superior package of services.

Because it offers the opportunity to serve specific populations with uniform quality services at standardized prices, the relevance of this idea to the once highly fragmented U.S. health care market cannot be overstated. In an integrated health system, physicians, hospitals, and other components share the risks and rewards—supporting one another, blending their talents, and pooling their resources. The network requires management of total costs, plus a focus on populations with common needs rather than on disparate individuals. Furthermore, it requires a data-driven, process-focused customer orientation.

A second innovative organizing principle at work in the VHA's transformation is the concept of the "virtual health care organization," which first emerged in the 1980s. It is based largely on experiences in the biotechnology industry, when businesses invented integrated capabilities by creating a wide array of discrete corporate partnerships, alliances, and consortia to either develop or market specific products. A number of private health care companies have used this approach to form virtual organizations that are held together by (1) the operating framework—that is, the aggregate of agreements and protocols that govern how patients are cared for, and the systems that monitor patient flow; and (2) the framework of incentives that governs how physicians and hospitals are paid.

Virtual health care systems invest substantial resources in developing their provider networks, which have a strong focus on community-based networks of participant physicians. The skills demonstrated by these virtual organizations are likely to become increasingly important in all facets of the economy and society.

CHAINED TO THE PAST

The VHA, at least in theory, was ripe for the application of the integrated service network and the virtual organization. And, in fact, all the necessary ingredients were buried within this monolithic, old-fashioned, hospital-centered organization. The first step was to liberate these serendipitous ingredients from their chains! It was clear that the VHA had to deconstruct its old organization simply to keep abreast of the frenetic pace of change in U.S. health care delivery.

Further pressure for action came from a Congress skeptical of the wildly skewed cost-benefits of the old hierarchical methods. Plus there were mounting complaints about inadequate and inconsistent VHA services from veterans' organizations. For years, these groups had been voicing their dissatisfaction over the long waits to see a doctor, being treated with a lack of respect, and long hospital stays for conditions better treated in an outpatient setting, such as the removal of cataracts.

The old VHA management was centralized to an absurd degree, and thus highly ineffective. Permission for leasing small amounts of space, or for such trivial expenditures as $9.82 for an individual's purchase of a computer cable, had to be approved at the CEO level. The center was so inundated with trivia that, by default, too much power had come to reside in the VHA hospitals. Given these handicaps, it's amazing that the VHA could have provided such a relatively good level of care and services to its constituencies.

But this is far more than a tale of a long-overdue cleanup of an inept government bureaucracy. This is a story of how we jump-started change thanks to a sweeping application of the integrated service network, and in the process lowered costs and improved services.

Contrary to popular belief, most of the nation's 26.1 million veterans are not eligible for care at the VHA. In essence, only veterans with service-connected disabilities or who are poor can receive care at the VHA. Nevertheless, the VHA grew to its present size in response to the enormous influx of wounded at the close of World War II. And fifty years later it was still trying to handle a completely different set of needs with the same structure.

Here's an idea of the magnitude of the problem: There are some 11.6 million eligible veterans who are sixty or over, and another 8.3 million who are between forty and fifty-five. Before its recent transformation, the VHA was treating some nine hundred thousand patients a year at the 173 VHA hospitals. The average length of stay in fiscal 1993 was nearly three times greater than the U.S. average—with only a small part of this difference attributable to the advanced ages of these patients.

The system was convoluted, fragmented, and self-defeating. It emphasized medical specialization, high technology, biomedical research, and acute inpatient services at a time when all trends in health care were heading in the opposite direction, toward primary care, or basic services.

Even more importantly, the VHA lacked the ability to adequately serve its aging customers, many of whom were on the edge of poverty and suffering from non-war-related illnesses—the two most common medical problems among all veterans being alcoholism and schizophrenia.

A "Vision" for Dramatic Change

The challenge was clear: The VHA had to transform itself from a hospital-based, specialty-focused health care system to one rooted in ambulatory care. Accordingly, in October 1995, the VHA consolidated its 173 independent and often competing hospitals, over 400 clinics, 133 nursing homes, over 200 counseling centers, and various other facilities into 22 Veterans Integrated Service Networks, or VISNs (pronounced "visions").

This new operating system emphasizes efficiency, collaboration and cooperation, and the quest for productivity by eliminating layers of bureaucracy and streamlining communications. The goal: To have all patients assigned to a dedicated generalist physician, or physician-led team of caregivers, responsible for providing readily accessible, continuous, coordinated, and comprehensive care.

No sooner were the VISNs up and running than a number of service improvements were pushed through. For example, in 1994 only a few VHA facilities had telephone advice services; within two years, all of them did. Adding to the new momentum at the VHA was the elimination of some 2,626 types of forms (64 percent of those in use), and the marked simplification and automation of the remainder. In addition, many tens of millions of dollars in savings resulted from an aggressive program to increase the number of goods and services acquired through bulk-purchase agreements, and a pharmaceutical prime vendor program.

Under the VISNs strategy, the basic budgetary and planning unit of health care delivery shifted from the autonomous medical centers to the networks—with each of these networks being responsible for all VHA activities in a specified geographic region. The VISNs promote better integration of resources and the expansion of community-based access points for primary care. The paradigm under which they operate is made up of strategic alliances between neighboring VHA medical centers, sharing agreements with other governmental providers, and other relationships, including direct purchases from the private sector.

THE HOSPITAL BECOMES PART OF A LARGER PICTURE

In this scheme, the hospital becomes a component of a larger and better-coordinated community-based network of care—embracing both ambulatory and acute and extended inpatient services. The superiority of the network is that it focuses on customer needs from primary to tertiary care.

The VISNs are a revolutionary organizational form, based on patient referral patterns, hospitals, and other VHA assets. Their mission is to conduct population-based planning, to increase patient access, and to pool and align local resources to provide a seamless continuum of care. The individual VISNs are like strategic business units. As the basic budgetary and planning components of the system, each one is measured against specific performance contracts.

The heads of the various hospitals and facilities report in to their VISN, which optimizes the networks and extracts the highest value for the resources allocated. All VISNs have procedures for input from the VA's internal and external stakeholders through a council that consists of facility directors, chiefs of staff, nurse executives, union representatives, and others. The council debates and makes recommendations to the VISNs directors.

The VISNs' big point of departure is that they are in part virtual health care systems—in that they may deliver services through contractual agreements with other institutions. Traditional, nonvirtual health care systems rely on ownership of assets and employment of their own professionals. In the new configurations, the once-central position of the VHA hospitals would be moderated by the needs of more coordinated, community-based care. The first outreaches of the network have already been built. The VHA has developed new joint-venture relationships with the Juvenile Diabetes Foundation, the National Cancer Institute, and the Shriner's Hospitals. Other such alliances are under discussion.

CHANGING THE PEOPLE—AND THE CULTURE

The VISNs had to be created out of whole cloth. As undersecretary it was crucial for me to have deep personal involvement in the networks' design, as well as in the recruitment of their leaders. I began by developing the questions to be asked of all candidates, and I personally interviewed all ninety finalists for the twenty-two positions. In the end, eight of these positions were filled by outsiders, some from private industry— a big break with VHA tradition.

The VISNs are the VHA's chief tools of transformation. In both image and substance, they are sweeping away the old view—prevalent inside and outside the VHA—that it was a kind of public works program in building construction and lifetime jobs. Such a culture of stasis is typical of large bureaucracies, which tend to focus on self-propagation at the expense of purpose. And in fact, even as the VISNs were being instituted, there remained the lingering attitude that, "Well, this too will pass. It won't be long before we get back to the old way of doing things." It took us a little while to stamp out passivity and negativity—much of it fostered by a reduction of staff from 205,000 to 181,000 and the elimination of seventeen thousand acute-care beds.

A New Role for Headquarters

If the VISNs are doing all the heavy lifting, what's the role of the Washington, D.C., headquarters? It has shifted its orientation away from hierarchical dominance to seeking ways to support the field—by offering governance principles and consulting advice, and by leading the system through the dynamic and turbulent changes ahead. To the degree that headquarters displays leadership capabilities and insights, the field managers will continue to seek its advice and counsel—not because of its position in the hierarchy. One of the chief missions of headquarters is to foster and demand new behaviors and attitudes that further the goals of the new overall structure.

A major block to change was a 1947 policy stipulating that VHA physicians could not be terminated for any reason short of malpractice. That law institutionalized complacency, and its repeal—which came in 1995 —was essential for the success of the reorganization. Another block was that the VA's research arms had splintered into isolated pockets that placed researchers' personal agendas ahead of customer service. Under the new network regime there must be a demonstrable link between research and patient care. In 1994, the VHA implemented its first-ever customer service standards, and patient surveys in 1995 and 1996 indicated statistically significant improvements.

A Work in Progress

Systemic change at the VHA is still a work in progress. Challenges remain. There still needs to be more managerial accountability, and there still needs to be more flexibility and latitude to make tough decisions. Some of the old culture of insularity remains—but the message is getting out.

This is an era in which the entire health care industry is in transition. It's our belief that by the time the transformation of the VHA is complete, it will be a fully integrated health care provider—one capable of competing with private entities.

KENNETH W. KIZER'S KEY PRINCIPLES OF TRANSFORMATION

1. *Clearly articulate your vision, intent and principles of change.* The VHA's statement is about "why," not "how." With a clear end-purpose in mind, we used certain principles of modern health care to lay the framework for transformation at the VHA, as well as the new managerial system that would implement it:

   - The VHA is in the business of health care, not of running hospitals.
   - Health care is now primarily a local outpatient activity.
   - The VHA's critical mandate is to provide good value.
   - The success of future health care systems will depend on their ability to integrate and manage information.
   - Health care must reorient itself to become more population-directed, community-based, and health-promotive.
   - Health care must become more accountable and responsive to those who purchase it.
   - Medical education and research must be accountable to the public good.

2. *The process of change should be broadly inclusive.* The top manager should allow all members of the organization to have their say in some form or forum—and what they say should be taken seriously and sincerely. However, that inclusivity should be flexible enough to embrace partnerships and outside associations that can facilitate the new vision.

3. *Change within an organization must move in harmony with environmental or externally focused change.* Top managers, particularly those in the public sector, cannot hope to stand against the "forces of nature"—this constitutes bad management. In the case of the VHA, that means being in sync with broad trends, such as the national revolution in health care, the explosion of biomedical research and knowledge, the shift to an "information society," and the aging of the eligible VHA population.

4. *The top manager must make key personnel decisions.* Bad hires stay around to haunt you; good ones make you look good. Here are seven key characteristics of the good hire:

- Committed to change
- Shares the vision
- Experienced, knowledgeable
- Innovative, nontraditional
- Respected
- Empowered
- Willing to get his or her hands dirty

5. *Set high expectations.* People will meet them—unless your system impedes their best efforts.
6. *Focus on rigorous execution, including minimizing errors.* Innovative, nontraditional thinkers will make errors because errors are inherent to trailblazing. These should be openly discussed without instilling the kind of fear that engenders complacency. However, stupid, careless mistakes should not be tolerated.
7. *Anticipate problems.* Change, by definition, is rarely neutral. It will create new problems—but they shouldn't come as a surprise.

13

A BENCHMARK THAT BROUGHT MANAGERS IN FROM THE COLD

Sir Richard Evans, British Aerospace

A British journalist has described British Aerospace's CEO Sir Richard Evans as an uncomplicated salesman type, "the sort of affable host you might find behind the bar of a friendly northern golf club." But behind "Dick" Evans's genial and uncomplicated façade there is a man with the survival skills of a chameleon. He came up through the company ranks as a supersalesman who pulled off a defense-equipment sale to Saudi Arabia that was Britain's biggest export contract ever and stopped the company from going down the tubes. Two years after his making it to CEO, the company was sinking again and had to take the then-biggest write-off in British corporate history—a billion pounds.

But after masterly divestments (including Rover the auto producer), downsizings, and shedding of assets and many thousands of employees, Evans sprang back from the brink. Whereupon he changed from a turn-around manager to an apostle of radical change, becoming the architect of an ambitious program designed to unify heretofore disparate divisions. Again, he succeeded brilliantly, infusing a new identity into a proud and yet in places demoralized organization.

THE PROBLEM THAT TRIGGERED a sweeping process of change at British Aerospace (BAe) is ubiquitous. Few large companies have escaped it at one time or another in their histories. It is the problem of runaway divisional and staff "fiefdoms." Lacking sufficient unity and internal coherence, these firms pay too heavy a price for decentralization. They fail to capture powerful synergies, and latent strengths and divisional competencies aren't shared throughout the company. In short, they're not firing on all cylinders.

BAe's fiercely independent fiefdoms spring from its historical origins in the late eighties as a holding company formed by the merger of disparate pieces of the British aircraft industry.

In 1992, when the curtain goes up on our story, BAe had just weathered a succession of deep crises, taken the largest write-off in British corporate history, and was in the process of creating a strong recovery. Profits were increasing, so were the order books, and investors' perceptions of the company had changed for the better. As for the future, each one of the fiefdoms boasted credible plans for further performance improvements. All in all, everything seemed rosy.

There was only one snag. I had a gut feeling that these plans lacked sufficient scope and momentum, considering the virulence of present and future competitive forces. Just how virulent was dramatically brought home to my top managers when our archrival, Boeing, announced a new version of its 737 with greatly improved operating characteristics at a price 30 percent below its earlier model. What's more, Boeing made this offer before it actually implemented the projects that would yield the needed savings on the factory floor.

Boeing's spectacular display of confidence created a crisis of self-examination in our aircraft division, where analysis showed that BAe could not immediately emulate Boeing. Elsewhere in the company dark clouds were also beginning to form—notably in defense. Since the end of the Cold War this had been a contracting market, experiencing many mergers.

Adding all this up, I concluded that the business units' competitive muscles were neither fast enough nor strong enough for the race ahead. The divisions would have to come in from the cold. There was no other remedy. This was a pretty tall order. Many BAe divisions had cherished histories and strong identities. They perceived themselves as being successful and in no need of interference from headquarters. Some had already experienced the change management bandwagon in earlier days—they would not relish another dose of that medicine.

As always, the wait-and-see arguments for doing nothing were persuasive. But my conviction was unshakable that our long-term success critically depended on a process, directed from the top, designed to get the divisions to mesh and enhance their capabilities, and to share the skills and competencies in which they were often brilliant practitioners.

Change programs come in many shapes and colors; many are based on theoretical models available from consultants. By contrast, BAe's is the result of home-grown innovation that springs from our particular circumstances. It began with the idea of sharing capabilities, but soon expanded to the idea of trying to excel in all the key functions of business. From this came the ambition to become a world-class player across the board. We envisioned BAe becoming the benchmark standard used by suppliers, customers, peers, consultants, and the media.

It was a wildly ambitious undertaking, since there were a number of areas where we fell well short of the benchmark class. This was to be expected after many years of fighting a rearguard battle and facing repeated survival crises. But although the vision was bold, it was also realistic. If BAe achieved its goal, the company's excellence would be reflected in its rising market share and higher rates of profitability and growth.

Thus was born the "Benchmark BAe" program—a product of intense and difficult discussion between the company's four executive directors and myself. Why difficult? Because while we all subscribed to the formal case for radical change, in practice each of us needed to express our own view of the company.

Finally we hammered out a defining statement that said BAe was "dedicated to working together and with our partners, and to becoming the benchmark for our industry, setting the standard for customer satisfaction, technology, financial performance, and quality in all that we do."

The next step was to figure out how this goal might be achieved. We began by asking the top two or three managers from each division to define those attributes that, if promulgated and shared, would create the conditions in which Benchmark BAe would flourish. After much discussion and soul-searching, these thirty managers isolated five key values: (1) People are our greatest strength, (2) customers are our highest priority, (3) partnerships are our future, (4) innovation and technology are our competitive edge, and (5) performance is the key to winning.

The simplicity of these statements masks the torture the authors collectively experienced in framing them. For instance, they had to work out a common definition of "values." But what their phrasing may have lacked in elegance was made up for by sincerity and conviction. The important thing was that these five key values reflected the thinking of powerful and highly credible line managers. They were easy to grasp, intellectually powerful, and allowed for many different adaptations and iterations.

We then ran these five values up the flagpole to a larger group of some 130 senior managers, who debated them, pulled them inside out, and then successively passed them down to a wider executive audience. At first glance, debating values might seem an easy assignment. Only an idiot would disagree with the premise that people are important. The question was, important in what specific ways, and is that importance latent or something that is measurable and communicable, and to be fostered?

In the give-and-take of these discussions, BAe's upper echelons found that the things we'd considered obvious weren't obvious at all. Areas of intellectual certainty suddenly developed cracks. New vistas opened up before us. After all, the objective of these discussions was to break the old molds, to release a ferment of questioning—out of which a new sense of identity and purpose might emerge. The heads of the major divisions freely challenged but ultimately agreed, heart and soul, to believe in and promote the goal of becoming a benchmark standard-bearer.

Very early in the process we recognized that putting the five values into practice demanded new forms of behavior. And one of these new demands was the need for openness and personal candor—attributes that had not been cultivated or encouraged in the upper reaches of our business. Like managers anywhere, those of BAe were pretty skilled at formal presentations and expressing themselves in officialese at meetings, reserving truth-telling for the corridors outside. Needless to say, authentic visions, missions, and goals—and authentic buy-ins to them— could only emerge from these sessions if the participants were to say out in the open what they were accustomed to holding back. The fact that they did was astonishing, considering the fact that the fiefdom mentality went so deep that many of them had never met before or even spoken on the phone.

To encourage more candor, I urged workshop participants to give me feedback by writing to me in total confidence. Initially, I didn't receive an overwhelming response. But slowly the need for self-expression, and trust in the process, won them over, and the "letters to Dick" became frequent and voluminous. In my initial request I had set a limit of one page per letter. But four and five pages became common because people had such a need to get things off their chest.

As might be expected, the contents of the "letters to Dick" ranged far and wide. Some of my correspondents said the pace was too quick. Others begged for simple marching orders and an end to the give-and-take. Still others said things like, "Dick I support you one hundred percent, but we'll never get anywhere so long as the people from X division are in the room." However, at first haltingly, then in a rush, the letters revealed a strong basis of support for change and a good analytic grasp of where, how, and why our company was substandard on a particular benchmark.

Ultimately, the letters proved to be my greatest morale booster. They removed any last traces of doubt I might have had about the Benchmark BAe program.

Discussion of the five values proved to be a powerful bonding experience for everyone involved, creating the sense of community that had been lacking. As the program cascaded throughout the businesses, the emphasis shifted from value definitions to a consideration of the behaviors and practices that would best support each value. For instance, in practice what does it mean to live up to the notion that people are our greatest strength? How should leaders demonstrate a commitment to this value? How do different parts of the company rate in acknowledging the power of people? What are the company's shortcomings in this area?

The program was now entering a new level of specificity. To come up with answers about people values, we selected a 12-member people value team from a pool of 130 top managers from all the businesses. Similarly, we created teams around the other four values, each charged with creating an implementation plan.

One of the major thrusts of the people implementation plan has been to demonstrate a stronger belief in the value of nonmanagers at BAe. To make this message clear, many compensation and benefit features previously reserved for executives have been extended to everyone. These include annual reviews by supervisors, a personal employee development plan, and favorable car leasing and health insurance deals. We continue to demonstrate the importance of people by twice yearly creating a video shown to all employees that reports on BAe's progress against the overall value plan.

Every one of the five corporate value plans, as well as the implementation plans for the business units, has to include an assessment of the actual behaviors that will help meet the plan's goals. The value plans have become the building blocks of the overarching benchmark system, acting as a kind of prism through which actions are weighed, strategies judged, and behaviors encouraged or discouraged. Since people need help and reorientation if they are to change behavior, we have invested heavily in a twelve-day skills training program to help some fifteen hundred executives act out the five primary values each day. The BEST program—Benchmark Executive Skills Training—sends the message that the values are not just for talking about, they must be lived.

That, in brief, is our story over the three years the program has been in place. However, our narrative has one drawback. It gives the impression of rationality and programmatic coherence, leaving out the messy and confusing parts, the moments of doubt, and the moments of sheer improvisation. Also, the spread and influence of the benchmark program has been uneven; it cannot yet be said that BAe has become the established benchmark that it seeks to be to the outside world, but BAe believes strongly that it is moving in that direction.

But what matters is that the benchmark program has succeeded in releasing strengths and synergies between divisions, and it has laid a powerful groundwork for the global benchmark goal. It has also brought in money. BAe's win of a £2 billion Nimrod contract in 1996 would not have been possible without a much higher level of interdivisional cooperation than had existed two years before. And when the company's turboprop division announced a large number of layoffs, its manager was inundated with calls from many other divisions offering help in relocating its former employees. That would have been inconceivable three years before.

What's next? More of the same. I realized at the outset that we were embarking on an epic journey. Even if the company succeeds in reaching world-class status on every benchmark, we still face the continuous pressure of seeking improvements to maintain that position. Some skeptics might see "Benchmark BAe" as overly ambitious, or say that because the process is open-ended BAe risks catching the well-known disease of "change fatigue." But that's not likely to happen, since the best remedy for "change fatigue" is "change opportunity"—successes that repeatedly build hope and the confidence to aspire higher.

Let's finish up by checking off some insights for CEOs that I've gleaned from my experience with our own change program and from observing others:

- *CEOs have to be visionaries, the initiators, and, to a very large extent, the implementers and orchestrators of an enterprisewide change process.* Anyone who thinks the initiative can be delegated to consultants or handed off to a change-management committee is pipe-dreaming. The program must bear the CEO's personal stamp, not just his or her authorization.
- *The process has to be all-embracing—excluding no one and no part of the company.* Therefore its ideas and programs must have wide applicability and also be easily communicated.
- *The CEO's commitment and sense of priority must be evident to everyone throughout the entire process.* If the CEO schedules a workshop to confer with senior associates, he or she has to arrive on time, not take personal breaks or rush off to make some phone calls. In short, the CEO must persuade by example, by demonstrating participation.

- *Patience is an essential quality for CEOs, and so is a tolerance for frustration.* They and other corporate leaders should never pressure people into blind acceptance. "Let us reason together" should be the motto above the workshop door. Participants should be given all the time they need to reflect, debate, and analyze.

- *A knack for accepting ambiguity is essential.* CEOs have to remain open-minded and flexible and be prepared to commit to outcomes without necessarily knowing in advance the road to be traveled. And they will have to improvise from time to time. If CEOs and their core group of managers try to agree on all milestones, paths, and deliverables at the outset, then it's a safe bet they'll never get off the ground. Creating change means flying through heavy cloud cover with poor instruments.

- *The CEO should be sensitive to some of the drawbacks that arise, because he or she is the spark and the catalyst.* For instance, some subordinates will think the program is just a personal and passing enthusiasm and that the CEO will soon tire of it. Others will find it hard to believe in the CEO's faith in building a sense of community, in sharing, and in the free expression of ideas. They will suspect some private agenda and think, "Why doesn't he bloody well say what he wants so we can do it and he can stop wasting our time?" When the light bulb finally goes on and they recognize there is no hidden agenda, no expected way to behave, then suddenly the floodgates open and everyone's energy and creativity are unleashed.

- *People can be very intractable when change is in the air.* Yet the change program must engage their own behavior. To get people to behave differently, everyone has to participate. Most people want others to change, and fail to see their own blind spots. A change program that fails to spark broad-based self-criticism is likely to flounder.

- *CEOs must impose some rigor on the whole process.* For example, in most cases it's probably a good idea to keep organizational issues out of the discussion, although people will keep trying to drag them in. Organizational change is merely a subset of far broader step-by-step change issues. So keep the spotlight on behavior and process—organization will come later.

- *CEOs must strive to develop momentum, excitement, and enjoyment in the process.* They must make certain the change program never falls far behind its targets. This is a commitment that cannot be undertaken lightly. Much is being demanded of people. Thus CEOs must have a clear grasp of the benefits of the process and the gains that will justify the inevitable pains and sacrifices along the way. There is high risk, because a failed change program and its busted hopes will result in a damaged organization that is even less effective than before. But there is so much more to be gained that it's worth the risk.

PART III
Leadership

GIANTS OF VALUE CREATION

Here's a fact to think about: In the last decade, the assets of the top ten world corporate giants have tripled in size. Meanwhile, the size of their CEOs' brains has remained exactly the same. As for more time on the job, it's the same story: No increase is possible. So we might well wonder how CEOs of very large enterprises stay in control. How do they captain a ship that has triple the old draft? As corporations have grown in scale and geographic range, it is surely no accident that the subject of leadership has caught the spotlight of much management literature as well as the business press. As William Steere, Jr., CEO of Pfizer, has observed, "As organizations grow in size, the importance of the executive as the visible representation of an increasingly removed or impersonal corporate structure grows accordingly."

The job description has also changed in the last decade. Today, a vigilant and demanding shareholder public, plus a vastly expanded business media, constantly measure the quality of projected leadership. Where they deem corporate leadership weak, they'll invariably ask, "What have you done for me lately?" In the same spirit, newly appointed CEOs are generally given a short window of opportunity to find their feet as leaders, while retired CEOs are less likely than in the past to hang around as board members and consultants.

"Leadership," wrote historian James MacGregor Burns two decades ago, "is one of the most observed and least understood phenomena on earth." Burns himself made an enduring contribution, with his distinction between "transformational" and "transactional" leaders. Today, every CEO worth his salt wants to be a transformational leader, in part because down in the canyons of Wall Street, a good leadership persona can add several billions to a company's market capitalization.

In the last decade we've seen the emergence of a handful of CEOs who cast a giant shadow. Hero CEOs like Chrysler's Lee Iacocca, GE's Jack Welch, and ABB's Percy Barnevik have demonstrated the power of a single individual at the top to create vast amounts of economic value. Which puts pressure on all CEOs to do likewise. It used to be that a CEO had only to be a good manager, recognized as such by his peers and his board. Nowadays the klieg lights are on the CEO to demonstrate leadership prowess, to show in thought and deed an understanding of the dynamics of value enhancement, to be aware of opportunity and impatient to exploit it.

CEO leadership is, of course, not just for public consumption. It must be a living thing inside the firm where it counts. Like Peter Drucker, we don't believe there is an ideal type of leader. "'Leadership personality,' 'leadership style,' and 'leadership traits' don't exist," he writes in *The Leader of the Future*. Suppression of personality is the essence of managerial discipline. The same leader should be able to adapt to all circumstances: growth-seeking, cost-cutting, strategic redirection, systems implementation. This said, we must also recognize that men and women get the opportunity to lead because their personal traits seem congruent with what needs to be done. In large corporations today, a benchmark of a CEO's leadership ability would surely include the following factors:

- *Ensuring that the company has world-class management processes— the best practices in strategic planning, marketing, human relations, and so on.* This should take priority over developing skills in such business processes as supply chain, finance, and the like. Topnotch management skills and techniques have the power to boost corporate self-confidence. They reflect well on the CEO, and they often have a trickle-down effect that fosters the best in process management throughout the organization.
- *Making the endorsement and support of core values a condition of employment for key managers.* All managers will fall into one of four categories of ability and congruence with values. One, high performers with appropriate values are the heroes. Two, those who are low on both scales should be canned. Three, people who rate high on values but have poor performance records deserve training and development. And four, the real litmus test of leadership— what the CEO does with high performers who do not support and may even be antagonistic to the core values; for example, with the head of a division who is an autocrat in a team culture.

  In such a situation, many CEOs are tempted to turn a blind eye because of the value added that this individual contributes. However, the strong leader does not hesitate to remove the individual even at the cost of some short-term losses. Speaking of GE's experience with counterculture executives, Jack Welch declared: "The decision to remove these managers was a watershed—the ultimate test of our ability to 'walk the talk.' But it had to be done if we wanted GE people to be open, to speak up, to share, and to act boldly outside traditional lines of authority."
- *Defining the corporation's boundaries—a challenge for leaders in today's environment that their predecessors rarely faced.* Leaders must determine which core competencies to retain and which functions to outsource or hand off to a joint venture. The CEO needs to be a mapper of the corporate topography.

- *Acknowledging and responding to the needs of the modern-day "knowledge organization," or the "learning organization."* This is what MIT's Peter Senge calls *"the* leadership issue of our times: How human communities, be they multinational corporations or societies, productively confront complex, systemic issues where hierarchical authority is inadequate for change." True leadership doesn't automatically arise from the position or power of the CEO. Leaders are judged—and will increasingly be judged in the decade ahead—on their capacity to recognize the limits and inapplicability of hierarchy, on the success of their experiments with authentic alternatives and their quest for the democratization of leadership.

- *Being a role model—an inescapable aspect of leadership for the CEO.* His or her smallest deeds send cues and signals down the chain of command about values and priorities. Not a difficult task, you say? Just try it sometime. To be a role model requires more self-awareness and self-discipline than many CEOs possess. For example, about a year ago the CEO of an international oil company declared with total sincerity that one of his chief priorities was people issues. However, an examination of his personal diary, and an analysis of how he allocated his time, revealed an embarrassing fact. Less than 5 percent of his time was devoted to people issues. He'd only imagined that he was improving the company's human capital. Henceforth, he vowed to do what he should have done in the first place—use his time in a way that reflected his goals.

- *Advocating new behavioral skills is a critical test of leadership.* These days, leaders are under pressure to create a noncoercive environment in which employees and suppliers are clear about the corporate identity and mission, and reflect this in how they conduct themselves day to day. Companies that have a "cult of the leader" are not likely to engender these abilities. The right environment is created by leaders with a keen understanding of the emotional impact of change and discontinuity, and the anxieties that new strategies, tactics, and policies can provoke. The result, when it works, is a community that has direction and purpose, a shared set of values and strategic priorities, and a common set of behaviors.

The power of independent thinking is an oft-proclaimed leadership trait. And surely one of the most independent-minded CEOs in the history of the air transport business is Sir Colin Marshall, chairman of British Airways. The company's initials, BA, stood for "bloody awful" at the beginning of his tenure, and for "bloody amazing" after he'd transformed it into one of the premier customer service organizations in the world. In chapter fourteen, Marshall reveals how his formative early experiences in business influenced his thinking and conduct as a leader.

A clear example of James MacGregor Burns's "transformational leader" is Compaq's Eckard Pfeiffer, who has a burning fanaticism for organizational renewal (chapter fifteen). Pfeiffer is the personification of the leader in a race against himself. Like a runner always looking to better his time, his life reflects a relentless drive to keep the fires of self-renewal burning. "No matter what industry a company competes in," he says, "it must live with one foot in the present and the other in the future. . . . There's simply no other way to build world leadership."

Somewhat different leadership qualities are on display in chapter sixteen, where Michael Kay tells how he took the helm as turnaround guru at LSG/SKY Chefs, the giant of in-flight food services. He recognized that he had one major shortcoming—a scanty knowledge of the industry and the company—and one major imperative, to revive the company before it turned into a corpse. His leadership strategy was to set audacious productivity hurdles and then cheer on his executives and employees to go out and leap over them.

Although the shy and intellectually brilliant Mrs. Sadako Ogata would never describe herself as a turnaround artist, that in fact has been her achievement as head of the Office of the U.N.'s High Commissioner for Refugees (UNHCR) over the last several years. In chapter seventeen, we learn that her organization's presenting problem was that its Geneva headquarters was not sufficiently plugged into UNHCR personnel delivering services in the field. She has remedied this shortcoming by applying business rigor to UNHCR's humanitarian mission.

If an important characteristic of leadership is the ability to go against the traditional hierarchy, then Monsanto's CEO, Robert Shapiro, deserves a medal for initiating strategy sessions with cross-sections of employees of different ranks, specialties, and geographical perspectives. Another major initiative is described in chapter eighteen, where Shapiro shows how he unbundled shareholder value and decentralized it far down into the business unit level in a bold effort to closely link individual managers' conduct and compensation to value creation.

At Pitney Bowes, CEO Michael Critelli has focused his leadership thinking on the problems of internal communication. In chapter nineteen, Critelli writes of his conviction that new technologies in communications do not displace old ones. What happens instead is that the old and the new coexist, sometimes uneasily. Although senior management at this corporate kingpin of the postage meter and messaging industry has come to rely more on E-mail and other technologies, Critelli argues that "electronic communications capabilities do not diminish the need for business leaders to communicate directly with their constituents. In fact, the opposite may be true." Critelli has gone to great lengths to cultivate the three C's in his staff: communication, candor, and collaboration.

What all these narratives have in common is a single theme: the personal will of the CEO to make a difference, to stand out in history. Achieving recognition for leadership qualities is the Holy Grail of CEOs, but there are clearly many diverse roads to the prize.

14

FROM APPRENTICE SHIP'S PURSER TO CEO: A JOURNEY IN SEARCH OF THE CUSTOMER

Sir Colin Marshall, British Airways

British Airways chairman Sir Colin Marshall is the architect of one of the most celebrated corporate turnarounds of the eighties. After a career in rental cars, where he became CEO of Avis, Marshall took the helm of Hunt-Wesson foods, where he learned more about the power of brands. In 1981 he moved back to his native soil to work with Sears, the British retailer and shoemaker, and in 1983 switched companies for the last time.

Marshall became an iconoclast in the airline business, famous for his independent thinking and his ability to get down to business basics. He also had to deal with Margaret Thatcher, who repeatedly told him there would be no government subsidies with the phrase, "Pennies do not come from heaven. They have to be earned here on earth." And earn them he did.

During the 1987 privatization, the company metamorphosed from a bumbling and arrogant institution—famous for its customer contempt— into a case study in customer relatedness and satisfaction. The world's largest and most consistently profitable international airline owes much to what Marshall calls his "evangelistic determination to strive for customer-service excellence." In this chapter he explains how that evangelism was formed and has evolved.

I'D LIKE TO BEGIN on an unusual note, by talking about some early influences and events that shaped my career as a manager. Experience has been my greatest teacher, perhaps richer than any formal management education might have been.

My first job was as cadet purser on the Orient Line, which in the fifties carried hundreds of thousands of British emigrants to the Antipodes. This was the first such voyage for many of the passengers, and during the six weeks at sea there were plenty of·possibilities for friction, dissatisfaction, and stress. This was also my first raw experience with the demands and behavior of customers in what were often tense situations. Seasickness has a deep mood-altering effect, and not for the better.

But I also perceived that my own behavior and my peers' could make a deep impression on people's awareness and understanding. So I set out to build buoyant relationships with passengers—through helpfulness, friendliness, and courtesy. I would make certain the children had the right breakfast cereal, before tantrums broke out. Or I'd help get those affected with mal de mer (or mal de bottle) discreetly to their cabins.

The approach worked. The passengers became aware of what was reasonable to demand of the crew, and we were scrupulous about meeting those demands. On those occasions when we went beyond the call of duty, we typically got an appreciative response. I didn't realize it at the time, but I was practicing what was to become known several decades later as "customer service"—the cornerstone of a future business strategy.

Some years later I emigrated to the United States to become a management trainee with the Hertz car rental corporation. One of the most significant first impressions the United States made on me was not, as I recall, the big automobiles, the high-rise buildings, or the frenzied pace of life—though these did impress, naturally. Rather, it was the quality of service at the average diner or humble restaurant.

I was repeatedly amazed by the fact that the coffee came unsolicited, like magic, the instant I sat down. And my cup was replenished automatically thereafter. For someone accustomed to the austerities and bad service of postwar Britain, this was rocket science in terms of customer service. So too were incredible things like valet parking, supermarket bag packing, and the "flub stubs" that guaranteed no-quibble refunds if the product or service wasn't up to scratch.

In crossing the Atlantic I'd traveled to a place where the customer is king—and a king he or she remained in my mind. Britain was a land of "Sorry, sir," where every sort of provider created and abided by absurd codes of conduct that often suggested the customer had no rights at all. The contrast was liberating. Thenceforth the task of satisfying customer needs, and the building of customer loyalty, became a core philosophy of mine.

Harold Geneen, the business genius who built IT&T, once told me, "You read a book from the beginning to the end. You run a business the opposite way—start at the end and then do everything you must to reach it." What he was saying is that you don't just sit around dreaming up new products. You go first of all to the customers, discover their choices and preferences, and deliver them as precisely as possible.

In the many decades since my talk with Geneen, customer satisfaction and putting the customer first have almost become clichés—the acknowledged goal of all businesses. However, I believe that many companies only pay lip service to the power and effectiveness of putting the customer first. In reality, I suspect that only a handful of global ccmpanies are 100 percent dedicated to putting the customer first.

I have often been asked why, after a pretty successful transatlantic management career, I opted to quit as deputy CEO of Sears in 1982 and take on the leadership of an overmanned, moribund, demotivated British government-owned airline. Especially since the airline industry was notoriously volatile and prone to high uncertainty. Among the factors that weighed in my decision was my experience as a British Airways customer.

Whenever I flew British Airways I could see that service standards were showing signs of severe fatigue, but I also recognized that there was a noticeable hidden depth to the people. It was clear that none of those I met regularly at the airports or on board the aircraft came to work to do a bad job. It was the system that worked against them. They were manacled by the company's perception of the needs of its own production processes—rather than the needs of its customers.

The task of turning around British Airways was something like an archaeological dig. Once the dust and debris of ages had been carefully brushed away, we uncovered the jewels. And the brightest of them were the very professional and highly skilled people of British Airways. I thought they were capable of being the best in the industry.

What they lacked were the right tools, the right motivation, and the right leadership. They lacked an environment in which their skills and experience could be freed up to respond to their customers, rather than remain constrained and frustrated. What they needed was a market-led, customer-sensitive organization. The results are there for everyone to see. I have no hesitation in saying that our evident success is almost wholly due to the commitment of the people of British Airways, whether they work behind the scenes or at the points of sale and service delivery.

Today, my deepest concern is for British Airways to continue to measure up to the challenges posed by liberalized trade in Europe and the world at large. In the freer global environment there will be fewer artificial barriers or structural inefficiencies that can be used as excuses for inadequate service. Although technology and innovation are obviously important competitive factors, it is customer service that will be the deciding factor in creating sustained profits. This is the age of marketing, and its core discipline is customer service. I'm convinced that the days of penny-pinching, accountancy-based business planning are coming to an end.

However, many companies don't fully recognize this new imperative. Instead they are underinvesting in marketing and customer-driven initiatives in preference to short-term, accountancy-led tactics. And even many of those espousing a strong customer orientation believe that structure and complexity and systems can substitute for a real hands-on approach, which is why they fall far short of their objectives. The leadership of many companies still doesn't get the fact that customer involvement means they must have a personal and intimate understanding of the customer-supplier interface.

Many of my CEO peers seem a bit schizophrenic about marketing, as demonstrated in a recent Marketing Council survey of British marketing professionals. They all agreed that marketing would increase in importance over the next five years. They felt that marketing know-how was necessary for the survival of companies. And they believed that the whole company, not just one department, needed to understand marketing and contribute to it.

That was the good news. But the bad news showed that there is a deep split within many corporations on the returns from serious marketing investments. Respondents to the survey felt their marketing initiatives were frustrated because they suffered from short-termism, lack of strategy, and inadequately trained people. They believed that most chief executives were driven by financial or production priorities, not those of the market. I suspect these views come as no surprise to marketers in the United States.

As a result, I asked the London Business School to investigate some of the dimensions of this problem. I suggested they look for models of excellence among market-oriented, externally focused organizations with a firm grasp of marketplace dynamics—including, but not confined to, an understanding of the expressed and latent needs of customers.

The research, which is still in progress, involves responses from four hundred British managing directors. It examines value systems and market-sensing behaviors, and analyzes their impact on different types of businesses. The study makes distinctions between standard marketing strategies, such as focus groups, in companies that have a deep marketing commitment, and compares them with those where marketing has lower priority.

I believe that while market sensing may be important, without a market-oriented value system driving and guiding an organization's behavior, activities like market research may get absolutely nowhere. One of the ways to remedy this is for management to rigorously test the depth, sincerity, and completeness of its value system and how it relates to the customer.

The findings of the study, which apply equally well to marketers in the United States, strongly indicate that high-marketing-value firms do better than less committed rivals. It supports the premise that the marketing concept as an underlying value system is much superior to a set of marketing behaviors.

The point is that marketing practices have limited power in themselves when they're not supported by the corporate culture. The distinction is between ritual and commitment: Marketing practices work best where they emerge from a deep, comprehensive commitment to the market. For instance, time spent by the chief executive with customers appears to be linked positively with business performance. This research is building up one of the most convincing pieces of evidence in favor of market-based business strategy. It demonstrates that a strong external focus is critical to success.

While the CEOs in the study indicated that they spend less than 15 percent of their time in direct contact with customers, I do sense small signs of change. I know of several businesses that have adopted strategies that encourage senior management to go out and actually talk to real live customers. In some cases this basic, obvious, but forgotten practice is driving formal market research and analysis.

In management literature we often see innovation praised and extolled. But innovation is not abstract; it has to be forged out of a concrete set of circumstances. I believe that the root of most innovation comes from the supplier-customer interface, not the lab. The most innovative companies are the ones that listen and that don't feel threatened or defensive about criticism.

If those of us who head companies don't keep our customers in sight and earshot all the time, we deserve to be passed over. This challenges the status quo in many firms where production and finance have the upper hand. To succeed in today's environment, customers have to be brought out of the back room and put front and center in every aspect of business activity.

In conclusion, I'd like to summarize my beliefs with a number of interrelated maxims that anyone taking over an operation, whether it's a company or a division, might find helpful:

- Never take an organization at face value—look beneath the hood to see if the raw material of human potential is there.
- Ask yourself night and day, "Have I created the right structures to liberate the skills and potential of the entire workforce?"
- Be candid. Do not dissemble, consciously or unconsciously. Too many bosses are hypocritical or get into states of make-believe. Cut out all lip service ideas.
- Remember, it's the customer who pays your salary and everyone else's. Embed customer service and accountability to customers at all levels of the organization.
- Do not be overly reliant on internal processes and systems. There is no substitute for direct, face-to-face interaction with customers.
- Know the strengths and limits of your organization. Don't overreach; don't promise subordinates or customers what you can't deliver.
- Keep your strategy simple. Don't overintellectualize. Leave exotic management ideas to business schools and consultants.
- Invite challenges. Dare your customers to make audacious demands.
- Let experience be your teacher. Ask yourself continually, "What lesson is staring me in the face? What are people seeking from my company, and what can I do to help them get it?"

There's no mystique about the objectives of serving customers and making money. The great thing about management is that it is truly democratic. Anyone can play. Anyone can break through the conventional wisdom and see what's crying out to be done.

15

FUTURE TILT: HOW AND WHY COMPANIES NEED A CULTURE OF CONTINUOUS RENEWAL

Eckhard Pfeiffer,
Compaq Computer Corporation

Few industries rival the information technology business for the enormity and velocity of the changes seen since the introduction of the personal computer. Those changes were just the beginning of the convergence of computing, communications, media, and entertainment that are fundamentally transforming our personal and professional lives.

Compaq Computer Corporation has been at the center of this transformation. Founded in 1982 in Dallas, Texas, as a manufacturer of portable personal computers, Compaq is the world's largest supplier of personal computers and the fifth largest computer company in the world, with revenues of $18.1 billion in 1996. Not willing to rest on its achievements, Compaq's new objective is to become one of the top three global computer companies by the year 2000.

Eckhard Pfeiffer joined Compaq from Texas Instruments in 1983 as vice president–Europe. By 1990 he had turned Compaq into the number two PC supplier in Europe (number one since 1994). Since he took the reins as CEO in 1991, Compaq's stock has increased more than eightfold, and its sales and net income have risen more than five- and tenfold, respectively. Compaq now stands as one of the most admired companies in the world. CNBC named Eckhard its CEO of the Year in 1994, and Forbes placed him on its short list of the Best Performers of 1995.

THE FUTURE IS OFTEN unpredictable and ambiguous. Most people know that change is inevitable. But since the leaders of some companies find trailblazing too risky, they have learned to keep their organizations moving forward by following the paths cleared by others. With a little luck they manage to avoid the challenges and uncertainties that create disruption. In short, the leaders of these companies are followers. As long as they follow well, they and their businesses may survive. But they will never control their destinies.

Then there are the organizations that want to shape the future. These companies learn to anticipate the possible directions the future may take and begin to blaze the new path without hesitation. The leaders of these companies encourage their people to challenge conventional thinking, to change the business dramatically, and to create continuous renewal and progress. These companies don't just want to survive—they want to lead. They want to write the rules that others will follow.

At Compaq, continuous renewal is more than a catchphrase, it's our culture. Renewal challenges the company to stretch and grow.

From its beginning in 1982, Compaq has produced innovative products of high quality. Our management team has always been aware that market leadership was impermanent and that corporate complacency was risky. But even savvy teams sometimes need a stern reminder. For Compaq, that reminder occurred in 1991 when we reacted slowly to fundamental changes in the computer business. Company revenue, profitability, and market position suffered a sharp downturn. It was a defining moment.

The crisis of 1991 burned itself into Compaq's collective memory as one of those events we would never forget—and never repeat. Our response to this crisis was to put even more emphasis on challenge and change at every level. This created a new corporate culture in which managers strive unceasingly to read the signs of change and to pursue new opportunities and ideas instead of clinging to old ones. Our people are continually challenging themselves to attain ever-higher levels of performance, while simultaneously creating the next wave of renewal.

The one good thing about a crisis is that it clears the way for organizational self-appraisal and sweeping change. Of course, the first step in this process is to perceive that a crisis exists. For some organizations, even this can be a major challenge. Denial is a common reaction to crisis, and it prevents many companies from recognizing and dealing with obvious and deep-rooted business problems. But denial isn't a reaction limited to companies in crisis. Even more often it afflicts those that are still riding high on earlier successes. It's up to the leaders of those companies to resist the natural tendency to relax by stressing that the next big challenge is still ahead.

SHAPING COMPAQ'S CULTURE OF SELF-RENEWAL: THREE GUIDING PRINCIPLES

The computer industry is not for the faint of heart. It is a rough-and-tumble business where being on top one year is no guarantee for the next. In fact, some observers have said that market leadership in this business is inevitably transient, in part because large organizations always lose the ability to keep up with the pace of technology and the constantly shifting requirements of customers.

We don't agree. Dominant firms can fight the inertia of success if they apply the following three guiding principles:

- *Attack your own business and financial models before someone else does.* Continually rethink every product, service, process, and activity. Question everything about your business. Make sure that you give your people throughout the organization the authority to challenge sacred cows and provide new strategic models and operating frameworks.
- *Be careful about focusing on your industry's market leaders, particularly if they're losing market share.* Your market intelligence needs to extend beyond the traditional boundaries of your industry and its current products. Your traditional competitors will often be the wrong place to look for signs of fundamental change.
- *Stretching the organization brings out the best in it.* People respond to a bold, well-defined vision and adjust swiftly to its demands. Don't rely on incremental steps—they're just an excuse not to change. When you reach one goal, pursue an even bolder goal.

In mid-1996, we put these ideas into practice at Compaq. Believing that the computer industry had reached a critical juncture, we initiated an internal "Crossroads" project designed to challenge everything about the company, especially the very strategies, operating assumptions, and business models on which we had built our industry leadership through the first half of the nineties. Crossroads' overarching aim was to redefine Compaq's future direction—goals, strategies, financial targets—to the year 2000 and beyond. While some organizations take years to conduct strategic reassessments, we took the boot camp approach: an intensive, compressed effort to achieve high-impact change. Crossroads fulfilled its mission in eight weeks.

Here's how it worked. We assembled fifteen cross-functional teams, each with eight to ten of the company's best performers, to develop an integrated set of recommendations. Top management deliberately limited its role in this phase and focused on facilitating the process.

The teams consulted among themselves and with their peers in Compaq. They analyzed technology, market, product, and process issues with channel partners, customers, and suppliers. They explored the implications of digital convergence and the Internet with experts outside the computer industry.

Eight short weeks later, these teams delivered their proposals. Their recommendations—both strategic and tactical—were broad in scope and profound in their redirection of Compaq. The teams identified:

- The potential impact of new technologies and competitors on Compaq's business
- Likely strategies of existing competitors
- Alternative distribution and manufacturing models
- New customer and channel requirements
- Potential market and product strategies
- Investments for the core PC businesses
- Investments in new markets

After some internal top management debate, these proposals gave rise to a new three-pronged strategy designed to (1) strengthen and grow Compaq's core businesses, (2) invest in strategic new products and markets, and (3) push harder for the development and professional growth of all Compaq employees. To implement this strategy effectively, the company reorganized itself into four customer-focused global product groups and created a worldwide sales, marketing, service, and support organization. Additionally, we began to focus our resources on reshaping the future direction of product distribution in the age of the Internet.

CREATING AND MAINTAINING A CULTURE OF SELF-RENEWAL

Compaq's success provides the opportunity to discover—or rediscover—several fundamental lessons about building an organization that embraces change and challenge. Executives or managers who want to lead a revolution of their own should take them to heart.

Challenges, Not Demands

Threatening employees isn't the same as challenging them. Unfortunately, this is a lesson too many companies have yet to learn. Experience should eventually bring them around.

While it is possible to use a crisis, fear, or unreasonable demands to generate a single wave of change, the effects are seldom long-lasting or self-sustaining. Executives, managers, and employees who have survived these tactics don't look forward to experiencing them again. The next time decisive action is needed, you can count on them to freeze.

People have to be willing to accept the risk of change to create a self-sustaining cycle of improvement and an ongoing sense of renewal. Compaq employees know that individual and collective success can only continue if they embrace change as an opportunity rather than reacting to it in a crisis mode.

I knew we would undermine the company's culture of renewal if we either compromised the independence of the Crossroads teams or ignored their proposals. Each member of my team sent a clear message to all managers and employees that the process used to create change, and the people involved in this process, were just as important to the organization as the actual outcome of the Crossroads analysis. This message about the importance of trust and commitment will pay dividends for a long time.

Communication

High-velocity, future-tilted companies use an array of listening posts to sense the future. These companies go through prodigious efforts to create and maintain open lines of communication with customers, business partners, industry analysts, and other organizations that can provide insight into market and technology trends.

For example, Compaq's Customer Satisfaction Council, a global organization chaired by the top manufacturing and quality executive, meets twice a month to review market information, customer feedback, and product quality and performance data from around the world. One of their chief information sources is the Customer Satisfaction Index (CSI), which examines how customers feel about the products they use and the service they receive.

Compaq analysts conduct over five thousand CSI surveys semiannually in key markets, channels, and product lines around the world. The CSI also includes data on key competitors, which leads to the development of external benchmarks. This information is tracked very closely by all levels of Compaq management, not just by the Customer Satisfaction Council.

Best Practice

Whether addressing key product development priorities or implementing sophisticated enterprisewide computer systems, the dismissive "not invented here" attitude has no place in a culture of challenge and renewal.

Compaq keeps its own research and development efforts sharp by sharing knowledge and innovations with business partners like Microsoft and Intel, and by investing in early-stage technology companies. This provides access to additional expertise in key emerging technologies and product development strategies. One example among many is Compaq's pre–initial public offering investment in Raptor Systems, a developer of network security firewalls that helps Compaq meet corporate Internet and intranet needs.

Team Genes

Some Compaq employees joke that the company has a gene for teamwork and team learning. Compaq knows that team IQ can be higher than individual IQ, and that teams may be better than individuals at piercing denial and facing current reality. A manager's ability to foster teamwork and collaboration is considered a critical personal competency, reinforced through performance appraisals, professional development plans, and job assignments.

Team technology and team aptitudes are the bedrock of renewal. At Compaq, cross-functional task forces are regularly assembled to address emerging issues. Team members are also responsible for selling their proposals within the organization, which speeds up the process of acceptance. Roughly 70 percent of task force recommendations are accepted by higher management—a testament to the quality of these ideas and how well they've been presented.

A Different Kind of Executive

Future-tilted companies require a different kind of manager than those found in inherently more stable industries. Boldness and imagination are at a premium in the information technology business. This is why

Compaq has created an Executive Competency Model that defines the key leadership characteristics important for professional success. Company executives use the ECM to help define recruiting profiles, create staff-development programs and succession plans, and establish job requirements.

Riding the Wave of Change

What about the companies that don't embrace self-renewal? They will never be more than followers; global leadership will always elude them. No matter what industry a company competes in, it must live with one foot in the present and the other in the future—responding to today's customer needs while preparing for tomorrow's by striving to find the future first. There's simply no other way to build world leadership.

16
MEMO TO A TURNAROUND BOSS

Michael Z. Kay, LSG/SKY Chefs

Michael Z. Kay had solid turnaround experience in the hotel business when in 1991 he took the helm as president and CEO of LSG/SKY Chefs (referred to as SKY Chefs), a leading in-flight food-service firm.

Although the company had been on a roll two years earlier, Kay found it in swift decline. Its end-product prices and operating costs were significantly higher than its rivals', and customers perceived its quality of service as just average.

Over the next three years, SKY Chefs' operating costs declined by $60 million, thanks to spectacular gains in labor productivity, backed up by overhead reductions at headquarters and a significant drop in workplace injuries. Margins soared as customers upgraded their perception of the company's quality of service.

Between 1992 and 1995, operating profits rose from $28.5 million to $64.7 million on roughly similar revenues. By 1995, SKY Chefs was healthy enough to make a dramatic acquisition. It absorbed Caterair International, a company that three years earlier had not only been bigger than SKY Chefs but ranked higher by nearly all measures of excellence—proof indeed that Michael Kay is a turnaround leader.

SKY Chefs is now a company with sales of $1.5 billion.

Dear Harry,

Warmest congratulations on being recruited as the new CEO of the Acme Pogo Stick Group. Rumor has it that Acme's a real junkyard dog, but you must know that already. However, to help you get started, I'd like to share some advice on the potentials and pitfalls of taking the helm of an organization that at the moment has short life expectancy—and may actually be terminally ill.

There are few situations where management know-how can create wealth and jobs and satisfy shareholders and customers more than a turnaround. The thrill that you might succeed at such an endeavor is worth the considerable risk that you could also fail. There's a low probability of succeeding because of the forces arrayed against you from the outset—lost momentum, red ink, poor morale, credit constraints, dissatisfied customers, et cetera. Then too there's the diagnostic headache: What really went wrong? And is righting those wrongs the path to follow? The causes of the company's present plight range from strategic misdirection, to environmental shifts, to a poor understanding by previous CEOs of the drivers of the business. The list is long on possibilities.

This memo will focus primarily on just one of the many-faceted challenges you face, namely, operational improvement: getting the actual business of the firm running at maximum efficiency. To be sure, there are situations where even a tightly run corporate ship needs a turnaround. But they're rare. Dysfunction is contagious in companies in decline.

In a nutshell, the key to better operations is unlocking the power within the existing upper- and middle-management teams. Chances are good that you will find know-how, insight, even managerial brilliance in those quarters—but it's locked away in peoples' minds simply because no one asked for it in the past. Granted, some companies are so rundown and atrophied that the existence of this untapped power may be open to doubt, in which case some reseeding of management skills will be needed. But nine times out of ten, the power is there, bound by chains the incoming CEO must remove. This is one of the first and most creative acts of the skilled turnaround CEO: liberating a company's knowledge, drive, and commitment that has been previously unused and perhaps even suppressed.

The CEO has to produce results fast or the whole enterprise will go up in smoke. So the first order of business is to understand the bare bones of the company and, in consultation with key managers, to set turnaround value objectives—for the company, for decentralized units, for processes, and for individual managers. These value objectives, or targets, should be tightly focused and detailed. But, above all, they should be breathtakingly bold—the most ambitious bogeys possible. Avoid thinking in terms of small steps and reasonable increments like a 10 to 15 percent improvement for this or that function or operation.

One way to approach the task of determining these high-hurdle goals is to ask what the company would be worth publicly if three-quarters of its operating inadequacies were cured. Another approach might be for the CEO and the top echelon to determine an ideal rate of return, on the order of two or three times the cost of capital. Another might be to look at the profitability of the most capable competitor.

More important than the actual method, however, is to create such ambitious value targets and demanding timetables that they result in that Everest feeling—the sense among employees that they are embarking on an endeavor that will demand their utmost. Meanwhile, it sends a message to those who want to keep on doing business as usual to consider seeking work elsewhere.

In short, the turnaround bogey and the high-stretch time frame should be dramatic enough to be both an inspiration and a motivator. Having a significant economic interest in the outcome helps fire up managers. And at SKY Chefs, middle managers collectively owned about 20 percent of the company. They were made aware that if the value target was achieved, the value of each of their shares would increase roughly tenfold.

An operational turnaround depends on keenly motivating and liberating the creativity of the people whose hands are on the levers of the operation—upper and middle managers. They, in turn, will unlock the knowledge and repressed motivation of the line workers under them. It's the managers' task to fire up the ranks with the new creative esprit and the quest for excellence in work tasks, flows, and structures.

Enhancing the productivity of the workforce is the main key to recovery. Gains arising from increments of capital or technology usually take longer to show up. They can be pursued when the turnaround is on its way.

Gains in productivity need not be perceived as a managerial enigma, difficult to achieve by even highly motivated ordinary mortals. But in practice this is often the case. All too often companies squander opportunities to achieve productivity gains, or they fail to uncover the potential lying buried beneath irrational practices and procedures that have become sacrosanct or that managers are afraid to change for their own irrational reasons.

CEOs can't get their arms around this problem by themselves. Their role is to swiftly mobilize various teams of middle managers and line personnel as primary agents of the company's new mission. These teams have to go back to square one. They need to ask the most fundamental questions about each task and subtask, identify those that add value, and compress or eliminate those that don't. They must challenge many cherished assumptions about the best systems and structures, and rigorously reconfigure the ends and means of work. They must also look outside the company to find models in other organizations that have made relevant breakthroughs.

The company has to make a commitment to this high-stretch goal from the outset, often before anyone has figured out how it can be achieved. You must believe absolutely in the underlying profitability of the business. And with equal conviction, individual managers and teams must believe in the value of new tools, concepts, and procedures that may have been ignored, shunted aside, misunderstood, or misapplied in the past. The key to breakthrough results is excellence-building tools that create dramatic operating changes.

Many businesses simply jog along, content to produce 2 or 3 percent annual productivity gains, and squeezing out economies here and there thanks to a handful of improved processes. Incremental gains have no place in a turnaround. What you must demand is major transformation fueled by explosive and revolutionary ideas.

In retrospect, it's hard to believe that such profound opportunities for productivity improvement existed at SKY Chefs. Especially since they operated in an industry where labor is the bedrock of profitability. Yet, once the productivity teams were up and running, this proved to be so. One of the principles around which SKY Chefs and many of its competitors formerly organized and structured work was the belief that the longer the lead time when delivering meals to flights, the greater the efficiency. However, when cycle-time management concepts were applied to this notion, it proved to be flat-out wrong. Once the company built a rapid-response production line, they discovered that long lead times tend to be a drag on productivity. The results speak for themselves. The redesign of work at SKY Chefs yielded a productivity gain of 25 percent within three years, and that gain generated the lion's share of the $50 million in savings the company had set as its goal.

The exceptional effort and imagination required of middle managers has to be backed up with tough-minded, ubiquitous, and unremitting accountability. Effective accountability systems not only create rewards for superior managers but also give them visibility. This sends a clear message throughout the company when they are then given tougher challenges and asked to shoulder greater responsibilities. You can safely assume that there are many unacknowledged stars in your company waiting to strut their stuff.

Many companies that fall into decline suffer from failures of accountability. When only lip service is paid to the concept, the result is a climate of accommodation. This, in turn, contributes to inertia among managers who have become resigned to working far below their potential. In the turnaround, everyone should have a clear answer to the following question: "What does it take to get promoted or fired around here?" People need to understand just what qualities it takes to make a recognized hero. This can be achieved through well-articulated and fully and relentlessly communicated goals, supported by an accountability system that is taken seriously.

Before a turnaround became imperative, managers at SKY Chefs wore blinders. They tended to rationalize both outstanding and below-average performance, and concentrated on one-on-one relationships with their immediate subordinates—often at the expense of the corporate mission. Meanwhile, their promotions were governed by fixed rituals, with all managers having to accumulate specific experiences and skills before qualifying for the next higher level in the hierarchy. During the turnaround, this strict progression was abolished, and sheer ability became the criterion by which managers were judged. At the same time, much of the harshness and inflexibility of the earlier system was discarded. It was replaced by three primary values that would transform behavior and drive the turnaround. These values became the leadership's insistent message:

- Always stretch beyond your comfort zone.
- Always ask for help when you're not achieving the goals to which you've committed.
- Always identify, promote, and motivate the best talent.

On the other hand, when disappointments and shortfalls occur, the accountability system should not be punitive. After all, you're demanding that managers stretch past their old boundaries and dream big. For the best of motives, some will overreach. In such cases they should be encouraged to ask for help—and all managers should be judged and rewarded on their willingness to give help to others. Many companies have informal federations of managers heading different business units who do in fact help one another in emergencies or crises. But typically these managers are not measured or compensated by the amount of help given. They should be. "Ask for help" is everyone's safety line. Here the Everest metaphor applies: Nobody makes it to the top unless the entire team pulls together.

Human relations practices emphasizing rank and authority based on seniority are out of step with the new collective ethic. To achieve the kind of massive transformation required by a turnaround, more than the top-down input from bosses is needed. You should be trying to create a democracy of intellect, based on the concept that everyone has innate managerial acumen and can contribute concretely to the value goals.

In most turnaround situations there is a clock ticking loudly. The CEO simply does not have time to use longer-term solutions. Some options will have to be discarded—for example, creating change through behavioral conditioning and modifications. By the time most workers start responding to attempts of this kind, the company is likely to be in Chapter Eleven. It's both swifter and less risky to trust the economic carrot as the catalyst for the changes that you're encouraging individuals to make.

If teams are the engine of the turnaround, what is the main task of CEOs? They must lead by example. They must be the chief architects and cheerleaders for culture change. Like politicians, they must go on the stump at all corporate locations, press the flesh, and exhort both middle managers and the rank and file to believe in their capacity for change. They must demonstrate in every way possible their own personal commitment to the new values.

This is why at SKY Chefs I knew it was important to reappraise headquarters' costs and functions. As CEO, I had to demonstrate that even at the corporate center dramatic change in outlook and process was possible. The team I entrusted with this mission found a number of routes for significant savings:

- Some functions, such as the corporate kitchens, were relocated in the decentralized units.
- Some processes, such as information systems, were outsourced to achieve significant savings.
- Some staff activities and functions were simply abolished.

At SKY Chefs, worker safety was another heavy cost burden. Injuries and lost time from accidents were staggering. In 1990, among some eighty-four hundred employees there were nearly two thousand injuries, generating a punishingly high lost-day cost per year. This was surprising in a company with an established safety program. Accordingly, a new special-purpose safety team of managers and line personnel—supported by a few outside experts—was convened and given a mandate to make rapid changes. Working with top management, this team created a goal of reducing injury-related expense by half within a year, again without any certainty that this goal could actually be achieved.

They soon discovered the flaw in the existing safety program: It was designed principally around the idea of identifying and tracking safety code violations, rather than encouraging on-the-job behaviors that would reduce accidents. The team made a number of dramatic recommendations, chief of which were that every kitchen should have highly active and responsive safety teams, and that a kitchen's good safety performance should comprise a significant portion of the kitchen manager's and management team's incentive compensation. The economic yield from these improvements amounted to about $10 million of our $50 million value goal. By 1995, SKY Chefs' lost days had declined by some 75 percent, injuries by 80 percent, and our bottom-line savings totaled over $11 million.

Some of the credit for this achievement belongs to individuals, and some to the team structure. Team effectiveness springs from the power released by collaborative and consensus solutions, backed by the collective will of a group when it is deeply focused on a problem area. When they operate as part of a team, people are more likely to think boldly and to commit to audacious targets and dramatic remedies.

When teams are ready with their recommendations, top management has to be ready to listen. At SKY Chefs, I needed to demonstrate my trust in my teams' dedication and intelligence by implementing their findings. Failure to adopt a team's recommendation can create a demoralizing precedent. Teams need to know that their solutions will not be second-guessed or countermanded, although of course they may be asked to agree to some modifications if there were facts that escaped them for some reason. CEOs should limit team assignments to major cross-discipline issues for which solutions are not apparent at the outset. The team's objectives should be stated with crystal clarity. When a team's mission is unambiguous, its recommendations for change are much more likely to be on target.

The reason for placing such enormous authority in the hands of teams is that the incoming CEO has been given the role of savior, even though he or she may lack intimate knowledge of the company and, often, of the industry. CEOs must lead without claiming to have any magic bullets. They should inspire, motivate, and sometimes astonish the middle managers who truly do have the details of the business in their grasp. The bullets they have to keep dodging are people coming to them for answers. The leadership style of successful CEOs depends on delegating authority to the special-purpose teams they create, alter, and dissolve as the turnaround progresses. Much of their effort has to be dedicated to exhorting middle managers to believe in the culture change they're sponsoring. They must encourage their managers to trust the new values of high goals, high performance, and constant accountability—blending a bottom-line focus with an astute perception of what it takes to motivate people to surpass themselves.

At SKY Chefs, I have focused on special-purpose teams because experience showed that they had the capacity to achieve rapid and dramatic operating improvements. But teams are equally important as the company's model of governance. Once our teams demonstrated their capabilities, everyone in management realized that this was a superior tool for managing the day-to-day business. The team approach promised to retain and extend our hard-won operating gains because constant improvements and refinements would clearly be necessary to sustain top performance. In the final analysis, teams are more than organizational structures. They represent a superior behavioral style—a way of tackling challenges large and small that virtually guarantee a company's capacity to respond to the demands of change and to command its own future.

So, Harry, wishing you all the best, we'll sign off. If you put these suggestions to work in ways that make sense in your specific operating environment, you'll have a good chance of accomplishing the turnaround you've been dreaming about. Just keep in mind the three operating principles of my core message:

- Change culture and employee behaviors by introducing new values along with high-stretch financial goals.
- Create teams that are accountable for analyzing and reconfiguring operations to yield dramatic transformations and economies.
- Propagate the new values relentlessly, and incorporate them into the accountability structure.

17

STAKEHOLDERS ARE A REALITY CHECK FOR WORLD REFUGEE GROUP

Sadako Ogata, The Office of the United Nations High Commissioner for Refugees

Sadako Ogata is a former academic, and her field of expertise is decision theory in international conflict and diplomacy. A one-time Japanese delegate to the United Nations General Assembly, in 1968, 1970, and 1975–1979 she served as chairperson of UNICEF's Executive Board.

In late 1990 Mrs. Ogata was appointed High Commissioner for Refugees. Since then, this soft-spoken woman with an unassuming manner has shown an iron will and enormous drive in her campaign to improve her organization's delivery of a vast range of services to refugees, whose numbers have increased during her tenure from nineteen million to twenty-six million.

Unlike some UN agencies, the Office of the High Commissioner for Refugees (UNHCR) gets little regular funding from the UN budget. Most of its $1.3 billion budget comes from voluntary contributions. This means that the United Nations High Commissioner for Refugees must establish and maintain a reputation for efficiency and effectiveness with a large population of donors and stakeholders. These include nation-states, non-governmental organizations (NGOs), and the governments of the areas from which refugees are fleeing, as well as those where they hope to resettle.

The number of donors and the size of their contributions is a direct reflection of their perception of the needs of the world's refugees. This in turn depends on the high commissioner's ability to project the desperation

of the refugees' plight, and to reassure the donors of her organization's ca-
pacity to deliver needed services.

Although Mrs. Ogata is more a politician than a manager, she has lever-
aged her experience in international diplomacy in a way that has made
her an effective leader for change in a previously hidebound organization.
The UNHCR presents a management challenge even more complex and
demanding than most multinational corporations.

With headquarters in Geneva, the UNHCR employs some fifty-five
hundred people, working out of 255 offices in 123 countries—typically
under conditions of great instability, anxiety, and often physical danger.
In turn, these staffers work in local partnership with over 450 NGOs to
protect, feed, repatriate, and resettle refugees in situations where what
can go wrong often does.

One litmus test for staff performance that Mrs. Ogata uses frequently is
to weigh an individual's capacity for professional growth and develop-
ment. She is convinced that on-the-job learning is a constant possibility,
regardless of a person's age or rank. She herself has grown and matured as
an initiator of change in the UNHCR, and she has accomplished this de-
spite having to deal with the inevitable degree of bureaucratization en-
demic to all intergovernmental organizations.

Early skeptics have been silenced by the sweep and breadth of her ini-
tiatives and achievements. They have also been impressed by her personal
commitment demonstrated by her frequent field trips to crisis spots. At a
time when the United States had been accusing the UN and its agencies of
featherbedding and managerial inefficiency, the UNHCR has been ac-
knowledged as a sound and continually improving operation. Mrs. Ogata
has been a beacon showing that reform is possible.

ONE THING THAT MOST private and nonprivate institutions share is that
they both have stakeholders. To serve these stakeholders, they have to
demonstrate (1) responsiveness in delivering on their mission, and (2)
operational efficiency and effectiveness. The lucky institutions are those
with stakeholders who demand high standards and are vigilant about fer-
reting out shortcomings. In this sense the UNHCR has been fortunate.
Our dependence on voluntary funding has kept us on our toes, since
every year the value of our work with refugees and the methods by
which work is done are reappraised.

In some ways this is analogous to the scrutiny of a corporation by its
public shareholders, only it is more exigent, since disappointed stakeholders can slash their contributions and thus drastically curtail the
range and effectiveness of the services UNHCR provides for people in
extremis. Under these circumstances, it is easy to forget that refugees

are first and foremost individuals, not an abstract problem. The "problem" approach tends to lead to insensitivity, inadequate refugee relief, and ultimately to disenchanted stakeholders. The UNHCR cannot afford to sacrifice a generation of refugees because it is trying to be efficient at a given time. It is our policy never to walk away from pressing human needs until the job is done.

I'd like to discuss two of the many recent initiatives and programs that have made UNHCR's stakeholders increasingly aware of the plight of refugees, as well as convincing them that their contributions are being deployed with maximum efficiency. Both of these initiatives are concerned with redeploying headquarters' resources and policies in a way that strengthens the efforts, morale, and productivity of the staffers in the field who are in direct contact with UNHCR's refugee "customers."

The barometer of stakeholder confidence has to be constantly monitored. In April 1991, three months after my appointment, the UNHCR faced a situation that could have seriously damaged donor confidence. Over a period of three weeks, 450,000 Kurds fled toward the Turkish border with the armies of Saddam Hussein on their heels. At the same time another 1.25 million Kurds moved toward Iran. As the refugees fled to this harsh, desolate mountain border range in midwinter, it quickly became clear that no agency was equipped to respond swiftly and effectively to this enormous crisis.

Unfortunately, the UNHCR was hamstrung by the internationally accepted definition that a refugee has to have crossed an international border. Since the Kurds were still within the confines of Iraq, we could not mobilize resources as swiftly as the need demanded, nor did we have the resources to cope with 1.7 million refugees.

As a result, in 1991 UNHCR created the Emergency Preparedness and Response Section (EPRS). This new unit has the ability to send fully trained operational teams to meet emergency conditions in the field within seventy-two hours. Every UNHCR section volunteers staff for the EPRS, which is run by a small core group. These volunteers are trained as a team and remain on twenty-four-hour standby for six months.

Since its creation, the EPRS has been deployed in many parts of the world whose names read like a checklist of humanitarian crises, from setting up the humanitarian airlift into beleaguered Sarajevo, taking a mere nine days in June 1992 and lasting more than three years, to organizing the relief effort for one of the largest refugee crises ever, namely the exodus of 1.2 million Rwandans into eastern Zaire in mid-1994.

By redefining global ideas of who a refugee is, and by creating in effect a relief SWAT team, the UNHCR has demonstrated its capacity to galvanize its forces with speed and effectiveness in response to emerging situations. These efforts have also helped focus attention on the underlying problem—the ongoing need to create a positive influence on world opinion to protect potential refugee populations.

A second field-empowering initiative gives relief workers in the field the tools they need to respond flexibly and swiftly on their own without all the checking back with headquarters that previous systems required. Changes are already being implemented across a two-year time frame. Project DELPHI, as the program is known, has been managed internally and has thus far involved most of the UNHCR staff. As a result, it has created a broad internal commitment to change.

However, empowerment initiatives are like loading a gun. The UNHCR must be sure that its field staff have the right attitudes and the right competencies to use their authority properly. In the past, there have been communication problems between headquarters and the field. There were also problems of delegating authority and resources. In response, there has been an effort over the past two years to implement a Career Management System that enables the UNHCR staff to align individual performance with overall agency strategy, as well as providing a clear framework for personal development. This scheme is built around six core competencies and six managerial competencies that outline the skills, knowledge, and attributes a staff member must have to be effective within the UNHCR—both at headquarters and in the field.

From an outsider's perspective, defining core competencies may seem a business generic. However, in practice they are difficult to define. It takes many hundreds of man-hours to secure ownership across a widely dispersed organization. On the other hand, a Career Management System has tremendous value in terms of encouraging cohesiveness, open communications, mutual trust, and delineating and sharing authority where it was not clarified before.

In any organization where the headquarters is removed from the action, these core values form the glue that binds field workers with headquarters staff. This policy expresses the one overriding reality that recognition and promotion will go to those who are predominantly successful in the field, not to those who stalk the apparent corridors of power in Geneva.

Another important action in recent years has been the formulation of the managerial competencies appropriate to UNHCR's mission, its management ethos, and style. The ultimate goal of listing such managerial skills is to drive home the importance the organization places on an indi-

CORE COMPETENCIES

1. Commitment to humanitarian principles and to UNHCR needs, priorities, goals, and values.
2. Ability to analyze, adapt to, and work effectively in a variety of situations; and the flexibility to cope with unforeseen or unexpected events.
3. Ability to work effectively with colleagues from different backgrounds and cultures to achieve shared goals and optimize results.
4. Ability to display initiative, to plan and manage one's own work; the determination to achieve results and to improve personal performance.
5. Ability to listen to—and understand—what people are trying to communicate; and the ability to express oneself in a clear and concise way.
6. Ability to demonstrate appropriate behavior in both professional and personal situations, as well as self-control, perseverance, and resilience.

vidual's capacity for self-development and for developing the potential of others. Today senior management at UNHCR must demonstrate their continuing growth as managers and leaders, and they are all expected to set an example by undertaking management training.

The core competencies provide a written expression of UNHCR's values and its underlying cohesion. But the managerial competencies promote true leadership by encouraging staff members to become models that exemplify those core values.

Since the office of high commissioner is a political appointment by the General Assembly, I will have no hand in selecting my successor. However, I hope to leave behind an important legacy—a career system that recognizes the inherent diversity at the UN and seeks to leverage that diversity for excellence.

MANAGERIAL COMPETENCIES

1. Ability to develop and communicate a clear strategic direction.
2. Ability to carry out the organization's vision, to manage change, to make timely decisions and be accountable for them, and to build, motivate, and lead a team.
3. Ability to create consensus with staff on objectives and competencies needed to achieve an overall plan, and to provide them with effective feedback on their performance.
4. Ability to provide effective coaching and to encourage staff development.
5. Ability to plan and use resources in accordance with guidelines and delegated accountability.
6. Ability to identify and understand relationships, constraints, and pressures affecting others, especially refugees.

18

SPARKING THE GROWTH ENGINE AT MONSANTO: USING SHAREHOLDER VALUE AS THE DRIVING FRAMEWORK

Robert B. Shapiro, Monsanto Company

Low-keyed Robert B. Shapiro could well have anticipated an easygoing tenure when he was made CEO of Monsanto in April 1995. Outsiders didn't think much needed improving in a company that was already a Wall Street favorite—thanks to a stellar chemicals business plus major sidelines in pharmaceuticals and biotechnology. But this former law professor and corporate counsel has surprised observers by the sweep and tempo of the changes he's instituted. In effect, he's fashioned a new identity for his company.

A milestone in this makeover was the 1997 spin-off of Monsanto's chemicals business with its $3 billion in revenues. The remaining $7 billion in life sciences revenues is expected to grow faster without the drag of chemicals. Growth projections for the biotech businesses are like giant beanstalks. Plant biotech alone should hit $2 billion in sales by the year 2000 and soar to $6 billion five years after that.

Shapiro's tenure at Monsanto has been marked by a large number of ambitious biotechnology acquisitions and the comeback of the G. D. Searle unit, which now boasts a promising lineup of new drugs. Shareholders have had a lot to cheer about: The stock has risen almost threefold in three years. Despite R&D outlays of 7.5 percent of sales, the average gain of earnings per share in this period has been 22 percent annually.

Perhaps Shapiro's greatest achievement has been in the field of ideas, specifically in promoting the concept of "sustainable development." Monsanto acknowledges the degradation that industrialization and population growth have caused to the earth, sea, and air, and offers the hope of developing technologies that extract more value while creating less waste with less punishment to the environment. "This new model of development," says Shapiro, "will impose two requirements. First of all, we'll have to produce much more with much less raw material and energy. Second, we'll have to make much wiser use of what we do make and waste much less of it."

Shapiro displays that rare mixture of vision and common sense, idealism and a strong bottom-line orientation. Just how strong is the subject of this chapter, which explains the merits of gearing managerial compensation to the profitable outcome of creating shareholder value.

BUILDING SHAREHOLDER WEALTH HAS risen inexorably in the last decade to rank at the top of management's agenda. Shareholder value creation is, of course, one of the foundations of the modern corporation. What's different nowadays is the intensity with which it's being pursued. The reasons aren't hard to find: the leveraged buyout frenzy, relentless competition, global market liberalization, and increased shareholder activism have combined to place intense pressure on management to serve shareholder interests with a vigor and determination never seen before.

There are three classic ways to grow shareholder value:

1. Enhancing operations through margin improvement and better capital utilization
2. Lowering the cost of capital
3. Growing the business profitably

In the early days of shareholder value, businesses pursued operational improvements through portfolio restructuring, cost reduction, capacity rationalization, and process reengineering. And they enhanced capital structures through prudent use of leverage and stock buybacks.

Today, the benefits of these approaches have largely been realized. The challenge ahead lies in achieving real growth at the high rates expected by shareholders in a global business environment characterized by explosive technological change and the emergence of markets of unprecedented size. All of this must be accomplished without losing focus on the bottom line. As the world clocks in a new millennium, the challenge for leaders today is to galvanize growth.

Because an organization is no more and no less than the sum of its people, pursuing growth demands the unleashing, to the fullest degree, of its employees' latent potential. Their commitment and motivation heighten efficiency and generate operational excellence. And their creativity ignites the engine of growth. In Monsanto's current industry environment—one that is ever-changing, ambiguous, and uncertain—it has become more important than ever for us to empower our employees. Self-motivated people know that much is expected of them, but they also know they will be rewarded for outstanding achievement.

The latent potential of most people is immeasurably vast. To develop this potential to the fullest, at Monsanto in 1996 we embarked on a five-pronged program to energize its people to create shareholder value. The five points of the program are:

1. Articulate a coherent vision.
2. Make clear what that vision means to Monsanto's people as individuals.
3. Provide innovative organizations, processes, and policies to help people succeed.
4. Align personal goals and incentives with corporate performance measures.
5. Communicate, communicate, communicate—effectively.

ARTICULATE A COHERENT VISION

Most large organizations need to articulate a vision that is simple, compelling, coherent, and logical. What follows is a compressed version of the Monsanto vision:

> We face a business environment that will change radically and unpredictably. Accordingly, we need to be flexible and responsive. Intense competition will make it unlikely that we can achieve price increases. Therefore, we need to achieve substantial and continuous gains in operational excellence, and increases in margin driven by eliminating waste, not value.

We have outstanding market opportunities, and the inherent growth potential of our businesses is just as outstanding. We need to seize these opportunities and grow at rates unprecedented in our history to create and fund an attractive future for our customers, our investors, and our people.

To accomplish this, we must unleash the creativity and entrepreneurial energy of all our people. We each need to take personal responsibility for operational excellence, idea generation, and building the business.

Growth is our new focus. And because we need to mobilize our energy and commitment to accomplish this goal, capital is not a limiting factor for us. We can, and will, fund all business ideas and improvements that increase shareholder value.

As we go forward, every idea and action will be judged by whether it increases or diminishes shareholder value. Shareholder value is the prism through which new insights are gained about improving the business. Because the primary method of creating shareholder value is generating returns above the cost of capital, everyone in the company must clearly understand this concept. Only then can individuals identify how they can best contribute to value creation at Monsanto.

An excellent example of this approach concerns three Monsanto plants operated by different business units. They had traditionally been run in isolation from one another, although they were only a few miles apart in the same metro area. However, once the managers of these plants got together to look for ways to enhance shareholder value, they saw that it was in everyone's best interests to run one shared maintenance organization instead of three. From there, they went on to amalgamate their purchasing, security, training, and utilities functions. This innovative example of teamwork has yielded annual savings of more than $3 million.

Make Clear What the Company's Vision Means to Individuals

A remote and uncommunicative vision is a dangerous thing. I have gone the limit in presenting and articulating the company's vision to our thirty thousand employees worldwide.

One example of "walking the talk": A recent three-day Monsanto Global Forum brought together a nonhierarchical, "diagonal" slice of employees. The delegates included senior management, plant operators, business unit presidents, field sales managers, secretaries, and staff function leaders. Together, we explored questions central to Monsanto's future success—anticipating future opportunities, maintaining operational excellence, and globalization.

The mix of people from all areas and levels of the company strongly conveyed the message of teamwork and the importance of each individual's contribution. By holding the forum on "neutral territory," away from corporate headquarters, no one was on his or her home ground. This way, everyone had the opportunity to feel summoned to lead, to manage, and to innovate. Rather than propounding solutions from se-

OPEN MARKET INITIATIVE: EMPLOYEES MAKING VALUE-CREATING CHOICES

Monsanto has adopted a new way of filling jobs internally, symbolizing the message that employees must take more responsibility for the skills they possess, the work they do, and the careers they pursue. The Open Market program does away with the boundaries and barriers that some internal job seekers once experienced. Employees who may once have felt constrained about seeking opportunities outside their own units now have the freedom to promote their capabilities for any Monsanto job, anyplace, anytime. They don't have to ask for their supervisor's approval before applying for another job, and similarly, managers seeking talent have the freedom to recruit throughout Monsanto.

In due course, the Open Market program will be supported by on-line listings of job openings and will circulate employee's résumés electronically. The important message conveyed to employees is that the Open Market represents a significant cultural change to a more partnerlike relationship. This way, employees enjoy the freedom to pursue their professional growth, and the company benefits by developing a resource pool of skilled employees capable of achieving the corporation's ambitious growth goals.

nior management, The Global Forum raised key questions that the thirty thousand people of Monsanto must resolve together to meet the challenges of tomorrow.

PROVIDE INNOVATIVE ORGANIZATIONS, PROCESSES, AND POLICIES TO HELP PEOPLE SUCCEED

When companies experience a big culture change, their CEOs must ask themselves and others, "What more can we do to help our people succeed in this new environment?" To liberate its people, to help them achieve their full potential, Monsanto has created new organizations, processes, and policies by:

- Organizing for growth
- Developing a new financial metric

Organizing for Growth

The new Monsanto emphasizes relationships and roles rather than structure. Gone is our ponderous, slow-moving group structure that until recently governed the hierarchical, headquarters-dominated organization. It has been replaced by thirteen small and nimble units that are able to respond more effectively to change and intensified competition, as well as to technological developments, political changes, and social trends.

This new corporate structure is designed to support the business units—the growth engines of the company. In addition to speed, flexibility, and responsiveness, these autonomous yet interconnected units have one additional characteristic: They offer a more efficient structure for motivating and inspiring workers because their actions can be clearly linked to value creation.

Further organizational evolution to promote teaming throughout the company is planned after the chemical business is spun off.

In order to spur its growth objectives, Monsanto has established "world area teams" for specific high-potential countries. Their roles are to address growth opportunities for current products and technologies across all business units; to develop new growth ideas based on market needs; and to identify strategic acquisitions. Other growth teams will be evaluating the opportunities that lie at the intersection of two or more

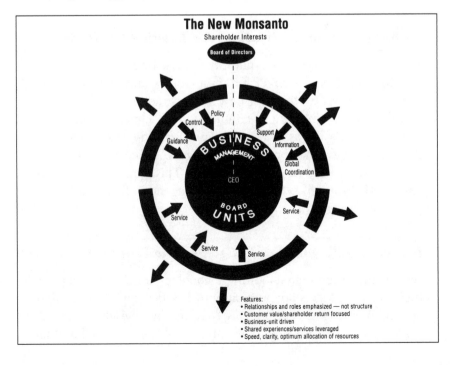

The New Monsanto

Shareholder Interests

Board of Directors

Policy

Control

Guidance

BUSINESS MANAGEMENT

Support

Information

Global Coordination

CEO

BOARD UNITS

Service

Service

Service

Service

Features:
- Relationships and roles emphasized — not structure
- Customer value/shareholder return focused
- Business-unit driven
- Shared experiences/services leveraged
- Speed, clarity, optimum allocation of resources

business units, or that emerge as a result of new forces in the marketplace. What's more, there is a Growth Enterprises business unit that incubates new product ideas and makes "seed" investments in promising new products that don't fit neatly into existing business units.

We are also addressing the question of what happened to so many past innovations within Monsanto that never saw the light of day. Our new Specialty Products business unit is exploring the business potential of at least a hundred promising inventions that languished for lack of attention in the old operating groups. There is also a new group studying issues and opportunities associated with environmental sustainability. In addition, we have an institute that scans the horizon and asks "what if" questions about the future. This institute is currently creating a worldwide internal network to detect trends and translate them into opportunities. In short, we have launched a host of initiatives to generate growth opportunities, to liberate thinking, and to enhance creativity, imagination, and innovation at Monsanto.

INNOVATION BLOOMS

The following three new product initiatives have emerged directly from the new shareholder value/growth paradigm:

Identifying New Applications for Existing Products

Monsanto has launched an innovative marketing effort to expand uses for Saflex, an interlayer for automobile windshields that prevents shattering. By thinking beyond the traditional auto market and focusing on lobbying for building code changes that would mandate interlayers as a defense against earthquakes, hurricanes, and explosions, the product's managers have generated the promise for significant growth at Saflex. This strategy fits hand in glove with Monsanto's proactive social agenda of preventing injuries and saving lives.

Leveraging Technology to Create New Products

By rethinking the manufacturing technology used in making NutraSweet brand sweetener, Monsanto has developed an entirely new product called Glacier. This is a safe, biodegradable, metalworking fluid that replaces conventional oils used to cool and lubricate parts being cut by machine tools. Today, Glacier is poised to capture a $500 million worldwide market.

Teaming for Nontraditional Product Uses

A group of new products—santosol dimethyl esters—sprang from an internal joint venture between two diverse business units. Waste streams from one of the business unit's processing plants are now being used to create new paint-stripping and hand-cleaning products that are biodegradable and low in toxicity and volatility. Once again Monsanto people have developed products that couple a positive social agenda with considerable growth opportunities.

Monsanto's Growth Enterprises unit is positioning the company for tomorrow's growth opportunities. One of its distinguishing features is that it's not simply an R&D product lab—people are a key ingredient in its success. For example in Project Liftoff, a company-wide growth initiative, Growth Enterprises honed thousands of ideas generated by Monsanto employees into sixty investment proposals for new business ventures. The goal? Making money for shareholders.

A New Financial Metric

All too often creating shareholder wealth remains a preoccupation of top management alone. However, when middle management is disconnected from this process, many opportunities to increase profits and rates of return do not get pursued or adequately exploited. This is why Monsanto has introduced a new financial metric—Economic Value Added (EVA)—to more effectively align all employee actions and business activities with shareholder value creation.

After exhaustively exploring the factors that drive share prices, we concluded that two forms of financial measurement—total business return and cash-flow return on investment—have the highest correlation with the market movement of share prices. These measurements were adapted and translated into simple but valid economic value-added measures. They can be used in day-to-day decision making at the business unit level for setting goals, evaluating strategies, and investing resources.

ALIGN PERSONAL GOALS AND INCENTIVES WITH CORPORATE PERFORMANCE MEASURES

"What gets measured gets done" may be an old adage, but it's a true one. Monsanto is now in the final phase of installing the new financial metric—aligning and integrating performance metrics and evaluations with incentive compensation. These moves are similar to ones taken to align executive compensation with shareholder value. The message is clear, internally and externally: Senior executives will not be rewarded unless the shareholders win. To give all our employees a greater stake in creating shareholder value, we have granted traditional stock options to all employees—not just our senior managers.

Some two hundred "change agents," ambassadors representing all functional areas of the business units, have been trained in EVA concepts and are carrying the company's message back to their units. Once shareholder value concepts have been embedded and applied at the business unit level and the results have been reflected in performance metrics, the business unit evaluation and compensation systems will effectively be linked. The metrics will determine both the normal compensation for expected performance and the extraordinary compensation due for achieving very high targets.

COMMUNICATE, COMMUNICATE, COMMUNICATE—EFFECTIVELY

Finally, of course, clear communication is what makes all this happen. Communication is greatly facilitated when the message is simple, powerful, and logical. Communication is also greatly facilitated when all the company's actions can be viewed in a consistent framework.

However, while it's important to keep preaching the company's message, facilitating two-way communication is a key requirement for implementing change. And two-way communication is encouraged when leaders continually point out that they don't have all the answers, that they're depending on the entire organization to come up with innovative approaches. When this attitude is genuine and clearly communicated, it promotes a climate of interaction that kindles energy and commitment.

At every opportunity for communication, whether with employees, customers, or shareholders, my management team and I consistently broadcast the message of "growth to build shareholder value." Using vehicles as diverse as articles in *Monsanto* magazine and sending E-mail to all employees, we are constantly challenging employees for their input on such questions as: "How can Monsanto grow to become a truly global company? How can we do this with discipline through EVA?"

People are responding remarkably. Thanks to consistent, continuous, clearly articulated communication at all levels of the organization, our employees know specifically how to contribute to the value-creation process.

In speeches to securities analysts, CFO Robert Hoffman has also been posing the Monsanto challenge: "How do we raise the bar? How can we create an entirely new level of shareholder value? How can we provide the motivation and incentives for our employees to do so?" In response, analysts are finding more and more reasons to become believers: A Bear Stearns report remarked, "We . . . expect considerable value realization from . . . the long-term strategy of the new growth-driven Monsanto."

In 1995, the traditional "Letter to Shareowners" in Monsanto's annual report launched the growth-for-shareholder value message. Key messages were reinforced about the "three areas we're developing to create additional value for our shareowners—operational excellence, growth, and sustainable development."

MONSANTO'S COMMITMENT TO CHANGE

Monsanto is a textbook example of the courage, drive, and energy it takes to create change in an organization. Day by day we are journeying along one of the most promising pathways for change now open to global organizations. Companies with tens of thousands of employees worldwide and long records of excellence often appear to be immutable entities. But this is an illusion. Their product stream and processes, their opportunities and inherent risks, need to be tended daily by committed individuals at every level of the organization.

Monsanto's people are not only looking at the necessary continuities in any ongoing organization, but also at the opportunities for momentous positive change. Creating a value and reward system that puts such individuals first ensures—as much as anything can these days—that the twenty-first century will be kind to Monsanto.

SHAREHOLDER VALUE METRICS: TOOLS THAT MAINTAIN MONSANTO'S FOCUS ON GROWTH

The heart of Monsanto's change strategy was the introduction of a comprehensive program to align employee actions and business activities with shareholder value. EVA was the key. The company's new financial metric drives decisions and evaluates performance to directly correlate business results with stock price or market expectations.

These expectations may be translated into minimum EVA targets for Monsanto and its business units. As a result, management has been able to set business targets to achieve or exceed investor expectations and translate those goals into actions that can be understood and implemented throughout the company. These tools allow mangement to focus on four value drivers: operational excellence, zero tolerance for underperforming capital, ensuring profitable growth that will add value, and optimizing the company's cost of capital.

To reinforce its commitment to growth, Monsanto aligned all executive compensation with the risks and rewards of shareholder value creation:

- Senior management's base compensation was frozen.
- Senior executives were required to purchase substantial amounts of Monsanto stock.
- A premium-priced option plan was established whereby Monsanto executives will not be rewarded unless shareholders realize a 67 percent improvement in share price over six years.

To secure the commitment of all employees to creating shareholder value, the company granted traditional options to all of its twenty-seven thousand employees. Finally, the company has issued additional shares to provide management with the flexibility needed to react quickly to strategic opportunities that promise economic value, as well as to split the stock and activate our share-repurchase program.

From planning, to measurement, to compensation, Monsanto's integrated shareholder value initiative has been widely and effectively communicated to the investment community.

19

COMMUNICATING IN THE INFORMATION AGE: THE LEADERSHIP FACTOR

Michael Critelli,
Pitney Bowes, Inc.

When Michael J. Critelli, chairman of the board and CEO of Pitney Bowes, Inc., was an undergraduate at the University of Wisconsin in the late sixties, majoring in communications, he took a course called "The Rhetoric of Campaigns and Revolutions." As a model for changing people's behavior and perceptions over time, the professor focused on Franklin Delano Roosevelt's four-year campaign to prepare the American public for World War II.

That model would serve Critelli well when he assumed the top job at Pitney Bowes in January 1997. A lawyer by training who joined Pitney Bowes in 1979, Critelli is spearheading the change that will prepare the venerable $3.9 billion maker of mailing and office systems, software, and services to compete successfully in the twenty-first century.

Founded in 1920 by an English addressing-machine salesman named Walter Bowes and his partner Arthur Pitney, who invented the postage metering machine, the Pitney Bowes company created the postage-meter industry. In the process, it emerged as one of corporate America's most consistently successful firms. For the past fourteen years it has registered double-digit dividend increases, and is the only office equipment company to be listed in all the editions of The 100 Best Companies to Work For in America *and* The 100 Best Stocks to Own in America. *Today, it has more than thirty thousand employees, with products, people, and services in over two million customer sites around the globe.*

In recent years, Pitney Bowes has expanded its offerings to include in-

novative technical solutions and services to meet the messaging and mail-
ing needs of its customers. It added to its portfolio addressing and other
message-management engines, paper/digital messaging interfaces, digital
copiers, customized facsimile applications, and other electronic technologies.
Even so, Mike Critelli is determined to move Pitney Bowes into new high-
growth areas such as the small office/home office (SOHO) and make this
solid company far more aggressive as it prepares for the future. To do this,
the recently appointed Pitney Bowes CEO is drawing upon many of the
lessons for effective communications he learned in his various management
roles at Pitney Bowes, and even during his student days at Wisconsin.

WITH THE COMING OF the Information Age, the CEO is potentially better able to communicate his or her company's message than ever before. New and established technologies and communications tools allow business managers and workers to share information and ideas electronically, and enable corporations to reach out to their global business partners, suppliers, and customers far more efficiently and cost-effectively than they have in the past.

Yet the explosion of message traffic in recent years has given rise to a communications gridlock that is adversely affecting productivity and making it more difficult to get the attention of the intended recipients. Today, more and more of the workday is consumed in reading, listening, and responding to a seemingly endless barrage of electronic, voice, and paper messages—often at the expense of profit-producing work.

Some of the consequences of this burgeoning message traffic were underscored in a study conducted for Pitney Bowes by the Institute for the Future, the Gallup Organization, and San Jose State University. Among the findings:

- More than 70 percent of *Fortune* 1000 workers feel overwhelmed by the growing number of messages they send or receive each day. Some 84 percent of respondents said they were interrupted three or more times an hour by messages. Most of these *Fortune* 1000 workers are already sending and receiving an average of 178 messages each day—often having to send the same message repeatedly to get through the message glut, which simply compounds the problem. As a result, it often seems as if communications demands are driving the conduct of business instead of the other way around.
- The selection of communications tools and methods is an extremely complex process integrally related to the business environment. There is no single blueprint for choosing communications tech-

nologies, nor is there any sophisticated or elegant rationale behind these decisions. At the same time, current workforce trends—such as geographically dispersed work teams, a growing dependence on telecommunications, and increased employee travel—make managing the communications process increasingly difficult. Even so, only 31 percent of those surveyed reported that their company had policies in place to guide and support their employees in making decisions about communications tools and strategies.

- Rarely do the new communications tools that are brought into the company replace the old existing ones. Rather, they are bundled as different electronic and paper-based media, and mixed and matched to ensure that messages get through one way or another. As a result, workers are using a variety of new and older proven communications methods and tools that include telephone, fax, PC, and E-mail.

- The growing demands of communicating in the Information Age have given rise to a new function within the *Fortune* 1000 workforce: "mission controllers" who act as organizational traffic cops. Typically, the mission control function is widespread, made up of high-level managers and professionals, as well as clerical and support staff, who have the knowledge and experience to help supervise the flow and reduce traffic volume, screen overloads, filter messages, and bridge uneven or incompatible communications infrastructures. *The mission-control function serves to bring some degree of order and supervision to the corporate communications process, and it is now emerging as a key office-communications role.*

- Finally, the study found that workers at all levels of an organization lack a clear understanding of the costs involved in communications. In fact, cost was seldom cited as a factor when making communications decisions. Hidden additional costs such as labor, phone line charges, supplies, or lost productivity are rarely factored into the decision process. In addition, communications costs are nearly always spread across department or individual accounts. *Rarely are the aggregate costs of communications even considered in terms of their comprehensive impact on organizational and financial performance.*

For CEOs, these findings present two distinct challenges. CEOs need to ensure that their organization's corporate communications are managed comprehensively to achieve maximum benefits at minimal cost. However, in addition, they must also ensure that the messages emanating from the CEO's office on down are consistent and have the desired impact on employees, customers, business associates, and supporters. Effective communication has always been the cornerstone of good management, and never more so than in the Information Age.

A Pragmatic Approach: Leadership Is Key

With more than three-quarters of a century of experience in helping businesses meet their communications needs worldwide, Pitney Bowes takes a pragmatic approach to corporate communications that mixes well-proven methods and mature media with innovative approaches and the latest in messaging technology.

What works at Pitney Bowes has proven effective for its customers as well. It's an approach that almost invariably hinges on the leadership factor. For instance, at Pitney Bowes and other leading-edge companies, the policies and principles that drive the organization's communications emanate directly from senior management. It is important for the CEO to serve as a role model, both in terms of his or her personal communications behaviors and in setting corporate communications objectives. The leadership factor is also critical in establishing realistic, workable guidelines for building comprehensive communications and messaging systems and processes that will provide the maximum business benefits and efficiencies needed to compete effectively into the next century.

Among the most important of these guidelines:

1. *Tried-and-true methods are often the most effective.* While senior management has recently come to rely more and more on E-mail and other new technologies and solutions to convey its message on a timely basis, face-to-face communications remain the standard for one simple reason: Electronic communications capabilities do not diminish the need for business leaders to communicate directly with their constituents. In fact, the opposite may be true, given the existing information and communications glut that exists within many organizations today.

    With face-to-face communications, CEOs can reinforce their message directly, correct any misconceptions or misunderstandings on the spot, and make sure their message has the desired impact—something that's not easily measured looking at a computer screen rather than the face of the person being addressed. At Pitney Bowes, for instance, I conduct regular face-to-face management meetings with the heads of operations worldwide. These meetings not only provide an overview of current developments, they enhance the participants' sense of responsibility and accountability, and create a better understanding of the company's integrated goals.

2. *Think before you send.* Too often corporate workers and managers are sent electronic messages that don't apply directly to them. Or consumers receive mail soliciting them to buy products in which they have absolutely no interest. In an effective corporate communications system, the communicator carefully thinks through both the message and its distribution, highlighting pertinent passages for individual recipients. There's no reason to blanket a distribution list with a massive body of data when each individual needs only a portion of the total communication.

3. *Focus on the recipients in your work circle as well as the outer circles.* Communications today are like the proverbial stone thrown into a still pond: they create patterns of concentric, ever-widening circles. It is important to understand and share communications preferences with your closest circle—the people with whom you most frequently interact. This can often eliminate significant duplication of messages. In addition, consider the impact of your communications on the outer circles. Ultimately, the communications process is all about moving an audience and getting recipients to react in the way desired by the sender or deliverer of the message. This is true whether you're communicating with your inner circle, your broader employee base, or your customer.

4. *Don't overreact to the latest technology trends.* For years we've been hearing about the paperless office and the letterless mailbag. People thought that TV would replace radio, or that PCs would displace TVs, or that videos would displace movies. None of these things happened. Today, for instance, paper-based communications are on the increase, with the higher volume of paper usage driven by new technologies such as faxes and copiers. As the study conducted by the Institute for the Future points out, new communications tools don't displace the old. Rather, they're folded into the existing communications infrastructure. As the need for global communications accelerates, we must continue to accommodate the different messaging habits and tools used by our business partners and associates in other parts of the world.

At the same time, change often creates a ripple effect that produces new uses for traditional media. For example, recent telecom deregulation should ultimately result in reduced costs for telephone use. As a result, customers, especially in large urban areas, are expected to add more telephone lines, which will create additional billing processes. This means more paper usage, more fax usage, and additional E-mail volume. In managing and planning for corporate communications systems, it's important to weigh these kinds of considerations.

5. *Take control of your corporate communications costs.* In many corporations today the communications processes are disparate. Typically, different people are responsible for the E-mail, voice mail, telephone communications, and fax functions. This is one reason why organizations often don't have a real sense of how much they're actually spending for communications. Accountability is frequently fragmented and delayed when you have one person buying network support, somebody else buying the security, and a third buying the workstations.

Another reason to rexamine communications cost is that the whole electronics communications industry has been built up around the model of low entry, or no entry, cost, where you pay as you go, or someone else in another cost center is footing the bill. The last thing many communications equipment and service providers want you to understand is how much you actually end up paying.

To get control of their overall communications costs, companies need to rethink management of this area. There is a huge management opportunity here that people haven't even begun to comprehend yet. However, to take advantage of that opportunity, companies have to reengineer their communications processes so that their entire communications budget falls under a single umbrella. Or, at the very least, companies must ensure that they have a process owner in place. You have to have accountability, and you have to look at your communications systems holistically.

SHARING DEFINING QUALITIES: THE CEO AS A CATALYST

In addition to acting as the role model in setting communications guidelines and standards, CEOs today are using communications to change corporate culture. Nowhere is the leadership factor more important than in influencing the evolution of corporate culture and in preparing businesses to meet the changing competitive landscape of the twenty-first century. This is certainly true at mature, highly successful companies. For example, my management team and I have been transforming Pitney Bowes from a company that was largely focused on retaining what it had to one that is aggressively reaching out for more.

Since Pitney Bowes has no "burning platform," no compelling issue that could be used to drive rapid change, the transition necessarily has had to be gradual. Nevertheless, in these instances, as well as in the more dramatic restructuring situations, CEOs must articulate a clearly defined long-term plan for what they want their companies to become. They need to be entirely consistent in their message. And they need to use constant repetition to get this message across. The impact in communicating the need for change is cumulative, and top management must take advantage of every opportunity and situation to inch people closer to the intended goal.

Relying on communications, CEOs can also help their organizations—particularly top management—define four crucial qualities and put them into effect: competitiveness, candor, collaboration, and accountability.

In traveling extensively to customer sites and operations worldwide—and in listening carefully to what customers are saying—CEOs are continually taking the pulse of the marketplace and communicating external market expectations back to the business units and frontline employees. In the process, senior management plays a key role in providing business-unit managers with the information they need to remain competitive and ensure customer and shareholder value.

For example, at Pitney Bowes I meet regularly with investors and communicate in detail with business unit heads what shareholders expect from their various units. Further, in an effort to communicate more openly about shareholder expectations, we now share the forecasts of the Wall Street analysts following Pitney Bowes with a large group of managers within the company. In the past, that information was restricted to a closed circle. As a result of this new practice, today there are continuous two-way communications providing the company with a clear and timely view of what the shareholders expect from their holdings in Pitney Bowes, and what the business unit heads can expect from the market.

This two-way communications process has benefited the company in other ways as well. For instance, our company's financial services group had an unclear image in the perception of shareholders. Now, every time I talk to a shareholder, I immediately phone the president of that unit and say, "Here's what this investor said about your division today." That kind of consistent feedback provides the financial services unit with a realistic and timely assessment of its value to stockholders.

At Pitney Bowes, candor is viewed as another important ingredient in achieving continuous improvement and fostering an open communications environment in which change can evolve. My team and I have espoused a policy of complete candor, within competitive limits; and this in turn encourages employees to feel they can and should be honest with each other about all aspects of the business.

Collaboration is also critical, again with CEOs acting as catalysts in modeling and implementing this capability. At Pitney Bowes, I have stepped up direct communications with board members, meeting with each individual member at least twice a year to ensure that the company's strategic planning objectives are conveyed at every board meeting. In the past, all of the company's strategic plans were presented at a one-day, once-a-year meeting.

In addition, I have facilitated communications between the board and other groups important to our business. I recently took the board to Europe for four days of meetings with European policy makers. This established a dialogue that helped the board better understand this important market and the communications issues associated with the European community. The result of such measures is that Pitney Bowes now enjoys a more collaborative relationship with the board than in the past, and this allows us to maximize the value of that resource.

Finally, in defining accountability, the role of the CEO is to empower the management team to be fully responsible for all its actions. This means creating an environment that encourages open communications and supports risk taking, which in turn fosters a feeling of personal responsibility among all employees for what happens in the company. Such an environment at Pitney Bowes allows our people to exercise the authority they need to deliver on the company's commitments to our customers and shareholders.

PART IV
Culture

W<small>HEN MANAGEMENT CONSULTANTS</small> T<small>OM</small> Peters and Robert Waterman pass away and arrive at the Pearly Gates, they may have some explaining to do. St. Peter is sure to ask, "Are you the authors of *In Search of Excellence,* the early eighties best-seller that popularized the idea of a corporate culture? Weren't you the ones who said that excellent companies are those with a strong 'unifying culture and shared vision'?"

"Yes," they'll say, looking demurely at their feet.

"Then you must be aware," St. Peter will continue, "that the concept of a corporate culture has completely dominated business thought management ever since."

The consultants will smile.

"Okay, Tom and Bob," St. Peter will say with genuine curiosity, "I'm willing to let you into heaven provided you can satisfy me on one point: What *is* corporate culture?"

Chances are that Peters and Waterman would be hard-pressed for a definitive explanation—as would many thousands of consultants and managers. "Culture" is a word as beguiling as it is ambiguous. That it exists nobody can doubt, but most of us are unaware of the cultural constructs that guide our actions and beliefs in everyday life. Corporate or organizational cultures are even more elusive and difficult to comprehend.

Fifteen years after its publication, it is clear that *In Search of Excellence* was a liberating event. Terence Deal's *Corporate Cultures,* published the same year, was also influential in getting the word "culture" into common business use. It was not a breakthrough, since academics had been on to the topic about a decade earlier. But after the splash made by the Peters and Waterman book, nobody could think about management issues without giving some weight to a company's unitary culture and its fit with strategy and structure.

Inevitably, some of the richness of the cultural dimension of business and organization has become trivialized. Inevitably too there is sometimes an excess of evangelism about the ease and appropriateness of cultural intervention and modification. Even so, there remains a sustained interest in a great number of organizations in acquiring accessible and usable concepts about their culture that can make a significant impact on the way they manage their business.

Corporate culture is the kind of abstraction whose meaning depends on who is seeking to define it, and why. It is so loaded with paradoxes and contradictions, yet so ubiquitous, that any questioner runs the danger of predetermining answers and losing objectivity. Corporate culture can be treated as a static thing or as a dynamic and holistic set of interrelation-ships; as a reflector of meaning or as a generator of behaviors. And if some of the more academic descriptions and commentaries on corpo-rate culture seem detached from reality, remember what McGill profes-sor Henry Mintzberg said on this subject: "There are times when we need to caricature, or stereotype, reality in order to sharpen differences and so to better understand it."

Here we will view corporate culture from the top down, and its utility as a CEO tool to implement change. Clearly, this isn't an all-seeing view, since how the members of an organization perceive its culture depends on their relative position. Clearly too the top-down approach to cultural change is open to abuse. In *Human Relations* (April 1997) Peter Hawkins warned that a "culture-change program can be an exercise in power and control by the dominant group, which if unilateral and insen-sitive will inevitably lead to reaction and often rejection by those on the receiving end of the new cultural imperialism."

But of course without CEO endorsement—or at least adoption of the terms of the debate—no culture change effort is going to get off the ground. Viewed from the top, corporate culture is a profound shaper of behavior, positively and negatively. Although many of the exemplars in *In Search of Excellence* turned out to have feet of clay only a few years after the book's publication—in essence, the correlation between cul-ture and performance broke down—common sense suggests that the notion of cultural aptness, of a fit with the business environment, is in-controvertible. At the most nuts-and-bolts level, a company's perfor-mance measures and rewards have a strong cultural reverberation. They are the genetic code of the corporate culture.

"Culture is the coding of values and deeply held beliefs that mold an organization's decision patterns, guide its actions, and drive individual behavior," according to Melvin Goodes, Warner-Lambert's CEO. In chapter twenty, Goodes discusses a values program in which a "Three-Sixty-Degree" employee evaluation system is used to make the com-pany's values real. Out of this synthesis, the company obtained a significant increase in the integration of employee behavior and corpo-rate values.

In common parlance, corporate culture has frequently come to mean anything and everything, as in "our culture won't [will] allow" whatever. And in countless employee opinion surveys and focus groups, it is the corporate culture that is fingered as the scapegoat for all sorts of short-comings and problems. For many workers, culture has become the very personification of the company, the fountain of its attributes. And even

CEOs who are skeptical of culture manipulation keep a weather eye out for the cultural consequences of major strategic moves. Or they will make a strategic move and subsequently claim that their intent all along was to reshape the culture.

Although there are more definitions of corporate culture than there are colors of the rainbow, from the CEO's perspective what matters is "culture as fitness"; to wit, its relationship to the bottom line. Sea changes in the external environment—globalization, convergence of technologies, and so forth—repeatedly come up on the CEO radar screen to beg questions like, "Does my company's corporate culture have the right ingredients to react to and succeed in this emerging environment?"

As MIT professor Edgar Schein said in *Administrative Science Quarterly* in June 1996, "If we carefully observe what happens to organizations when they attempt to improve their operations in response to new data from the economic, political, and technological environment, we discover the critical role that culture and sub-cultures play." Schein, one of the academic pioneers in this area, goes on to define culture as "the set of shared assumptions that a group holds and that determines how it perceives, thinks about, and reacts to its various environments."

The spotlight on corporate culture today has much more to do with the environmental turbulence of recent years than with the impact of a management best-seller. CEOs are looking for cultural meanings that add to competitive strengths. And while the CEO's basic tool kit of mission statements, vision declarations, and core value statements may seem frail when juxtaposed against the magnitude of cultural inertia, let's remember that often the best way to achieve cultural change is with hard-edged performance measures and rewards, and people practices with predictable cultural impacts. In other words, indirection may succeed where a frontal attack on a "cultural" problem with culture change weapons will very likely fail.

A fine case study of the indirect method is to be found in chapter twenty-four, where Javier Herrero, CEO of Iberdrola, a Spanish power utility, shows how the introduction of Activity-Based Management (ABM) disciplines is having a sweeping effect on his company's culture. Although the ostensible target was the value chain, better processes, a better customer interface, and cost shrinkage via reengineering, in the end Iberdrola management came to feel that, in Herrero's words, "ABM is a powerful shaper of values and not simply a different approach to cost accounting."

Great strides have been made in the last decade toward understanding all the many shapers of corporate culture. Here are some of the principal ones. Incidentally, these are not watertight categories; rather, they are overlapping, with many feedback and interactive effects among them:

- *Leadership*. Leaders consciously and unconsciously communicate beliefs, values, and assumptions by their style of leadership and how they exercise authority. Culture change requires a clear examination of leadership traits and their likely impact, and of the ability of leaders to express the need for change and carry it off.
- *Performance measures*. Every corporation has a vast range of choices in what is measured, how it is measured, how clearly, and how frequently. All such accounting is in fact cultural communication, since it defines winners and losers. There is a deep level of symbolic communication in measures that emphasize individual versus group contributions, or emphasize the short term or the long term.
- *People practices*. People are not just passive containers into which the CEOs pour their version of corporate culture. Organizations clearly express their character and expectations by the way they set recruitment practices and parameters. Their profiles of desirable skills and attributes, the amount of training and intellectual enrichment offered, the pace of and criteria for advancement—all of these affect culture. No sophisticated company today will alter the symbolic language of its personnel practices without looking at the possible cultural impact. For instance, no company will abolish merit pay structures and substitute broad banding and profit sharing without considering their effects on the culture—both internally in terms of human interaction and behavior, and also at the corporate borders with suppliers, customers, and communities.
- *Structure*. The structure of an organization defines its realities and meaning, not only in terms of personalities (who reports to whom), but in terms of texture, form, flexibility, and duration. Most culture change programs modify old organizational forms and create new organizational vehicles.
- *Competitive context*. Different industries have their own sociological mores, often dependent on the amount of technology involved, or where products stand in the life-cycle chain. To a large degree, corporate cultures reflect those industry characteristics. The interesting questions are those that probe differences from industry norms. Even more than that, every company needs a culture that is able to ask the right questions. In a fast-growth industry, for instance, the ability to envision future scenarios is more important

than in a slow-growth business. So the question then might be, "Does our culture foster frequent and intelligent assessment of future scenarios?"

- *Time.* Culture change is not for managers with a short-term focus. Most of the powerful levers of culture change operate with the speed of a supertanker navigating a narrow channel. Cultural impact has to be measured in years, and redirections may be required along the way.

- *Transparency.* Depending on its character, corporate culture may or may not foster community. Those that overstimulate internal rivalry and competition for advancement diminish the potential of community. Clearly a sense of community can reinforce cohesion and help change to flourish. When the disseminated logic of culture change is transparent, community is strengthened. That logic should be rooted in history and a widely shared consensus of the shortcomings of the old culture and why the new must take hold. In addition, everyone needs clear milestones on the long road to culture change.

- *Resistance.* All culture change produces opposition and resistance. Management can ignore it, dismiss it, suppress it, or let it come bubbling to the surface and deal with it constructively. Very often the virulence of the opposition frightens the change managers. It makes them inclined to sidestep the tough issues and avoid engaging in those areas where the weight of the past is heaviest or where powerful executives are protecting their turf. This timidity can have disastrous repercussions: Often a company will react with a "soft" communications program that merely urges people to adopt values. Unfortunately, this inability to confront points of resistance may ultimately destroy the company's capacity for change and breed cynicism.

- *Change measurement.* One of the most frequent causes of failure in culture change programs is lack of rigor. In many firms the practices and tactics adopted by culture change managers reflect the characteristics of the culture itself: fluffy diagrams, vague accountabilities, ambiguous time scales, and poorly defined outcomes. What is needed is the same rigor companies apply to capital appraisal or budgeting. In culture change, as in everything else, the maxim holds: "What gets measured gets done."

One area in which perceptions of corporate culture have unequivocally added to management competence is in the merger and acquisitions field. In retrospect, the older generation of CEOs was pretty callow about the effects of combining large enterprises. Today, however, there are some CEOs who have made their sensitive handling of the cultural aspects of mergers into a competitive weapon.

Walter Shipley, chairman and CEO of Chase Manhattan, for example, so brilliantly executed one massive bank combination (Chemical and Manufacturers Hanover) that when a few years later a second big money-center bank (Chase) sought a merger partner, it turned to him as a kind of father figure. In chapter twenty-two, Shipley discusses his skills at "inclusive," nonhostile mergering. As a result of his two big experiences as a smooth consolidator, his bank now boasts widely acknowledged mergering skills that will be an important asset as mergers rationalize the banking industry in the years ahead. According to Shipley, "Mergers present many eye-opening lessons in how dramatically different both cultures and procedures can be in rival institutions. At the operational level there were startling differences of approach and philosophy at Chase and Chemical."

Many mergers today simply would not have happened without a consideration of cultural variables. That was surely the case with the creation of Fairway Filamentos, a Brazilian joint venture of two mature businesses owned by non-Brazilian interests, one German, the other French. "The revolutionary fusion of a German- and a French-run operation presented an extreme case of adaptation and new corporate culture creation," writes Fairway CEO Dirk Blaesing in chapter twenty-three. Fairway started with two strong cultural legacies that had to be modified and, in some cases, demolished.

Blaesing tells a story of corporate self-invention, of taking people and processes, bureaucracies and customary styles of behavior, and welding them into an organizational unity. As he says, "this goal had to be achieved under severe time pressures. The longer the joint venture took to find its identity, the more ground it would lose in the marketplace. Thus the fusion process was driven by a genuine sense of extreme urgency. Companies with long histories of stability can fine-tune their cultures over many years. Fairway Filamentos had to get a viable culture up and running in only a few months."

Internal and external change are primary drivers of cultural adaptation as companies try to catch up with shifting realities. In 1994, the National Australia Bank Group surveyed about twenty thousand employees. As CEO Don Argus points out in chapter twenty-one, "Those first findings from the surveys were a shock! They showed clearly that while we were trying to pioneer new territory, we were still relying on old skill sets and capabilities to carry us forward." His organization's "'steady-state' operating environment was unable to deal with the rapid, continuous change it was experiencing." Result: A reconfiguration of values was prescribed.

Yet another strand in today's rich tapestry of culture modification comes from the steady internationalization of previously domestic business environments, in both developed and underdeveloped economies. There is a rising imperative everywhere to act against some kind of global benchmark. This, in turn, has spread the ethic of professional management—along with its enormous baggage of values—to the farthest corners of the earth, shaking up old customs, traditions, and cultural values based on family ownership and control. In chapter twenty-five, Tanri Abeng, CEO of Bakrie & Bros., describes the nuances of such a delicate takeover from family patriarchs. Professional managers, he warns, "need to penetrate the old structure and culture, not overwhelm it with strange new practices. If they don't take care, the whole restructuring process will backfire on them and provoke stubborn resistance to change."

Rudyard Kipling once said, "It is better to travel than to arrive." That's a good perspective for culture change. There is no ultimate peak on the mountain where a CEO can stand and say, "I did it!" Because nobody can know what "it" is, or might have been. Corporate culture is not an artifact but a dimension. And cultural change is both better understood and realized in the quest—in the sifting through of its many variables, and in the CEO's determination to extract meaning from the process and the journey.

20

TRANSFORMING THE CULTURE OF A GLOBAL ENTERPRISE . . . ONE EMPLOYEE AT A TIME

Melvin R. Goodes, Warner-Lambert Company

In 1991, twenty-six years after joining the company in Canada, Mel Goodes became chairman and CEO of Warner-Lambert at a time of deep uncertainty.

A global company with three diverse core businesses—pharmaceuticals, consumer health and personal-care products, and confectionery—Warner-Lambert found itself confronted with the need for essential and extensive restructuring if it was going to overcome Wall Street's perception that it was a prime takeover candidate.

By 1996, Warner-Lambert was a dramatically changed company. Marketing its products in 140 countries, and deriving nearly 60 percent of its revenues outside the United States, Warner-Lambert sales had grown by 36 percent, and earnings had more than quadrupled in five years. At the same time, the company was emerging as a major force in the pharmaceuticals industry, with a growing investment in research and biotechnology, an expanding pipeline of new drugs and therapies, and strategic joint ventures with global companies such as Glaxo-Wellcome. The rising value of Warner-Lambert shares reflected this momentum.

Goodes's tenure with the company had been spent largely outside the United States in operating manager positions in Latin America, Europe, and Asia. Because of Warner-Lambert's slow-moving bureaucracy, he had frequently resisted promotion to corporate headquarters. So when he took the reins as CEO he was determined to push for deep and far-reaching changes everywhere.

His first task was to address the capabilities of the existing agents of change—from top management to the most junior employees within each operation. What he found was a culture of entitlement that had to be transformed into a culture that expressed, stimulated—and rewarded— individual and team performance.

THOSE WHO STEP INTO the top jobs of the world's largest companies soon learn that their lives have become much like the heroes in myths. In fact, their task bears a strong resemblance to the labors of Hercules. They're only given a few years—never enough—to make their mark and to triumph. Then the Fates whisk them off the glittering stage.

In practice, this means an incoming CEO has a unique but quickly evaporating opportunity to redirect an organization suffering from the inertia inherent in employing many thousands of people around the world. He or she only gets to be the new CEO once, which means swiftly establishing leadership, defining the new direction and strategy, and getting everyone into the sprinter's blocks. After the CEO has created a clear vision and set of goals, there can be no second thoughts. You can't risk changing the message for at least five years—it takes that long to change behavior in massive global organizations.

SUBTLE LINKS OF CULTURE AND BEHAVIOR

For most CEOs, the principal lever for change is the company's culture. Culture is the coding of values and deeply held beliefs that mold an organization's decision patterns, guide its actions, and drive individual behavior. Culture acts as the backbone of behavior in most organizations. Like the genetic coding hidden away at the core of every living cell, it shapes and models the decisions made by an organization.

Visibly, it's "the way we do things around here." Less visibly, it functions in depth as the matrix of the beliefs, values, and attitudes that permeate an organization. Durable and deeply embedded, the corporate culture provides continuity, which is an important asset. But it also creates a major drawback. Because it is so deep and powerful, a company's culture is inherently difficult for a CEO to modify during the limited time of his mandate.

The values that drive an organization's behaviors are potent. They can block a company's strategy or catalyze it. Strength and fit are what matter. A strong culture can be an enormous advantage if it's in sync with the organization's strategies. On the other hand, if the fit is flawed, the strengths of a culture are also likely to be its greatest weakness—all of those beliefs and norms propel the company toward mediocrity, or worse. It's the strong cultures with a good fit to strategy—and the business results or potential to prove it—that attract the best people.

Typically, culture change is triggered top-down from the chief executive—but it is actually achieved from the bottom up. Enduring cultural change is created with practical tools such as measures, rewards, and carefully structured people practices. One key tool is a strategy for superior performance based on a cultural analysis of the way people work, followed by appropriate reshaping of those practices and attitudes. However, this requires a deep and sensitive understanding of the ways in which individuals interact with the corporate culture.

Such an analysis must discern how individuals perform in order to help them not only work smarter and more productively but also to enable them to adapt to a continuous succession of new challenges and market demands. By first communicating and then demonstrating these new expectations, rewards, and disincentives, cultural transformation becomes a process of stimulating change one employee at a time.

There are many ways of approaching this task, and the path chosen depends on each corporation's individual circumstances. At Warner-Lambert, two of the tools we used in the 1991–1996 transformation of individual employee behavior could not have been more down to earth. First, we embarked on a program of defining, articulating, and propagating five core values. Second, we adopted a "Three-Sixty-Degree" program for the evaluation of all managers and many supervisory and support personnel. The name of this new program was chosen to suggest that every point on an individual's compass, every aspect of behavior, needs to be brought into the assessment.

Articulating corporate values crisply and communicating them consistently is a well-established management practice. The problem is that too few companies pay much attention to their vaunted values beyond that initial exercise. Even fewer employ a formal Three-Sixty-Degree evaluation program to help their managers evolve. While both tools have obvious merit, Warner-Lambert cultivated change at the intersection of the two programs, each reflecting and validating the other. Instead of the traditional direct review by a superior, employee performance would now be evaluated by subordinates and peers as well as by supervisors— and the employee himself or herself. The reviewing group includes everyone to whom an individual provides significant services within the company.

THE FIVE CORE VALUES—THE CATALYST FOR CHANGE

Values exist in abundance, and acceptable statements of values can be cranked out at the drop of a hat by communications departments. However, real cultural transformation cannot be created through slogans or aspirations. Values must be based on actionable practices that everyone can recognize and emulate. They must be rooted in what actually goes on in a company day to day, and embody the best practices distilled from the way people actually work. At Warner-Lambert, the effort to crystallize the company's most valued practices—what the company stands for, how it operates, and how it treats others inside and outside the organization—led us to target five critical attributes:

1. Focusing on what's important: sound science, providing consumers with superior products at attractive prices, speed of action, excellence in execution, and constant readiness to seize opportunities globally
2. Being fast and first to exploit new opportunities, from strategy to implementation
3. Rewarding the true successes of individuals and teams
4. Being open and candid in all our dealings with each other, our suppliers, and our customers
5. Prizing creativity and prudent risk taking

Added together, these core values go a long way toward defining the new Warner-Lambert. They give the company a distinctive personality in the eyes of employees, customers, partners, suppliers, investors, and the communities around the world in which the company is situated. Merely stating these core values, however, was only the first step. We also had to go the extra distance and make certain that our employees understood all the dimensions of these values so that their behavior meshed with corporate expectations.

LEADING, NOT PREACHING. ASKING, NOT TELLING.

To support its five "most valued practices," Warner-Lambert launched the Three-Sixty-Degree evaluation system among employees worldwide. Surveys were distributed to more than ten thousand employees, asking them to give confidential evaluations of the managers and team members with whom they work—and to evaluate themselves as well.

The Colleague Survey

A series of twenty-five straightforward questions asks respondents to provide rankings of individual traits on a scale of 1 to 7, in which 1 indicates "almost never," and 7 indicates "almost always" or "without fail." Each question focuses directly on the behaviors manifest in one of the five core values, as the following examples demonstrate:

Value: Prizing Creativity

To what extent does this manager . . .

- Support new and creative ideas, even if some of those ideas run the risk of failure?
- Encourage innovation?
- Show impatience with the status quo?

Value: Being Open and Candid

To what extent does this manager . . .

- Share all information in an open and candid way?
- Encourage and listen to alternative points of view?
- Constructively confront poor performance?

Value: Being Fast and First to Exploit Opportunity

To what extent does this manager . . .

- React quickly and decisively to new opportunities and challenges?
- Instill a sense of urgency and the need for action, while fostering an environment of rapid information exchange?
- Actively seek, identify, and exploit new opportunities?

The evaluations require a second step: a review meeting with a direct manager or supervisor to develop an action plan for progress.

Feedback would come from four perspectives: supervisors, peers, direct reports—and oneself. This approach was distinctively different from the "soft" agenda of a personality assessment. Its goal was to arrive at actionable results, with specific targets and a base against which both individual and team progress could be measured.

These evaluations were designed around the newly articulated core values. They forged a visible link between the new evaluation process and the company's commitment to building ongoing change in its culture worldwide. Thanks to the design of the evaluation, it clearly tied individual performance to company performance. This, in turn, provided managers and employees with the empirical evidence they needed to make certain that their interests were identical with the company's. They could see that what was good for Warner-Lambert was good for them as well, because a high value score cleared the path for advancement.

DO WE WALK OUR TALK ?

One reason these values are taking root and changing the culture of Warner-Lambert globally is the company's commitment to walking the talk. Rewards, promotions, incentives—and disincentives—are now aligned with the company's most valued practices and with employees' Three-Sixty-Degree evaluations.

This change produced culture shock: Things were now very different than even the recent past, when reviews were perfunctory. In those days, few performance distinctions were made—virtually every employee got a C. As a result, there tended to be only narrow differences between the compensation of outstanding performers and marginal ones. In the end, performance reviews provided no incentive whatever for employees to excel.

Under the new Three-Sixty-Degree program, the company introduced a forced ranking system that graded each employee's contributions. Today, the spread in compensation between top and bottom performers in the same job can differ by as much as 60 percent—a powerful incentive for all individuals to rank well and to continually improve their performance against expectations.

ACTING ON THE EVIDENCE

In our experience, peer-evaluation programs provide a credible and candid means for developing the individual. This is particularly true when the exercise is done without attribution, as a private and personal matter. Afterward, employees receive appropriate coaching and an individualized follow-up program.

The Three-Sixty-Degree program was designed to overcome the serious lack of candor in most traditional superior-to-subordinate evaluation processes. Few of us are rigorously honest counselors. Most of us are uncomfortable in counseling unless the burden of our messages falls at one extreme or the other—either praising staff for their accomplishments or admonishing them for error or failure. Few of us are skilled at giving clear, actionable advice about characteristics or skills that need improving—especially when we like the individual and overall performance is satisfactory.

However, these deficiencies in counseling skills can be remedied by a carefully thought out peer review in the Three-Sixty-Degree evaluation process. The lack of attribution frees people to offer honest and candid views about others' work and work relationships. Those on the receiving end of this analysis are forced to confront the reality of their behaviors. As a result, this approach gives employees a better grasp of how and why senior management arrived at key decisions.

Although the Three-Sixty-Degree evaluation program bears a superficial resemblance to the run-of-the-mill peer reviews that have been around for a long time, this program is in fact different and much more powerful. Why? Because of the linkage with the five core values. Without this linkage, a peer review might lead to an interesting observation about employee performance, but it does not translate into a vehicle for cultural change. When observations are scattered all over the lot, they can't help but be unactionable and unmeasurable.

Aggregating the results of the Three-Sixty-Degree survey provides an additional and highly valuable management tool—the ability to measure the composite performance of divisions in the United States and affiliates throughout the world. With this information it becomes possible to explore a number of hypotheses and questions. Do higher-performing groups behave differently? How can these differences be factored into the company's most favored practices and spread across the entire organization?

This material gives us valuable insights into the distribution of the strongest and weakest support for the five basic values. The result has been global benchmarking and the dissemination of superior practices throughout Warner-Lambert. The aggregation study provides a means of tracking the progress of different operating units year by year.

Warner-Lambert sees the heart of the matter as the need to drive these core values and practices down through the company. Actionable core values and the new performance evaluations are mechanisms for keeping people focused. This is a vital and constant challenge in a company with a diversity of businesses and product lines and a global reach.

A WARNER-LAMBERT VICE PRESIDENT COMMENTS:
ROBERT TODD, LATIN AMERICA–ASIA SECTOR

Price Waterhouse (PW): How often do you implement Three-Sixty-Degree evaluation surveys in Latin America and Asia?

Robert Todd (RT): We do one every year. They're a vehicle for putting across our core values and getting people to understand them. They also make our people understand that they are personally accountable against them. By doing an evaluation each year, we're showing that we mean it, we take it seriously. These surveys are our best means of sustaining commitment and reinforcing company values. Doing evaluations annually also means that we're able to track progress from year to year and provide feedback to employees.

PW: Can you see a payback for what is clearly a substantial investment of time and resources?

RT: There is implicit evidence that our program is very valuable to us in creating behavioral change and that it is making us a more responsive organization. Warner-Lambert has many lines of business—and they all exist in each country—so focus is a constant challenge for us. This program is working. Employees are buying in to its goals and purpose.

PW: How do you gauge employees' responsiveness?

RT: There's a lot of empirical evidence. If you ask employees, they'll tell you that these values—and the expectation that everyone will strive to perform against them—are sinking real roots. People now challenge each other on whether they're being practiced in specific work situations. In Venezuela, on their own initiative, employees have printed these messages on the cafeteria tray papers.

PW: How do you use the colleague-survey results?

RT: First, we communicate the results—not for individuals, because those are strictly confidential, but for affiliates in each country and divisions in the United States. This spurs some competition and cross-fertilization in which effective strategies are copied. Second, we require an action plan from each subsidiary company and division about how they intend to move forward in the next year. This makes it all very real.

PW: *What results were least expected at the outset of the program?*

RT: We're finding that not just managers but employees at lower levels are showing increased understanding of the core values and their purpose—and they're putting them into practice at work. We can see this growing from year to year. There is real penetration through the ranks and through the organization. People aren't satisfied with just principles. They want to know what those principles look like in action. They want examples. They want to know how values work on the job, so that they can *learn* them and use them. If the company is committed and demonstrates that commitment through a sustained effort, employees will figure a lot of it out for themselves. They'll work through what it means to be fast and first to market and how you go about making that happen in actual work situations.

As might be expected, the Three-Sixty-Degree survey evaluations are deployed somewhat differently by different operating groups. For example, Warner-Lambert Colombia has developed five training modules. Each is built around one core value and practice to deepen employee understanding of how the values apply to their particular work situations. In Venezuela, hourly employees on the plant floor are being exposed to the core values and responding favorably with changes in attitude and behavior.

MANAGING LIVING CULTURE

Without clear top management direction, the identity of large organizations can become confused—the larger the organization, the smaller the degree of clarity about who we are, where we're going, and how we get there. Headquarters may know "who we are" and "why we are the way we are," and the business advantages of that identity, but this corporate self-knowledge gets diluted in subsidiaries, divisions, and branches. This, in turn, leaves managers and their subordinates to improvise the form and shading of the corporation's culture and values. The result is not necessarily a happy one. The vast technological and economic powers of a global giant may never be fully deployed in the business arena because, quite simply, there are no road signs and trail markers inside individual employees' minds. As a result, employees become much less productive and self-empowered.

The management of culture—unheard of even two decades ago—constitutes one of the great new advances in the art of management. Yet, in recent years, managers have soberly learned that culture is in many ways one of the most intractable and elusive targets of transformation. Too many companies fail to come to grips with the challenges and merely pay lip service by issuing a statement to the effect that "our culture is thus or thus." This reduces what may be a vital business culture to a slogan that soon becomes empty and exhausted. Culture is a living thing. It should continually animate the hearts and minds of workers, spur them to greater self-development, and give them a more productive and rational environment.

21

FOCUSING LEADERSHIP THROUGH CORPORATE VALUES: A KEY DRIVER FOR SUCCESS

Don Argus, National Australia Bank Group

The National Australia Bank Group has been one of the outstanding success stories of the Australian corporate sector over the past decade. Transformed from a domestic bank into a major transnational financial services organization with a retailing presence in five countries and broad representation in Asia, the National owns banks in Australia, New Zealand, the United Kingdom, the Republic of Ireland, and the United States.

In the nineties, the National has grown its profits from $AUD 0.3 billion to $AUD 2.1 billion, a rate of 23 percent per year (compound average). It has grown its assets at a compound rate of 17 percent per year. Today, the National is Australia's most profitable company, its largest bank, and its second largest listed company, with total assets of over $AUD 173 billion, and a market capitalization of over $AUD 21 billion.

In 1990, Don Argus became group managing director and CEO of the National. Recognized as Australia's leading banker, Don Argus began his career with the National at a small branch in the state of Queensland. He progressed through a variety of branch and state management positions before being appointed general manager of the Credit Bureau in 1986, and general manager of Group Strategic Development in 1988.

Corporate values represent a key item for the National in managing its growth, and they are part of the learning the National Australia Bank Group has experienced in recent years. They're a major part of the philosophy that underpins the efforts of Argus and his senior management team to build an integrated, globally focused financial services group.

THE CHALLENGE FOR THE National Australia Bank Group has been to manage rapid corporate growth in the swiftly evolving banking and financial services sector, where globalization, technology, and deregulation are increasingly influencing industry change.

In 1994, we found ourselves in a situation where the pervasive changes taking place in the industry were escalating the need to make our own internal organizational changes. This has both accelerated the pace and added considerable complexity to the task of transition.

This complexity has placed a great deal of pressure on our traditional management and operational processes—in fact, it has redefined the nature of a contemporary banking and financial services group. Some of the issues that have surfaced are what types of product to offer, distribution channels, market profile, and image. In response, the National has adopted a new approach to selling and marketing.

Naturally, these internal changes have had a tremendous impact on our people. New demands are being made concerning the types of skills they need, the nature of training required, and the attitudes and behaviors they must exhibit to successfully meet customer needs. However, with over fifty thousand employees spread over four continents, we have had to overcome a certain degree of organizational drag. It's one thing to identify needed reforms, but making them happen at all levels and in all parts of the business takes considerable time and effort—and in today's competitive environment, time is in short supply.

As have many large organizations before us, we assumed that the implementation of common systems and the transfer of best practices could be quickly achieved. It didn't take long for us to realize that our task was far more complex than we had first thought. Existing organizational protocols and behavior needed to be recognized, and international and functional boundaries had to be overcome.

We gained critical insights into these and other issues when we surveyed twenty thousand of our people in 1994, and then followed this up in 1995 with a review of twelve thousand more. Through a combination of one-on-one interviews, focus groups, and a quantitative survey involving over nine hundred managers, this review studied the corporate cultures in the various banks that comprised the National in Australia and internationally. The scale and scope of these surveys was a new experience for us, and it provided me and my management team with the base of information we needed to create the new values-driven organization.

Those first findings from the surveys were a shock! They showed clearly that while we were trying to pioneer new territory, we were still relying on old skill sets and capabilities to carry us forward. It was now obvious that the National's "steady-state" operating environment was unable to deal with the rapid, continuous change it was experiencing. We were going to have to totally overhaul our management attitudes and practices.

The surveys also showed that we had imposed a values system on our people without involving them in the validation process. Even more importantly, the findings showed that there was widespread skepticism due to perceived differences between the values managers were espousing and their actual behavior in the workplace.

These were sobering findings for an organization that had set aggressive performance targets for its burgeoning global business activities. My management team and I realized we had to create a collective focus for this large and diverse organization across the globe. But success soon proved to be elusive because of underlying issues that needed to be addressed before the full benefits of globalization could be realized.

My team quickly shifted its attention to "people issues," beginning with a comprehensive reappraisal of our management style and corporate values. Taking stock of the situation, we responded quickly and positively, providing a strong focus on the issues and the leadership the National needed to ensure its future success.

LEARNING POINTS

As our review process progressed, it generated significant learning points. The five key issues were:

1. An organization's core values have to be validated by all employees and made relevant before they can achieve widespread acceptance.
2. The articulation of values has to be matched by a concerted effort to train managers and other employees in the behavioral changes necessary to make sure the organization lives its values.
3. These agreed-upon behaviors need to be seen in a global context and be flexible enough to cope with national and regional cultural differences.
4. Establishing a values-driven culture requires the organization's senior executives to shift from a purely managerial focus to a leadership focus.
5. An organization needs to continually renew its stock of leaders, and to entrust them with the task of sustaining its core values.

LEARNING POINT 1: DEFINING CORE VALUES

Values are the core beliefs and accepted habits of an organization. They form the basis of the corporate culture. I recognized that the National's values needed to be expressed simply to ensure rapid understanding and acceptance throughout the organization. My team also recognized that the core values not only needed a buy-in from our people, they had to be relevant and meaningful for the business as well.

As a result, we developed seven core values. They are simple and to the point, but provide a powerful, focused direction for all the National's employees:

- Service to our customers
- Quality in everything we do
- Professionalism and ethics in all our actions
- Competitiveness and a will to win
- Growth and development of our people
- Continuous productivity improvement
- Growing profit for our stakeholders

These core values were tested across a range of our people to make certain they were understood and seen as relevant.

LEARNING POINT 2: COMMUNICATING CORE VALUES

Describing the core values in framed wall plaques wasn't enough. After all, they're not a wish list, but an integral part of the leadership that is expected throughout the National. So we set up a concentrated program of training and development to help drive the values home. This was the only way real change could occur in the way we did business.

The seven core values form the basis of an integrated series of programs we call our "Leadership Model." Since it was crucially important for our people to fully live these values, senior management has begun a major communications and development program that will ultimately involve all employees. These programs are designed to proceed in tandem with our business strategies and operating performance objectives.

For our managers, we developed several additional programs. One of these is "Excellence in Leadership," a new form of performance assessment that defines, measures, develops, and rewards key leadership behaviors. Each participant is assessed by a number of sources, including the manager, direct reports, and peers. Since most of us tend not to see ourselves exactly as others see us, this kind of feedback can be a powerful source of information. It gives us a basis for deciding if we need—or want—to change any aspect of our behavior.

Initially involving around a thousand managers, the program will eventually be used across the National by all our managers and supervisors. Strategically, we needed it to drive organizational change and to align the behavior of individual managers with our changing business environment.

LEARNING POINT 3: THE GLOBAL PERSPECTIVE

Over 40 percent of our asset base lies outside our home country of Australia, and this global business reach has added a further dimension to the development of values throughout the National. Managing globally means our values must be relevant in the United States, the United Kingdom, or Asia, as well as in Australia or New Zealand.

This need has been met by carefully blending our core values with local requirements worldwide. The values aren't different, but their application may be different in some areas. For example, customer service styles may vary from country to country, and customers' expectations may vary. And while our values relating to customer service won't change, day-to-day services will be tailored to meet local needs.

Nevertheless, the seven core values have imbued the National with a global focus and a commonality of purpose. We all share the same values, and we all feel part of one team and operate accordingly. Over time this will become an extremely powerful management and operational tool.

LEARNING POINT 4: A NEW LEADERSHIP FOCUS FOR MANAGEMENT

Implementing the core values across the organization meant that managers had to develop a different mind-set. Traditionally they had been very focused on managing—on assessing, controlling, and reporting. But for the future, the National needs its managers to be far more focused on developing and providing leadership.

The core values offer a basic road map for the organization to move ahead, and a template for the leadership style needed to make that happen. However, while values provide a strong foundation for a business, they can be difficult to communicate and even harder to implement. To meet this challenge, we developed a number of highly innovative communications programs, ranging from the traditional group video and publications and presentations, to business television and strategic mapping.

It wasn't easy to make the shift from a managerial to a leadership focus, and the process of developing stronger leadership is still in process. Nevertheless, the seven core values are becoming pervasive throughout the business and deeply influencing the way daily activities are conducted. Our managers are beginning to experience the successes brought about by these core values, and this is inspiring them to reach for greater heights.

LEARNING POINT 5: THE CONTINUING LEADERSHIP CHALLENGE

As we grow, the National faces the challenge of renewing and refreshing the leadership throughout the organization. To meet this challenge, we have developed a "Transformational Leadership" program to identify and develop a strong core of senior management talent capable of leading into the future in an environment of change and complexity.

The three-year program, which began in 1995, is designed to help individuals fulfill their potential as leaders. The program centers on two major themes: personal mastery and business leadership. The philosophy of the program is that effective leaders create quantum change throughout their circle of influence. The strength of that influence is a function of their skills and personal values. Measurement criteria for our "Business Excellence Model" include leadership, policy and planning, information and analysis, people development and management, process and product management, business results, and superior customer value.

The program focuses on self-directed learning and offers a series of residential workshops in Australia, Europe, and New Zealand. It also involves the formation of transitional teams working collaboratively with their peers from various parts of the National on projects of strategic importance. This is an exciting initiative because it is creating a core of influential and knowledgeable young leaders and is supporting succession planning.

Not only has our business strategy evolved over the past fifteen years, so have our organizational development priorities. The modeling and planning that used to be the province of operations, finance, and marketing has now been extended to human resource management. This signals a major shift in focus as well as an emerging change in our values.

NEW DIMENSIONS FOR THE NATIONAL

These learning points made clear that the traditional local bankers' way of managing was not going to work for us in the future. We were now a global business in a global industry, and change was inevitable for our continuing success. I also realized that bone-deep shifts in corporate values didn't happen automatically. We were going to have to continually define, communicate, and propagate the core values across the organization.

These changes also meant a head-on challenge to our managers' traditional expectations—away from the old task and managerial orientation toward providing real leadership. This was especially difficult for the many individuals who had grown up with a very traditional banking focus.

It certainly meant a selling job. While top management buy-in was important, I knew that to be truly effective, this spirit had to be instilled in all levels of the organization. Everyone had to be singing from the same hymn sheet, so to speak.

The core values experience has been a very positive one for us. Along the way, we discovered the need to be proactive in developing values that underpin all organizational activities. We learned that living these agreed-upon values is critical for our success—but that this is challenging to implement. Along with the rest of my team, I discovered that we had to be prepared for a few real shocks and revelations along the way.

One key to the success of the Leadership Model has been the way we've implemented it. Strong commitment from me and the rest of the management team has been essential. It has also required widespread involvement throughout the National. And above all, it has demanded openness in acknowledging our problems, and a willingness to confront and address them. Another key to its success is constant evolution. Since we are continually changing, our Leadership Model must respond accordingly.

The National Australia Bank Group has been extremely successful financially over the past decade. In tandem with an ambitious but orderly growth program in Australia and around the world, we have now embarked upon an equally ambitious yet very focused program to make certain that the values of the organization are consistently understood and applied across the organization.

The future success of the National depends on our business and human resource strategies converging seamlessly. It is clear to me that to create a world-class network of integrated financial service organizations, human resource needs are key. This is why we place such emphasis on the ongoing development of strong leadership through our corporate values.

We are confident that the work begun with the introduction of our core values program has provided an extremely strong focus on corporate values and strategy, and that this in turn will provide a firm foundation for the continued growth of the National.

22

THE ART OF THE INCLUSIVE
MERGER

Walter Shipley,
Chase Manhattan Bank

In 1959, Walter Shipley, chairman and CEO of the Chase Manhattan Corp., had a searing experience. The bank he worked for was taken over by Chemical in such a domineering way that, as he said later, "I lost all of my role models, and it took me between five and ten years to feel that I was on the first team of the new organization." Privately, Shipley vowed never to treat another human being like that, hardly imagining that he would later play a leading role in three acquisitions (Texas Commerce, Manufacturers Hanover, Chase Manhattan), every time making sure "that neither side is denigrated or downgraded." Although he's aware that his sensitivity in this area isn't shared by everyone, he has never wavered in his belief that the truly effective mergers aren't done with a big stick.

No CEO in power today has personally been the architect of more asset combinations than the six-foot-eight Shipley. The result is the largest American bank, with a balance sheet worth $340 billion, and a capitalization of $45 billion. Its annual technology budget of $1.8 billion is close to 10 percent of all technology spending by U.S. banks. Scale aside, another justification for these mergers has been the enormous economies in the cost of operations. When the final tally is made of the savings from the Chase-Chemical combination, some $1.7 billion of costs will have been extracted from the expense base of the two banks—much of it coming from the elimination of some twelve thousand jobs. In the following chapter, the amiable Shipley explains how he's been so successful at mergers while remaining true to convictions formed thirty-eight years ago.

WHEN MERGERS DON'T WORK out well, there are doubtless many contributing causes. I venture to say that one of them is the style in which these transactions were carried out. Too often you have a CEO who wants to dominate the process and who operates from a philosophy of acquisition that says, "We're going to do it our way—our accounting, our financial reporting, our management structure, et cetera."

But there are alternative ways of proceeding that can lead to better results, and for large service companies may be essential to fulfilling all the goals of such transactions. These alternatives are not theoretical; rather, they're the fruit of hard-won experience in two of the largest bank combinations ever seen in the United States: Manufacturers Hanover and Chemical in 1991, and Chemical with the Chase in 1996. These mergers conclusively demonstrated that a partnership among equals yields the best results for employees and for shareholders. Why? Because partnering captures all the benefits of rationalization, and of systems and process integration and consolidation, while retaining the loyalty and effectiveness of the employees of both institutions.

We call it the "inclusive" merger style because it seeks to extract all the economic value from a combination of banks, while respecting and honoring—but not getting hung up on—the history and character of the merger partners. There is both an ethical and a practical motive behind this approach. The cultural aspects of big service companies run very deep and constitute a significant part of their service delivery. Damage the cultures with internecine conflict, or with employee resentment of the merger, and the potential for efficiency diminishes. The customer suffers, and this impairs the value of the company. Merger partners need to remind themselves often that "this is our merger, not our customers'." From the clients' perspective, the combining should be accomplished without a hiccup, and service delivery should be seamless. Meanwhile, in the background the functions and systems are melding together, and an entirely new culture is forming from the seeds of the predecessor institutions—adopting the best characteristics of both.

A key ingredient of the inclusive merger is that it must have a rational basis that is easy to explain, and whose logic is powerful, succinct, and irrefutable. This is important as far as regulators and shareholders are concerned. However, it is absolutely critical when it comes to getting personnel to support, endorse, and carry through the transaction at all levels, despite the turmoil and possible glitches it may create in their careers. Making a logical case for the Chase's mergers was not difficult. Because of previous regulatory law, banking in the United States today is one of the country's most fractionated industries, one that urgently needs to restructure into more efficient and larger-scale units.

In 1991, on the eve of the merger with Manufacturers Hanover, it was obvious that Chemical did not have the size or strength to support the reach of its business portfolios. Ditto for the scenario in 1995. And in 1997 this is even clearer. Both the Chase and Chemical needed the operating and customer scale that flow from market leadership in all major segments. Individually, they were in too many businesses where they did not have leadership positions, and even after valiant efforts to downsize and focus their product lines, neither had the financial resources necessary to fix itself. They also needed deeper pockets to continue to play a role in further industry consolidation.

There was yet another factor behind these mergers—the opportunities offered by modern information and systems technology. The Chase's chief information officer, Dennis O'Leary, has said that technology is "the genetic code for the evolution of business," meaning that its intelligent application is a key to competitive success. But for maximum effectiveness, technology needs to be embedded in large institutions. In banking, this means that the competitive advantages of operational and customer scale are far greater than they used to be. It's hard to believe that any other industry has felt the transformational power of technology more than banking.

At the Chase there exist enormous opportunities for driving a greater volume of products through more efficient processing and distribution pipelines, as well as enabling a much higher level of product standardization. Once these megagains are demonstrable—for example, when $3 billion in funds move through the Chase daily, when global syndicated lending is just under half a trillion dollars a year, and when total foreign exchange equals 10 percent of the entire global traffic—employees are far more likely to accept the pain involved in a merger's layoffs and redundancies. And those who remain will put heart and soul into making a more powerful institution.

By contrast, the authoritarian, "my way," style of merger can demotivate the staff of the acquired institutions. It can debilitate people's potential, sap their energy and self-confidence, and leave a bad taste in their mouths. All of it unnecessary—and poor strategy besides. Many sources have commented on the smoothness of both the Chemical/Manufacturers Hanover merger and the Chemical/Chase merger, which were of historic size and complexity; on the discipline and good tactical execution; and on the way in which all key managers had a chance to express their points of view.

As a result, the Chase is widely perceived to have a core competence in this area. Indeed, the inclusive values demonstrated in the Manufacturers Hanover/Chemical deal played a significant role in persuading the Chase to sign on the dotted line. And when it came to the nitty-gritty issues of integration, the old Chase people recognized that Chemical was further along the learning curve, and that this meant a minimum delay in effecting rationalization and capturing bottom-line gains.

To be candid, the gains from the Manufacturers Hanover/Chemical combination in 1991 did not come quickly enough—as some security analysts impatiently observed. This was in part the result of not yet having a core competence, particularly in technology integration. One mistake we made was in deciding to evaluate the ingredients of the two banks' systems at a high level of detail and then selecting the best subsystems from each. Making this determination, and then integrating the pieces, proved to be time-consuming and it generated excessive complexity. The second time around, management opted for larger suites of systems. While all the ingredients might not have been perfect, this was offset by the gains in speed, efficiency, and costs.

Another thing the first merger taught was the benefit of crisp decision making. It isn't necessary to wait until 100 percent of the information is assembled and checked—often 70 percent is enough to move on. Slowness creates uncertainty, and uncertainty—especially in the stressful environment of integrating a merger—can be corrosive and eroding. Uncertainty also breeds conflicts. You're better off making decisions quickly and later reversing mistakes, rather than letting decisions drag on too long.

Accordingly, in the Chemical/Chase combination, the bank created a well-staffed team to plan the integration steps, to track developments, and to report on progress. Their Merger Overview Model (MOM) was highly detailed as to the timetable of events and major milestones, and had very coherent plans for managing interdependencies. It also had a review process for adjudicating areas of contention between different staff groups. MOM had no less than 56 different integration plans, 3,308 major milestones (72 percent accomplished in the first post-merger year), 13,000 tasks, and 3,820 interdependencies. In all, some 500 "financial events" were charted—each one a step toward integration that would yield specific dollar savings by a specific deadline.

MOM is a powerful and disciplined engine for setting goals, for tracking them, and for making sure that all the components of the merger deliver against expectations and on time. But its powers are limited. The strategic decisions for each line of business—credit cards, capital mar-

kets, custody, and the like—were the responsibility of the line executives. The heads of the different units from the Chase and Chemical sat
down and mutually decided on the strategy as well as the most talented
individuals to carry out that strategy. The fact that the present Chase is
staffed from a pool of the best people from three leading banks is no
small part of its strength, and one that emerges directly out of the inclusive culture. Top executives at both banks understood that they would be
judged by their adherence to the value of inclusiveness.

Mergers present many eye-opening lessons in how dramatically different cultures and procedures can be in rival institutions. At the operational level there were startling differences of approach and philosophy
between Chase and Chemical. In some cases, the exact same functions
were done with different nuances. In the making of loans, for instance,
the two banks' processes looked nearly identical. But a couple of months
after the combination, some subtle differences in their structure of authority became clear. They just didn't work the same way.

So management probed a little deeper and began asking questions,
such as, "Who approves the salary increase of the decentralized credit
person? Is this done within the unit, or is it shared with the central office? Who initiates the review? Who okays it?" Another point of difference was the fact that, at the Chase, loan officers had a voice in
determining if a particular loan was priced appropriately. However, at
Chemical they merely approved the credit, not the pricing. Similarly inconsistent practices had to be uncovered, negotiated, and resolved a
thousand times across the entire bank.

With each resolution, every link in the chain grew stronger. This sense
of strength and momentum spreading through the organization acted as
a counterweight to the negative feelings that many employees had toward the merger—especially those who'd worked like hell to make
"Manny Hanny" and Chemical come together just a few years earlier.
More important, however, was the distress of those scheduled for re-
dundancy.

An inclusive approach to a merger should not deny that there are
some very tough people issues that require sensitive handling. Mergers
create stress, discomfort, disruption, and anxiety. This emotional atmosphere will get a great deal worse if the unemployed aren't treated with
fairness and compassion, and if their abilities aren't given the proper respect. This is why the Chase took pains to benchmark severance programs
against the highest standards of cash compensation, outplacement, and
educational grants.

Chase also went the extra mile to be responsive to the emotional needs of those who stayed on: first, by making sure that the logic of the transaction was perceived deep down in middle management; and second, through communication programs designed around employee preferences. Initially, management had thought the best medium for communicating aspects of the merger would be videos and written communications. However, surveys indicated that people preferred small groups in face-to-face contact with their supervisors. So the videos were scrapped.

These, in brief, are some of the main characteristics of the integrative merger as practiced at the Chase. We recognize that not all merger-minded banks subscribe to this point of view. However, applying this approach in two historic mergers has provided credible supporting evidence that this is the best of many possible alternatives. It yielded fast economic gains, while maintaining the esprit de corps that delivers the best product and makes for contented customers.

23
A JOINT VENTURE THAT FOUND MORE THAN SYNERGY

Dirk Blaesing,
Fairway Filamentos

Dirk Blaesing is that classic modern type: the seasoned, globe-girding executive. In 1995, this twenty-seven-year veteran of Frankfurt's Hoechst Group became CEO of Brazil's newborn Fairway Filamentos. He'd worked for Hoechst in Brazil in the seventies, then in India for six years. But the apogee of his career has been the creation of a new corporate synthesis in a Brazilian context of two large companies, one German, the other French. Almost overnight, workers were "shifted to a new company they hardly knew," he recalls. "Many thought they'd lose something. Yet the company could not change operations on Day One." Read on and follow Blaesing through the transformations and the creation of a new corporate culture and a new identity.

COMPANIES GET INVOLVED IN joint ventures for a hundred different reasons. Usually, as with any marriage, both partners have something that makes the other more complete. And typically, joint ventures are start-ups. However, there is another type—the joint venture that combines the existing facilities, people, capital, and technology of two very seasoned companies, neither of which can overcome difficult market obstacles alone.

In this case, both sides of the fifty-fifty venture were Brazilian subsidiaries of world-class chemical and pharmaceuticals rivals—the French Rhône-Poulenc and the German Hoechst (known locally as Rhodia S.A. and Hoechst do Brasil S.A.). Neither parent company was happy with the profitability of its Brazilian synthetic filament businesses. Fairway Filamentos, the revolutionary fusion of a German- and a French-run operation, presented an extreme case of adaptation and new corporate culture creation. The joint venture's culture started from a base of nothing—or, more correctly, it started with past legacies of each operation that had to be radically modified and, in some cases, completely demolished.

Our story is one of corporate self-invention, of taking people and processes, bureaucracies and customary styles of behavior, and welding them into a unified organization with a single guiding philosophy and a common approach to problems and opportunities. What's more, this goal had to be achieved under severe time pressures. The longer the joint venture took to find its identity, the more ground it would lose in the marketplace. Thus the fusion process was driven by a genuine sense of extreme urgency. Companies with long histories of stability can fine-tune their cultures over many years. Fairway Filamentos had to get a viable culture up and running in only a few months.

A French and German *Entente Cordiale*

What precipitated the marriage were seismic changes in the Brazilian marketplace in 1994. These were brought about by the government's launching its new economic plan, which introduced a new currency scheme, lowered or entirely eliminated barriers on imported products, and decreased government spending in favor of industry privatization. Suddenly there was a surge in imports of synthetic fibers that drastically undercut local producers. Hoechst and Rhodia decided to spin off and combine their synthetic fiber units to give them a far stronger platform to expand their capacity and market presence. Meanwhile, the two parent companies would continue to compete in all other areas.

Although well over 90 percent of the workers in both companies were Brazilians, the two corporate cultures reflected their parents' very distinct identities. Not only are the French and Germans very different people, their corporations are different to an unusual degree. The French tend to be more decentralized in organization, but they invest a lot of resources on cross-linking communications, such as workshops and lots of internal liaison. Another factor that influenced the outlook of the Rhodia people was that they worked for the largest chemical company in Brazil. They had a lot invested in the prestigious image of being the greatest. By contrast, the people from Hoechst were accustomed to a more hierarchical and centralized operation. Most of them had spent their whole working lives in this kind of "command and control" operating style.

On Day One of the life of Fairway Filamentos in mid-1995, both cultures showed up for work, coexisting uneasily at the start. The same was true for systems, procedures, and protocols. For a while all of them ran on a double track. This duplication was felt to be healthy up-front because the joint management didn't want to intervene and pick favorites. There was also an excess of people, since all three thousand Rhodia and Hoechst filament employees were transferred to the new entity. This meant that all functional areas were initially overmanned.

HAMMERING OUT A NEW IDENTITY

There are at least two ways of arriving at a corporate identity. First, impose it by fiat—or try to. Or second, get all the key personnel into a room for several days and have them talk it through. Encourage them to express their needs, anxieties, orientations, define their goals, and, in short, forge a new identity through self-revelation, conflict resolution, and by hammering out strategic directions.

This second option was an easy choice for us, given Fairway's location. Brazilians are confessed addicts of discussion and debate (*batendo papo*, in the local idiom), and they are wonderful at expressing themselves freely. The Future Search Conference was convened only a few months after the merger took place. The company bent over backward to make certain that the demographics of this milestone gathering represented workers of all ranks. Of the seventy-three participants, fifty-seven were elected by employees in sales and marketing, quality control, R&D, plant operations, administration, and operations. The conference was also attended by a couple of consultants, including an anthropologist, as participant observers. And, much like a political convention, the affairs and deliberations of the conference were communicated to all employees every day.

"Not *another* conference," you sigh. But put yourself in the position of the typical employee, who expected to continue doing his or her job much as before and assumed that the culture of the old parent would prevail. The idea that a totally new culture was necessary came as a fresh revelation. The conference's agenda included a discussion of four distinct principles:

- *Principle No. 1: Market crises can create positive change.* People bond in crises. External threats and challenges tend to foster internal cohesion and a sense of community. Under such conditions, people are more willing to rethink assumptions and values, and this helps them identify the common ground they need to proceed.

- *Principle No. 2: The real enemies are outside the company.* One of the major challenges at Fairway was defusing the aggression and suspicion that stemmed from more than a decade of fierce competition between the Rhodia and Hoechst people. Even more critical, the company had to engender a climate in which workers not only didn't withhold information from their new colleagues, but shared freely of their background information, insights, and interpretations.
- *Principle No. 3: The company and top management are here to stay—permanently.* Shareholder commitment to Fairway's future had to be expressed in many ways. The first was to quash any speculation that top management might be transient—that they actually "belonged" to their previous masters and might soon be recalled. So we took great pains to demonstrate our strong identification with and allegiance to Fairway Filamentos—the new entity whose name very deliberately avoided identifying the original parents.
- *Principle No. 4: Equality in human resource approaches.* Differing styles of compensation and benefits for the ex-Hoechst and Rhodia employees were blended together. This gave everyone a level playing field. Many workers in fact experienced an improvement in their benefits. For example, one factory didn't have dental health coverage—now all do.

OPENNESS AND OVERCOMING GLITCHES MAKE FAIRWAY WORK

Perhaps the single most powerful demonstration of the forging of Fairway's new identity came in January 1997, when a common pension plan was established. Up to that point, because of legal difficulties, two nominal companies had been responsible for pensions. Their unification sent a very clear symbolic message that further encouraged worker identification and trust in the operation and its future. Another symbolic milestone was the opening of the first factory planned and completed by the new regime.

A new vision, however, is not a magic wand that can instantly erase the alienation many workers instinctively felt in the early days. Imagine a person's feelings arriving at work one day and finding a strange new boss in charge. Your first worry is whether he or she is going to make life difficult from now on.

The only obvious counterbalance to such anxieties is candor, openness, and good face-to-face communication. It also helps to establish rapport and pave the ground for new ideas when people admit the shortcomings in their previous methods and approaches. For example, even though I am German-born, I freely criticized the organizational template of German companies. This helped spur the evolution of our company's unique organizational structure and culture, which is far less hierarchic and more team-based than was Hoechst's. At the same time it is much less bureaucratic than Rhodia had been. The new organization has been flattened, and shop-floor operations have been redistributed among the five plants to streamline production costs.

The importance of speed in creating a new company persona was vividly dramatized after only a few months of joint operations. The Brazilian fiber market took a nosedive, in part due to a jump in local interest rates. Suddenly all the premerger sales targets had to be thrown out the window, and Fairway began to operate at a loss. The profit-index bonuses of managers shriveled to nothing. On the other hand, the resulting hardship and suffering created a deep sense of solidarity and strengthened the resolve of our teams to build their competence and competitive abilities.

Not all employees were able to march to the new drummer—there were failures of adaptation. The men and women who lacked the capacity to see or contribute to the new culture were offered transfers back to the parent companies, or dismissed. These redundancies helped to reduce the unwieldy size of the payroll.

Over and over again management reinforced the new focus on sharing and thinking positively. Obviously there were a number of glitches, but Fairway needed people who could overlook these shortcomings and concentrate on the external market threats to the company's continuity.

PROGNOSIS: LONG LIFE

So where does Fairway go from here? Research suggests that joint ventures are short-term relationships, lasting seven years on average. Two likely explanations for this are that shareholders push and pull in different directions; or secondly, that the joint venture's managers and employees never emerge from the shadow of those shareholders.

The prognosis for Fairway Filamentos is for a much longer life span. This is because the parent companies have truly integrated all their Brazilian nylon and polyester fiber assets and all their know-how in this one operation. The new company has evolved a unique identity that is fueling significant market gains in 1997.

24

Shaping Culture with Activity-Based Management

Javier Herrero, Iberdrola

Iberdrola is Spain's largest private company, the third-largest power provider in the European Union, and twenty-first in the world, with revenues in excess of $8 billion. The company has been active on privatization and modernization projects in Central and South America and former Soviet Bloc countries, and is based near Bilbao in northeastern Spain, home of most of the country's hydro sources. As general managing director, since 1993 Javier Herrero has charted Iberdrola's course through the tangles of Spanish deregulation. Previously he'd been the company's manager of planning, regulation, and investment.

CORPORATE CULTURE CHANGE IS a relatively new discipline. Some of its tools are known and understood, but there is still much room for experimentation and innovation, and for testing the approaches that yield the best results. At Iberdrola we are using the framework of Activity-Based Management (ABM) as a lever for culture change. At first pass, this approach may seem a little dubious, since culture change is often brought about through charismatic and forceful leadership or through a compelling vision, sheep-dip immersion training, and corporate brainwashing.

By contrast, our more programmatic method seeks to change the way in which our people see and understand the business. This approach should give them deeper and sharper insights, change their thinking processes, and eventually change their attitudes toward improving performance. The logic of this ABM-linked culture change lies in Iberdrola's unique circumstances.

The company was created by a 1991 merger of Spain's two largest privately owned electric utilities: Hidroelectrica Española, operating in central and eastern Spain, and Iberduero, operating in the north and west. Until now, Spain has been a difficult place for private capital in the power business because of heavy government regulation of prices, and restrictions on diversification out of power into ancillary lines of business. According to the European Energy Directive, the Spanish government has set January 1, 1998, as the effective date to start the liberalization. In this new arena we had to maximize shareholder value from our strategic advantages.

Our new management team felt that a radical culture change was essential because of:

- Intense regulatory surveillance of costs and end-user prices in a mature marketplace
- The diversity in operating styles, service delivery, and cost performance of the two wings of the company

ABM—THE CORE OF CULTURE CHANGE

To confront these challenges, we have devised a three-pronged strategy: improving internal efficiency, redesigning our commercial activities, and generating profitable growth. One of my first steps was to launch an all-out program to improve our understanding of the value chain, to map business processes and the delivery of customer services, and also to wrest some cost benefits through process reengineering. I next set out to reshape the design of the organization—from a structure based on functional specialization to more decentralized strategic business units, with support services provided by centrally organized staffs.

A major stumbling block to the effective implementation of these changes was the existing information and accounting system. It was simply too rigid to provide accurate and timely data, particularly about costs. Fine detail and consistency of information were simply not available.

That's where the ABM approach came in. It provided the platform we needed to integrate costs, activities, resources, and objectives. ABM proved to be the core of our transformation process, and it quickly became the center point of all other change projects in the company.

Like the word "culture," Activity-Based Management means different things to different people. It's a first cousin of Activity-Based Costing (ABC), an approach that is slowly gaining popularity. It attaches costs to activities, pinpointing cost drivers and tracking activity costs wherever those activities flow throughout the business. ABM applies a wider management philosophy and broad information framework around ABC techniques. Its goal is to enable people to view organizational activity and performance in radically new ways—to look at costs and profitability by customer, segment, product, or service, by product family, geography, business line, and so on.

The sharper insights available through ABM enable managers to make concrete links between resources, activities, costs, and productive output to customers. This powerful information delivery system can then be used to shift resources to create better returns—such as targeting more profitable customer segments, killing off or taking action on unprofitable products and services, and investing more in high-margin geographical markets. Without such insights, suboptimal activities that result in losses in one dimension are often obscured by better performance in another dimension.

Implementing ABM at Iberdrola

Three of ABM's characteristics make it central to the evolution of culture at Iberdrola:

- It cuts information at different hierarchical levels, so that accountability is pushed to the new business units.
- It speeds up and improves understanding of the linkages and cost drivers between one part of the business and another.
- It allows for linkage between many different types of performance measures.

Thanks to these benefits, individual managers can clearly see the relationship between inputs and outputs, as well as the consequences and impact their actions have on other parts of the business. This, in turn, makes it possible for them to act with maximum effectiveness. In fact, the whole culture change program at Iberdrola is based on the assumption that this information helps people radically reappraise their individual roles and gain deeper insights into the full range of the business environment in which they're operating. This is why I felt that ABM is such a powerful shaper of values and not simply a different approach to cost accounting and profit and loss allocation.

The ABM program illuminated the many facets of Iberdrola's business:

Vision, Purpose, and Strategy

When vision, purpose, and strategy are crisply articulated and reinforced, they have a powerful impact on culture. Muddled vision and strategy usually contribute to muddled results that have a negative impact on the business.

We began our change process by redefining and clearly communicating our new vision, purpose, and strategy. We emphasized the importance of delivering enhanced value for shareholders, and explained how this would be achieved. We also reached an agreement with an American power company to use its existing ABM model for Iberdrola projects because it was a benchmark of good practice. This proved to be a pivotal point in operationalizing the strategy, and it helped improve both the quality of the process and the credibility of the ABM project within the company.

Structure

Structure is the vessel that carries people and thus has a powerful impact on a company's culture. We redefined our structure to reflect the new behavioral values, shifting from a primarily functional perspective to one spun around discrete business units. The new structure moves autonomy and responsibility and decision making from the center to the operating units. And because it is less monolithic, it provides sharper accountability.

Leadership Actions

I gave the ABM program the highest priority and personally sponsored and directed it from pilot program to full-court press. From the beginning, I emphasized the central importance of the project to give it maximum visibility among all Iberdrola's top directors and managers. It may be a popular myth that all successful change requires powerful and consistent commitment from the top, but it certainly doesn't hurt.

Performance Measures

Performance measures—their focus, number, metrics, and application—are key drivers of behavior. They provide powerful leverage for active management. At Iberdrola the whole thrust of ABM has been to gain access to new, more meaningful measures that provide sharper accountability, more insightful performance, and the exploration of hitherto underexploited opportunities.

The remuneration of individual employees is now closely correlated to performance measures and targets. Before ABM, 80 percent of our measures and targets had been based on dates of accomplishment and meeting deadlines. With ABM, we switched from 80 percent qualitative measures and targets to 80 percent quantitative. The new measurements of achievement are now based on service quality and financial outcomes.

What was especially important to the success of the process was ranking the different measures. For example, profitability and other financial targets now became much more important than technical ones. Historically, engineering sophistication and prestige had always prevailed over considerations of commercial viability.

Competitive Context

By redefining the competitive context, we also changed the rules for middle managers and expanded their perceptions. They are now much more aware that they're operating in a global marketplace, and are prepared for deregulation whenever it comes.

Iberdrola also has a growing number of interests abroad, covering activities in power generation and distribution of electricity and gas in South America: Argentina, Chile, Bolivia, and Brazil.

Our vision was framed with market liberalization in mind. To reinforce it, an advertising campaign was launched in the press and TV, carrying the message: "In coming years electricity tariffs will be lower." Did this help generate a more positive image of Iberdrola in public opinion as a future supplier of electricity services at lower prices? Probably. But the campaign had its most profound effect on our employees. It helped everyone understand that the company was facing increased competition, and thus there was a profound need to reduce costs and to improve profitability and customer service.

People Practices

The way a business treats its people influences its culture through such factors as training, reward systems, and organizational communication. At Iberdrola we made a heavy investment in communicating our new ABM-based vision and values, in skills development, and in educating our managers to the ways in which performance-based financial rewards demand a shift of focus to new goals and objectives.

Empowering the Individual

Empowerment is a natural and potent way of dealing with complexity. With ABM, the responsibility for acting on relevant, segmented information is more widely distributed within the organization. Everyone at Iberdrola now receives relevant information about the financial results of their operational performance, with a focus on where, and how much, resources have been used. And they are expected to act on it. The fact that they can see how the information is assimilated and aggregated from their own data helps them own this information and gives them a sense of responsibility for doing the best possible job. In this way, management information quickly becomes a tool for promoting action deep in the business.

PUTTING ABM TO WORK

We encountered some difficulties in implementing ABM because the immune system of the old culture provided considerable resistance.

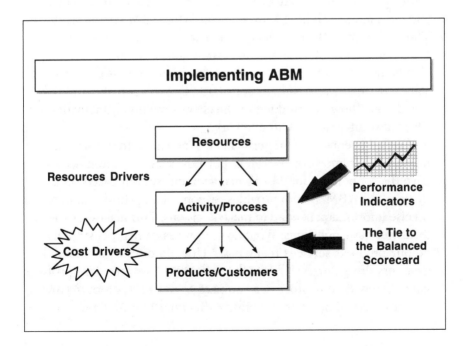

First of all, the traditional power structures did not take kindly to the devolution of their power to the business units. And then the widely held belief that the organization's overriding purpose was building power installations rather than delivering shareholder value didn't simply lie down and die. Another problem was that the basic quality of information was found to be wanting, a fact that was used as an argument to halt or postpone the implementation.

The opponents of change used the theory advanced by Italian sociologist Vilfredo Pareto that 80 percent of results come from 20 percent of the effort, so you might as well forget the rest.

Nevertheless, even though the total ABM program is only halfway to completion, results are already in. Improvements are clearly evident in the cost performance of our businesses. These have come through a

---

ABM AND ABC

ABM is a new business management approach based on Activities Management and supported by Activity-Based Costing (ABC).

Traditional accounting/management systems are based on cost center accounting by departments of the organization that are the owners of the resources. ABM's principal framework states that resources are driven by activities that in turn are driven by products and customers. Exhibit 1 shows how an ABC/ABM system works. The three main ABC elements are activities, resources (personnel, assets, financial, et cetera) and cost objects (products/services, clients/markets). Linking these three groups of entities are the resource drivers (the resources consumed by each activity) and the cost drivers (how the products or the clients execute the activities). This constitutes the ABC framework.

If we add economic and performance indicators to the activities in the ABC framework, as well as objectives and benchmarks, we have the foundation for ABM's management system based on activities. The ABM system provides responsible, up-to-the-minute, precise information needed to make decisions. This makes it easier to answer basic questions: What do our processes really cost? What do our products/services really cost? How do our customers and suppliers drive our costs? Which products/clients are more profitable? How do our processes compare to our competitors? How do our process-improvement efforts affect our bottom line?

sharpening of accountabilities, a better understanding of interfaces and linkages across the business, and streamlined processes for budgeting, planning, and performance review. Also bubbling up from all levels of the organization, there is now a stronger focus on shareholder value and the primacy of customers. If that isn't full-bore culture change, what is?

25

FROM "DYNASTY" TO RULE BY MBAS

Tanri Abeng, Bakrie & Bros.

In an economy dominated by the ethnic Chinese, Bakrie & Bros., one of Indonesia's largest conglomerates, stands out because it was founded and is largely owned by pribumi *(indigenous Indonesians). It stands out for another reason too—it is one of the few local enterprises to adopt a modern professional management ethic. In the early eighties, Aburizal Bakrie, son of the founder, took the helm and sold shares to the public. And in the late eighties he hired Tanri Abeng, a locally prominent U.S.-educated manager. Born to a poor farming family, Abeng earned an MBA from the State University of New York at Buffalo on a scholarship to the United States. His first job was in finance and later in marketing for Union Carbide; his second was turning around the local operations of Heineken beer.*

Dubbed by Indonesians the "billion rupiah manager" after the size of a reported $500,000 sign-on bonus from Bakrie, Abeng is the man "many regard as the best CEO Indonesia has produced," according to Asian Business *of June 1994. Thanks in part to his efforts, Bakrie Bros., with a workforce of fifteen thousand, is today a leading blue chip on the Jakarta and Surabaya Stock Exchanges. Since Abeng's appointment, the company's stock has risen by more than double. Other Bakrie family interests are privately held and separately managed.*

THE INJECTION OF PROFESSIONAL management into private companies that have grown too complex, too ambitious, or too inefficient happens thousands of times around the world every year. In the United States this transition is often masterminded by outside investors and venture capitalists seeking to charge up the company for greater growth, or to cure some of its weaknesses—or both. In less-developed economies, the same transition is often sparked by the members of the founder families, who foresee new circumstances that demand change and organizational reform, but who also recognize their own managerial shortcomings.

For all its ubiquity, the transition to professional management is nonetheless hazardous, complex, and often slow to achieve results. This is because of the weight and sanctity of the past and the lingering power and prestige of the owner or ownership group. The new, professionally trained leadership is often in an ambiguous position. As Peter Drucker has written, "There is entrepreneurial work and there is managerial work, and the two are not the same. But you can't be a successful entrepreneur unless you manage, and if you try to manage without entrepreneurship, you are in danger of becoming a bureaucrat."

Each type can be myopic about the other's virtues. Managers often see entrepreneurs as undisciplined risk takers, while entrepreneurs often typify managers as timid bureaucrats in love with procedure. These stereotypes get in the way of the mission of professionals, whose task is to rationalize the firm and take it to a higher level of performance. However, in order to do this, they must dismantle and replace the existing management style and structure, which are often the creations of powerful founding personalities.

Because of the eminence and prestige of the founders, as well as their relatives and heirs, the professional newcomers in gray flannel suits have to tread warily. When making changes in the status quo, they must be careful not to create the appearance that their predecessors have lost face—especially since they are frequently still powerful shareholders. At the same time, the new managers must also avoid creating friction with, and between, family members.

This means that the incoming professional managers must have negotiation and consensus-building skills, or develop them quickly, so they can inject new processes and new ways of thinking without doing violence to the fabric and continuity of the firm. Professional managers must guard against arrogance or excessive pride in the new structures they're creating. Ideally, they need to penetrate the old structure and culture, not overwhelm it with strange new practices. If they don't take care, the whole restructuring process will backfire on them and provoke stubborn resistance to change.

SLOW-MOTION LEAP TO PROFESSIONAL MANAGEMENT

This in fact happened in previous regimes at Bakrie & Bros., where attempts to change the culture failed. However, the latest attempt has succeeded nearly 100 percent. And because Bakrie has safely negotiated this slow-motion leap to total professional management, we believe that other companies—even those in a quite different cultural setting—might learn some pointers from our transitioning experience.

The transformation of Bakrie & Bros. into a complex, multifaceted enterprise did not occur without some pain and sacrifice. In the name of greater efficiency some of the old-timers had to go. In some cases these dismissed workers were personal friends of the founding family. This made the decision harder for the professional managers—and tougher on the workers involved, since many of them believed they'd be employed for life. Among the many new and challenging performance measures that were adopted, one of the most significant was a new human resource recruitment policy. It demanded that all employees, including family members, had to meet essential criteria in skills and aptitudes.

THE FAMILY ENTREPRENEURS VS. THE PROS

Not only were people divested in this turnaround, so were entire lines of business—such as a shoe factory, an apparel joint venture, and some mining operations—because their future looked problematic. In the past, all proposals for new investments had been approved by the owner, but the incoming professional management group created an entirely new process. New capital expenditure proposals were reviewed by an Investment Steering Committee, which had total authority in the matter.

As it happened, the changeover of authority in the firm occurred at a time when the economic situation called for a cautious approach to capital spending to conserve resources during a difficult time. Instead of making new investments, my new management team focused on greater market penetration and lower production costs in order to improve cash flow in the company's strongest units—steel pipe, rubber plantations, and telecommunications.

We adopted a strategy of vertical integration of Bakrie's core businesses and strategic investment in high-growth sectors. And we also decided not to diversify its portfolio of businesses any further. This is a fairly typical aspect of change from private to professional management in formerly privately held businesses, since family dynasties typically seek portfolio diversification by putting all investments into the firm. While this approach has merit from the family's point of view, it can often lead to stumbling blocks to efficient management.

On the other hand, in the changeover from a family-run company to one that is professionally run, the new management may discover it's necessary to accommodate the entrepreneurial vitality of some key family members. There is always the danger that professional managers will be—or will be perceived to be—too cautious about taking risks. The entrepreneurial spirit of the firm must be preserved, along with its aggressiveness in finding new opportunities for profit and in adding new businesses. This means that a balance must be achieved between untrammeled entrepreneurialism and the more systematic approach of the professional manager, who focuses on improving the performance of the current business and is often skeptical of the value of new ventures.

One way around this is for the company to build a dual organizational structure that fosters both the entrepreneurial and professional drives in the company. The entrepreneurial personality is heavily focused on opportunism, on developing business ventures that could be the seeds of great growth. However, it typically underplays the problems inherent in managing start-ups. This approach may create chaotic situations during implementation due to lack of preparation and insufficient knowledge of the managerial backup needed for the new venture to succeed.

By contrast, the professional personality is heavily invested in retaining and growing the existing business portfolio. It focuses on improving performance based on sound management principles and systems, on planning and controls and accountability, and on the growth and enhancement of skill sets.

At Bakrie & Bros. the solution to this dilemma was to put individuals with entrepreneurial qualities in business development, and those with professional abilities in operational functions. An entirely new stand-alone subsidiary, Bakrie Investido, was created for new and entrepreneurial ventures, and it has recently made high-risk property and television investments that would not have been appropriate for a publicly listed company such as Bakrie.

One of the perils of founder-manager companies is the charismatic magnetism of the patriarch. Far too many decisions, from the trivial to the serious, must bear the stamp of the founder, which means that he is often powerless to reduce or filter the flow of issues that cross his desk. Even when professional managers are hired, some people continue to sidestep them and report directly to the founder, under the impression that this will curry favor. In this kind of climate the danger is that too many people end up looking inward, trying to "manage the boss," instead of looking outward to the marketplace and the competition.

This used to be the case at Bakrie. However, the new professional group changed this by focusing on managing the system and managing the market. This was brought about in part by analyzing the ingredients of the old centralized power structure and deconstructing them into rational categories and specializations.

INDONESIA OR INDIANA—THE FUNDAMENTALS ARE THE SAME

These are some of the factors to bear in mind when a company is making the transition from private owner-managers to professional management. In the former environment, successful management is mythologized as a personal attribute of the founder and his lineage. In the latter, success is based on discipline, control, rationality, and freedom of action. However, the journey from one form of management to the other varies in both difficulty and speed depending on different family circumstances and different national cultures.

Indonesia is not Indiana. Most commerce in Indonesia is controlled and run by families. There, the belief in the power and rightness of family management is very strong, while the belief and trust in nonfamily, professional management has not yet found widespread favor. So for Bakrie, the transition came about more slowly than, say, a situation in the Silicon Valley, where the founders give way to professional outsiders. And yet, the fundamentals remain the same.

PART V
Innovation and Creativity

No Finger Painting, Please

"CREATIVITY, I FEAR, IS a void in many of our organizations," says Robert Galvin, former CEO and architect of today's Motorola. "We simply don't know how much more creative we can be."

"Lots more," you might think. And indeed widespread dissatisfaction among executives over the degree of innovation and creativity in their companies is more common these days than the gray flannel suit.

Sigmund Freud believed that at bottom all dreams are about wish fulfillment. If we could tap into the dream life of CEOs, we would find that the dream they all share every night is the wish for innovation. There is really no other activity that so quintessentially represents the achievement of the modern world than its amazing fertility in scientific and economic discovery. But CEOs should be careful what they wish for, because few companies are in fact equipped to recognize real from delusional creativity and innovation. Feel-good enhancement programs grow like crabgrass on the consulting circuit, most of them sidestepping the really tough question: What is the link between individual creativity and innovation and corporate success?

It is important to make very clear what we mean when we say "creativity" and "innovation." The distinction between them is key. In business, "creativity" can be deemed to be the generation of ideas within an organizational context that is capable of understanding, amending, and then taking those ideas to a further level of sophistication and adaptation. That is much more than just having a Eureka moment or a blinding insight in an otherwise humdrum meeting. Ideas are cheap. To be effective, they have to be in context, they have to be transmissible, and they have to have weight in terms of either known tactics or strategies. A handful of executives sitting around brainstorming is, at best, a prelude to creative possibilities. Creativity, as we see it, is a business skill, a vital competitive variable in thousands of industries: advertising, fashion, entertainment, biotechnology, software, publishing, and more.

"Innovation," however, is present when new methods, constructs, and ways of thinking result in significantly new products and services—and, sometimes, whole new markets. The innovation label does not apply to me-too products, to extensions, to new product and market segmentations. Very often we don't see the greatness of true innovation until some time after the fact. If it's not in some whizbang R&D product, then most people figure it must be the result of innovation in business processes, or perhaps in the way a successful company organizes its teams. Loose, after-the-fact attributions of innovation that are unsupported by evidence are simply part of our race's collective romance with technology.

What business really benefits from are instances of deliberate prepared-ness for creative innovation, followed by results.

In short, managers should try to think concretely about innovation and creativity, not take a pie-in-the-sky approach. Should you complain that what your company needs is a shot of creativity, try to imagine the scenario if a genuine blockbuster, once-in-a-lifetime discovery were to be presented to the executive committee. Does your company have the experience base and/or the financial resources to fully exploit all the pos-sibilities? After five companywide reengineering initiatives, is there any-one left in top management who still has the time and energy to champion the new discovery? How well does the product fit the company's strat-egy, or does it not fit at all? What are the economic and political forces arrayed (as there always are) against the adoption of this product?

Most of us worship innovation from afar because it is so rare. Man-agement thinkers who believe that innovation is a source of competitive advantage are right in terms of the history of an Apple Computer, a Xe-rox, or a Polaroid, but wrong when this precept is applied to most corporate situations. Writing in the May/June 1997 issue of *Research-Technology Management*, Greg A. Steven and James Burley point out that "across most industries it appears to require 3,000 raw ideas to pro-duce one substantially new commercially successful industrial product. In pharmaceuticals, the number is much higher."

Of those 3,000 ideas, they compute that 300 will merit some further experiments and/or a patent filing, of which 125 advance into full-fledged projects. These then get whittled down to 9, then to 4 at the fi-nal state of maturity, out of which 1.7 products are launched, of which one (or 59 percent) is successful. They further calculate that only 5 to 10 percent of all patents issued by the U.S. Patent Office have *any* com-mercial relevance, and only 1 percent of them actually become prof-itable innovations. Steven and Burley observe that "many companies lack good benchmarks to guide expectations of innovation outcomes" and add that "a significant improvement in the innovation process at a company could still be interpreted as failure because the number of out-right winners may not increase much."

The management of expectations is the beginning of wisdom about innovation. It is essential to define in advance what kind of innovation, or creativity, is sought, and why. So the issue comes down to one of focus and the creation of scenarios that must be industry- and strategy-specific. If your company makes stuffed animals and souvenirs, there's one type and degree of innovation that's needed; if it makes data ware-house software, it'll be another.

There is a lot of commentary in the management literature on the so-called race to innovate. But only a few contenders at any one time are racing. The others are just ambling along behind, preparing a me-too response. Once again, it's a question of strategic posture. As Shakespeare once said about timing, "Ripeness is all." The innovation that arrives too soon is no better than one that's too late. Consider, for example, the Internet. That it is a revolutionary new dimension is incontrovertible. But whether the first wave of fledgling publicly owned Internet companies have their timing right is being seriously questioned.

A focus on innovation has become one of the demands of the shareholder value movement. However, security analysts are quick to penalize companies that are beguiled by innovations outside their special niches. There have been several cases in recent years in which companies have made announcements of big slashes in their R&D infrastructures and personnel. Wall Street showed its approval by bidding up the price of their stocks—a reflection of skepticism about the value added by these firms' earlier research outlays. The logic of shareholder value thinking is not to diminish R&D outlays, but to ensure that they move from weak to strong hands, from wannabe innovators to those with the strategies that can get the most out of these expenditures.

In today's competitive environment, companies are under pressure to come up with credible, communicable, and tightly focused innovation and creativity strategies— whether they be a continuous process or a "Big Bang" innovation, whether they spring from internal company innovation of processes or systems, or whether they're the result of partnering with suppliers or customers. By definition, a more competitive climate heightens the impact of a product or a service with exceptional features that may have been the brainchild of innovation.

But companies clearly have many pathways to the achievement of innovation. Let's look at two divergent examples. Hallmark Cards has a celebrated program focused on boosting the creativity of its artistic group, whose visual and language skills are a key competitive resource in a business with continuous new-product introductions. Accordingly, the company has segregated its "creatives" and allowed them lots of personal management of their time. It also provides them with annual courses in creativity, and offers them special stimulating events—like a trip to the museums of Paris.

Quite the opposite approach has been taken by Dana Corporation in chapter twenty-six. The auto supply parts company has taken a leaf from the Japanese bible of continuous improvement. Instead of ivory tower "creatives," everyone at Dana is involved in and enthralled by one of the most ambitious and relentless employee idea-generation programs in U.S. manufacturing. And the premise of this effort precisely echoes the thoughts of Motorola's Robert Galvin: Since "we don't know how much more creative we can be," let's find out!

Dana's employee suggestion initiative bears no resemblance to the classic dust-coated suggestion box stuck along the corridor to the bathroom. Dana, says CEO Southwood Morcott, has a "formal, organized approach that provides a way for people to submit ideas; sets out how they will be recorded, evaluated, and implemented; and, importantly, explains how employees will be rewarded." In one case, Dana was in the midst of planning a several-million-dollar expansion when an employee submitted the idea of adding workstations to the existing assembly. Result: For an investment of $70,000, Dana eliminated a third shift, reduced the workweek from seven to five days, and simultaneously boosted productivity by 23 percent.

Of all the wish-fulfilling dreams a CEO might have, none can be more glittery than the notion of massive transformation by innovation, of getting rich on needs and wants undreamed of by anyone before. This is the innovation jackpot. But creating a market before customers express a need or desire is the rarest form of innovation. An uncommon example appears in chapter twenty-seven, the Enron story. In deploying some very run-of-the-mill technology to create gas-powered generating units for industry, this large natural gas utility set off a whole chain of deregulating events in both natural gas and electricity. Enron demonstrated strategic appropriateness and focus. Not only did it have uncommon foresight for a utility company, it had the help of economic scale plus the political connections it needed to create a unique opportunity and to make a bold plan happen.

In the popular imagination, innovation and creativity are the agents of the new. In reality, most corporate innovation is defensive—a reaction to external forces and shifting trends and patterns in the customer environment that continuously demand fresh strategies and approaches. Chapter twenty-eight shows how one division of Philips, the Dutch electronics behemoth, is responding to major shifts in customer preferences. A decade ago, all of its output was marketed as product. Today, its customers look to the manufacturer to supply integrated applications and turnkey solutions and systems, not just discreet black boxes. This has forced Philips to invent new operating styles and organizational structures, as well as to enter into partnerships with erstwhile rivals. Its changing market has forced Philips to explore a whole new level of complexity of service in order to get maximum revenues from its production lines. This tale reflects one big strand of innovation around the globe: the integration of service elements with hardware, so that the dividing line between a product and a service is increasingly blurred.

Strategic appropriateness is also at the core of the innovations at the MIT Sloan School of Business in chapter twenty-nine. Leveraging off MIT's acclaimed computer and science skills, Sloan innovated its way to an improved ranking among its business-school peers.

By this point, you must be thinking that success in innovation is like climbing Everest. It is. But say a CEO gets our message about focus, understands that strategically disconnected creativity is as useful as a party balloon, and knows the sober truths about the uncertainty of innovation as a competitive weapon. Yet, like our dreamer, this CEO still says, "I want to see more innovation—in the whole company, or in Department X, or in strategy formulation, or in supply-chain linkages: Will somebody please help me get it?" He or she should read the inspiring story in chapter thirty in which David M. Kelley, CEO of IDEO, a company that lives by the daring and the relevance of its creativity, shares a few how-to secrets.

That chapter leaves no doubt: Creativity and innovation can be nurtured and stimulated. But even when it is well focused and rooted in strategy, it's no panacea, and it certainly can't compensate for competitive disadvantages in other areas. If you doubt this, ask Intel, ask Honda, ask 3M, or any of the other icons of corporate innovation. One of the difficulties stems from the fact that innovation is a multistage process. It requires (1) generating the idea, (2) planning its execution, and (3) turning the plan into action. Some 80 percent of ideas fail at the second stage. Getting over this hump is the problem most innovators face.

It's important to recognize that innovation occurs at the boundaries of an organization just as often—and maybe more often—as it does in the R&D labs at its center. The boundaries are those regions where the organization intersects with competitors, customers, and suppliers. A study at British Aerospace in chapter thirteen found that 90 percent of its innovations were a direct result of these interactions at the boundaries. Similarly, the benefits to the British automobile maker Rover from its five-year strategic alliance with Honda were enormous—a 30 percent drop in production costs, a 50 percent improvement in time-to-market of new models.

Innovation won't happen without strenuous attempts to foster it in the right strategic context. Significant amounts of top executive time must be dedicated to innovation. British Aerospace attempts to do this by having fifty top managers get together twice a year with nothing on the agenda except innovation. And then there's the well-known case of 3M's allowing its research people to spend 10 to 20 percent of their time in skunk works outside the regular organization. But while top management clearly sets the agenda, they shouldn't personally try to innovate. We believe that some 80 percent of innovations come from people at least three levels below the top management team—a point of view that is clearly shared by Dana Corporation.

What about CEOs? Should they personally strive to be heroic innovators? The answer is probably not. There are too many other claims on their time for them to be rolling the dice. What's more, innovations by CEOs are unlikely to get the heavy screening that any novel concept requires. The key role that a CEO can play is interpreter—both analyst and judge of an innovation's economic relevance.

26

IGNITING A FIRESTORM
OF CREATIVITY

Southwood J. Morcott,
Dana Corporation

On the surface it looks as if Southwood J. Morcott, CEO of auto parts maker Dana Corporation since 1989, has set himself a quixotic goal. In an industry famous for its cyclical swings of demand, "Woody" Morcott is bent on making Dana a growth company. And so far he's succeeded. Dana has racked up a five-year run of uninterrupted increases in revenues and profits, backed by a steady stream of productivity enhancement.

What's his secret? Morcott believes that Dana reaps all the advantages of a large global presence, but acts like "an entrepreneurial company in the way it handles human resources." Few CEOs have gone as far or have worked as hard as Morcott to adopt the Japanese-inspired "continuous improvement" philosophy, or to invest in worker motivation and training.

Says Maryann Keller, the celebrated auto analyst with Furman Selz: "Woody Morcott has gone a long way toward creating a strategy that brings consistent growth in an industry typically marked by feast and famine." In this chapter, Morcott vibrantly shows how that growth is engendered by the flood of productivity-enhancing ideas from Dana people, and how to make this work for your company.

WHEN WAS THE LAST time you directly asked your entire workforce for their ideas? Sure, there's that column in the company newsletter where you say that you welcome ideas for improvement. And maybe you encourage creative thinking among your management team and in the meetings you conduct. Perhaps you even have a suggestion box system in place. But no one really cares or pays attention, and precious little effort is made to genuinely solicit ideas from every person.

This is a big mistake. A colossal waste. An overlooked opportunity.

Dana Corporation is taking a substantially different approach and we're generating thousands of new ideas every year from most of our forty-eight thousand people worldwide. The stated goal of Dana's idea-generation program: Two ideas per person per month—expected from the chairman no less than from the new hire on the plant floor. Dana's goal is to have 80 percent participation companywide, and to implement 80 percent of the ideas submitted.

Dana wants every idea it can get, big and small, from both individuals and teams. Ideas that identify a better way in all areas of the business, whether you work in an office or on the assembly line. We're looking for ideas on *combining* operations, functions, and processes. On *improving* accuracy, quality, customer service, system techniques, storage, shipping, production control, machine performance, materials handling, house-keeping, working conditions, paperwork, plant and office efficiency, and security. We want ideas on *reducing* rework, scrap, tool breakage, personal or property hazards, waste maintenance, repairs, downtime, person-hours, cost. On *saving* time, space, material, and manpower. On *simplifying* design, procedures, forms. Dana is serious about this.

How serious? Look at these numbers from our Parish Light Vehicles Structures Division based in Reading, Pennsylvania. There are approxi-

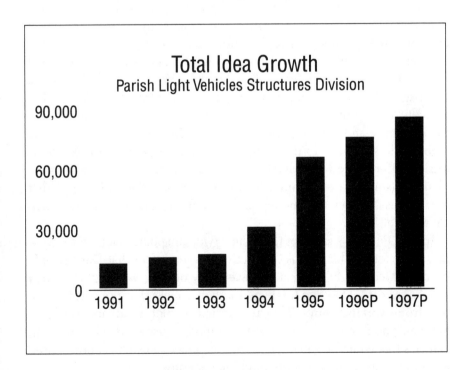

Total Idea Growth
Parish Light Vehicles Structures Division

mately 3,600 people in the division. Idea growth has exploded from 8,941 submissions in 1991 to 63,981 in 1995 (see figure, "Total Idea Growth").

Not coincidentally, during that same period division profitability increased by 40 percent and productivity by 13 percent. Morale is higher than it's ever been—people at all levels feel empowered to make a difference. They are, and they do. And the most interesting thing of all is that they're motivated to contribute ideas not because they expect financial gain but because of the personal sense of satisfaction they get by making a difference in the way things are done. More on this later.

While the Parish Division is clearly one of the pacesetters within Dana, the entire company is dedicated to achieving the same idea-generation goals, and each division is making substantial progress. The process yields a great many benefits, both tangible and intangible, and generates relatively modest costs.

THE "DANA STYLE"

If there is one value that characterizes this organization, it's the recognition that Dana's people are our most important asset. "Sure," you say, "I've heard that one before." Not at Dana. Here, the words are backed up by a clearly defined management approach, and policies and practices that drive it home. Walk into a Dana plant anywhere in the world and you'll see the motto: "People Finding a Better Way."

Dana has a highly defined corporate culture, and people are aware of it from the moment they first walk in the door. We've summarized it in a one-page list of key management concepts called the "Dana Style." Essentially, these nine points express the beliefs, values, and attitudes of the company and act as guides to action. Management perceives the Dana Style as crucial to the company's global success, and it is relentlessly reinforced and modeled by top management during their frequent plant visits around the United States and abroad. The philosophy that business is "10 percent money and 90 percent people" is firmly entrenched at Dana.

In the "People" section of the Dana Style, one point reads: "Experts—25 square feet." This means that in the 25 square feet that Dana people occupy at least eight hours a day, every day of their working lives, *they* are the experts. They see firsthand the bottlenecks that prevent the system from working better. They're the first to spot accidents waiting to happen. The first to detect flaws that could be corrected. They see efficiencies that could be gained. But without a mechanism to capture those expert insights, improvements would never come to light.

For this reason, another element of the Dana Style is, "Four magic words: What do *you* think?" This recognizes the need to actively solicit employees' ideas. It sounds simple, yet it's rarely done effectively. The vast majority of the world's workforce is never asked for its ideas. Friends, spouses, bartenders—everyone but the employer—learn what's wrong at work and how it could be done better.

Even the companies that ask for ideas usually do so in a halfhearted way that tells people loud and clear that there's a low corporate priority attached to the request. Typically, little thought is given to what kinds of ideas are needed. No incentives are offered. People may be intimidated by having to justify their idea with a sophisticated business analysis. There is often substantial lag time between the moment when an idea is submitted and the moment when a response is received. Even if a response *is* received, it's usually: "Thanks for your idea. The committee considered it, but we're sorry to inform you that we cannot take any action at this time." In other words, "Thanks, but no thanks."

THE IDEA BEHIND THE IDEA SYSTEM

So how does a company develop an idea system that actually works? First, let's define "idea system." At Dana, this is a formal, organized approach that provides a way for people to submit ideas; sets out how they will be recorded, evaluated, and implemented; and, importantly, explains how employees will be rewarded for implementation. Formality is kept to a bare minimum. At Dana we make submitting an idea as easy and uncomplicated as possible. It's the critical first step that drives everything else.

How do you make an idea system part of your culture? No question, it helps when your preexisting culture is people-oriented. At Dana Corporation, for example, idea generation goes hand in hand with education—our goal is to provide forty hours of classroom education per year per person. We believe that educated people are good idea generators. And in South America, where Dana people receive the most company-sponsored education, the average idea output per person is higher than anywhere else.

Ultimately, people should be empowered to have real influence over standards of quality, service, and business effectiveness within their areas of responsibility. In our experience, it all boils down to trusting and respecting your people and recognizing their unique expertise within their sphere of responsibility. People will help you achieve quality and customer satisfaction, higher sales and profitability, whatever goals you want to achieve— *if you're willing to make the investment in them.* A company that truly empowers its people will:

- *Improve decisions* by promoting decisiveness, speed, flexibility, and responsiveness, particularly with respect to customer needs.
- *Gain flexibility* by leveraging the innate versatility and resourcefulness of people to respond to an environment of continuous change.
- *Capitalize on the full potential of the human spirit* by creating a highly charged, high-initiative workforce motivated to overcome big odds in order to achieve the organization's objectives.

An idea-generation system can be tremendously empowering—if properly designed and implemented. Let's look at how to do it right.

FROM INCREMENTAL TO MONUMENTAL SUCCESS

In the seventies and eighties, Dana's idea system was paying modest dividends. It was already more successful than similar systems in other companies, and participating people received various forms of recognition. Yet it still had a long way to go. People's overall awareness level was mediocre. The old system hadn't motivated them to establish the habit of generating ideas.

In the early nineties, Dana revamped its idea system. It was transformed from being incrementally effective to being the best-practice model it is today. Our first task was to set, and institutionalize, our goals for the program. At the outset, we established the goal that each and every person at every level would be responsible for generating at least two ideas per month. Some effort would be made to channel people's thinking into certain categories of workplace issues and specific problem areas or bottlenecks, but any idea on how to be better would be accepted.

Why pursue quantity over quality? Because quality is subjective, and "little" ideas can often have a big impact. Even more importantly, we didn't want to inhibit the flow of ideas.

Among the most powerful aspects of this program's implementation are its measurable goals: 80 percent implementation, and 80 percent participation. Our creative bias was very clear—whether or not to implement an idea would normally be settled in favor of implementation. In effect, Dana was betting on the likelihood that when people saw the high rate of implementation, they'd realize their ideas were being taken seriously and momentum would build. We hoped that as people got into the habit of generating ideas and received proper recognition for their contributions, a brush fire of ideas would turn into a firestorm.

These goals were institutionalized by becoming part of the Dana Style. This meant that they were being communicated and implemented worldwide. However, making real progress meant that the message had to come from the top down. We had to assure all our people that they were now empowered to think creatively, and encourage them to play an active role in continuous improvement. We had to make clear that innovation and creativity—embodied in concrete ideas—would not only be *welcomed* but *expected*. We had to underscore that action would almost invariably be the result of their efforts on the company's behalf.

As senior management visited Dana plants around the world, they continually reemphasized the importance of two ideas per month per person, followed by 80 percent implementation. Division managers and plant managers quickly started singing the same tune—for them, idea generation was tied to an annual bonus. And Dana people responded enthusiastically. Some people even began submitting an idea or two every *day*.

Soon, more formal systems were developed throughout the organization. New ideas became topics of discussion at monthly division quality meetings—not at the bottom of the agenda, but at the top. Company bulletin boards became a forum for posting newly implemented ideas, and these in turn led to other ideas. Company newsletters started carrying stories about the idea system and recognizing workers who had submitted ideas that were successfully implemented. Raffles were held to choose and reward the best ideas submitted in the course of a month. Premiums were awarded to people who surpassed their idea quota. Word of mouth spread: "This thing's for real."

INFORMAL IS GOOD

At Dana, submitting an idea is as straightforward as jotting it down on a piece of paper. The company provides a form, but ideas come in on cards, napkins, and the backs of dry cleaning receipts. As for implementation, all we ask is: "Can your idea be implemented for $50 or less?" If so, you're empowered to do it—just be sure you document it. If not, submit the idea to your supervisor and you'll receive a written response within forty-eight hours. If your idea is rejected, you'll be told why. But odds are, it won't.

Dana's Reading, Pennsylvania, plant continues to be "idea central." From 1990 to 1995, Reading established an implementation rate of 77 percent (see figure, "Ideas Submitted and Implemented"). As a token of appreciation for people exceeding expectations by submitting more than two ideas a month, Reading established a premium system that offers various gifts based on the number of ideas implemented.

The gifts range from a Thanksgiving turkey for twenty-five ideas to a Dana leather jacket for a hundred. Of course, once you prime the pump, the ideas just seem to flow from certain people—like Reading's Wess Seltzer, who in 1995 submitted nearly 550 ideas (see sidebar). Wess will never need another leather jacket.

IDEAS IN ACTION

At Dana Corporation, we receive beneficial ideas every day. The majority yield direct, tangible financial benefits, either in cost savings or cost avoidance. For example, record-high customer demand had created a capacity challenge on an assembly line. We were seriously considering spending millions of dollars for facility expansion when an idea was submitted to add workstations to the existing assembly line.

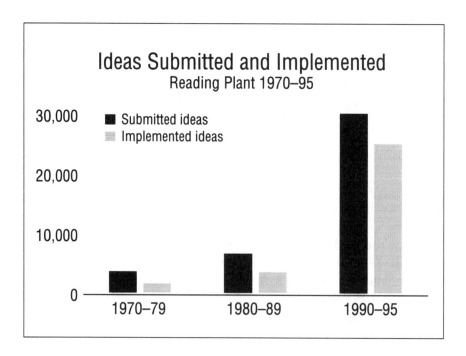

Wess Seltzer: Idea Man

On average, Wess Seltzer, a Parish Division fixture specialist based in Reading, submits more than two ideas a day, every day he reports to work. Roughly half of his ideas deal with safety and the other half with manufacturing process issues. True to the corporate ideal, 80 percent of his suggestions have actually been implemented.

Seltzer says that his years as a welder on the plant floor honed his insight into manufacturing processes. "During downtime," he told us, "the guys would all get together and talk about how to make things run smoother. But we didn't always have a lot of help in getting changes made." Now he's developed such a reputation for troubleshooting that workers seek him out for input on their ideas.

In Seltzer's view, the best idea he ever submitted was based on nothing more than common sense. A chain conveyor designed to transfer auto frames from one unit to another frequently broke down due to the weight of the frames passing over it. "It got to the point where I just started troubleshooting with Dave Hartman, and we came up with an idea to install an arm on the conveyor to get the frames through more efficiently.

"One lunch hour I pulled a steel part out of inventory, persuaded the tool man to put some holes in it, and Dave and I installed it." It worked. A solution that cost about $300 saved the company more than $10,000 a day on downtime.

Seltzer's ideas keep flowing. His goal now is to encourage other people to increase their idea flow. At the Reading plant, that means qualifying for increasingly valuable premiums as the idea count increases. He says he recently told a team of workers, "I don't want to be the only one here getting a jacket. There's no reason you can't come up with at least a hundred ideas. There's one guy now who's right behind me."

For a minimal $70,000 investment, we were able to eliminate a third shift, go from a seven- to a five-day workweek, and at the same time boost line rate productivity by 23 percent. The plant has since achieved record annual production volumes and is in a much better position to satisfy future increases in customer demand.

There have been equally good ideas aimed at the office environment as well as the plant floor. One of the most spectacular came from an accounts receivable supervisor at Dana's Superior Electric Division in Bristol, Connecticut, who devised a brilliant idea for streamlining customer-ordered drop shipments to reduce man-hours and ensure timely billing and payments to customers and vendors. The change not only reduced the number of people in this accounting process from three to one, it uncovered pricing problems on the vendor side that resulted in our receiving thousands of dollars in credits.

Other ideas have yielded more intangible, "quality of life" benefits that are creating a safer, saner, more productive workplace. For instance, by installing a lift table to control the height of a parts carrier, Dana reduced back and arm injuries. Since each back injury costs about $11,500 in workers' comp claims, this idea saved the company money and made the job both safer and easier.

"WHAT'S IN IT FOR ME?"

Generally speaking, what motivates a person to generate ideas? It's not necessarily financial reward. Almost all people want to do their jobs well—producing quality products or services that help their organization succeed in the marketplace. At Dana, we've found that being committed to idea implementation empowers people to do their jobs better.

Suggesting ways in which the company can continuously improve gives people a powerful sense of contributing to Dana's success and enhances their personal growth, pride in their work, and the feeling of truly making a difference—for themselves, their co-workers, and the company at large. Implementation helps them see that they're accomplishing their goals—an important reward in itself. Dana's culture recognizes that the more a company helps its people accomplish their goals, the better off that company will be.

Recognizing people's contributions is also a powerful motivator. People who find a better way through good ideas deserve to be recognized by their managers and co-workers. The company employee newsletter need not chronicle every single implemented idea, but it should summarize the best ideas on a regular basis. Other forms of internal communications (E-mail, bulletin boards, Intranet, et cetera) should be used wherever appropriate.

Does your department/group/team/unit have regular meetings? If so, make time to discuss new ideas and to recognize ideas that have been successfully implemented. Perhaps throw every idea implemented in a given week or month into a hopper and draw raffle winners. Or follow Parish Division's example: Offer premiums increasing in value for increasing numbers of ideas submitted and implemented. The premiums needn't be extravagant—at Parish they include tickets to ball games, certificates for a free oil change, and a book of discount coupons good at local restaurants and theaters. In essence, their value is symbolic. It's the company's way of saying thanks, added to the other motivators.

How do Dana people view the idea system? Judging from the exponential growth in numbers of ideas submitted and implemented, they value it highly. A sampling from their written comments confirms this:

> "I like to see that I'm making a difference in the quality of life on the production line, the quality of the product, and the satisfaction of the customer. There's nothing more gratifying than coming up with an idea and seeing that idea in place and working."

> "We all feel that we're empowered to make changes. . . . Without a suggestion system, top management wouldn't notice that what's good for its people is also good for the company."

> "I take pride in knowing that when I turn in an idea, it will be read, discussed, and considered by staff. . . . If my ideas are good enough to be used, they will affect me, my teammates, the plant, and eventually Dana as a whole."

As the last comment implies, it's very important for large organizations with idea systems in place at multiple locations to have a plan for sharing good ideas that might have relevance for more than one location. A process improvement on the assembly line in one plant might easily be adapted to others. At Dana, "best practice" ideas are shared informally from plant to plant and division to division every day; and they are shared formally at the annual three-day Quality Conference.

LIGHT THE TORCH!

All people in your organization have ideas about how they could function more effectively and how the company could be more successful. But most companies simply never ask for this information, and those that do tend to be halfhearted about it. With this attitude, any benefits will be haphazard or nonexistent.

Why not tap into the vast potential of the human mind? Leverage the

CRITICAL SUCCESS FACTORS OF AN "IDEAS" PROGRAM

- *Structure the idea-generating process,* but keep the mechanism(s) for submitting ideas informal to facilitate and maximize submissions. Accept every good idea, no matter how insignificant it may seem. The key is to encourage all people to develop the habit of generating ideas no matter whether they're big or small. Small ideas lead to bigger ideas, and they all add up to continuous improvement.
- *Set goals in terms of numbers of ideas expected,* implementation rate, and participation rate. Make clear that people at all levels are expected to submit ideas. To make the idea system credible—and thus effective in the minds of people—set the idea implementation rate high. Allow people to implement their ideas themselves if they require only a minimal financial investment. And constantly measure the effectiveness of the system. If you don't measure it, you can neither control nor improve it.
- *Communicate the process* by making it part of the cultural fabric of the organization. Individuals should be made aware of the organization's idea goals and expectations before they're hired, and they should feel called upon to generate ideas from Day One right through to retirement day. Commitment must be evident from the top down. Idea generation should head the agenda at every meeting.
- *Focus on bottlenecks* or problem areas.
- *Respond quickly to all ideas.* If an idea cannot be implemented, provide a written explanation of why not. Keep bureaucracy to a minimum.
- *Keep the internal awareness level consistently high.* People need to be kept up to date about implemented ideas because it spurs their creativity. Continuously strive to build on good ideas to make them even better. Use all internal communication vehicles at your disposal to recognize individuals for their good ideas.
- *Share best practice ideas* throughout your organization.

intellectual capital that every one of your people possesses. Consider putting in place an idea system that empowers your people to think creatively, that adds more value, and that contributes directly to continuous improvement. Given this kind of supportive environment, your people *will* find a better way. Once people begin to see the positive results their suggestions bring, momentum will build, and they will be motivated to search out more and better innovations.

Ignite the intellectual firestorm smoldering within your organization. Let it blaze!

Typically, a Dana first-line supervisor can approve $10,000 of capital without anyone else's authorization. Some plants allow people $500 in capital expenditures without even the foreman's approval. It's notewor- thy that Dana people are very careful about how they spend that money.

27

COMING SOON TO YOUR HOME AND BUSINESS: THE NEW ENERGY MAJORS

Kenneth L. Lay, Enron Corporation

Natural-gas and electricity companies are rapidly becoming "energy companies." Deregulation and privatization are driving the convergence of energy sources, the restructuring of the industry, and the emergence of new players. While major change has sent some companies into a tailspin, Enron has been in the driver's seat, creating energy solutions worldwide. The Houston-based company has become one of the world's largest integrated natural gas and electricity companies, with approximately $15 billion in assets.

Among its many businesses, Enron operates one of the largest natural gas–transmission systems in the world. It is the largest purchaser and marketer of natural gas, and sells natural-gas liquids worldwide. It manages the largest portfolio of fixed-price natural gas risk-management contracts in the world. Enron is also the largest nonregulated marketer of electricity in North America and is one of the largest independent developers and producers of electricity in the world. It is also among the leading entities arranging new capital for the energy industry. Enron owns a majority interest in Enron Oil & Gas Company, one of the largest independent (nonintegrated) exploration and production companies in the United States; and it owns a majority interest in Enron Global Power & Pipelines L.L.C., which owns and manages power plants and natural-gas pipelines around the world.

In this chapter, Kenneth Lay, Enron's chairman and CEO, describes the transformation of the energy industry and projects what lies ahead. Even more, he shares critical insights for companies in any industry undergoing sweeping change.

GAS AND ELECTRICITY DISTRIBUTION companies in the United States are undergoing their first revolutionary change since becoming regulated public utilities earlier this century. For the first time in history, households, commercial establishments, and large industrial customers will be able to purchase a brand of natural gas and electricity in much the same way they do their long-distance telephone service.

In these transformational times, incremental change and management bureaucracy are giving way to major industry discontinuities, new "best practices," and transformed supplier-customer relationships. The result will be the "new energy majors," a category of megacompanies in which the generation, transmission, and distribution assets of the old industry are being reconfigured with the knowledge-based assets of the new industry to create energy solutions for an increasingly sophisticated marketplace.

OPEN-ACCESS RESTRUCTURING WITH GAS AND ELECTRICITY

The ability of end users to directly purchase natural gas and electricity is a relatively new concept. Traditionally, a franchised public utility sold a product with the commodity and all its associated transmission and distribution services "bundled" into one price. By contrast, under open-access restructuring, the end user buys the commodity from competing suppliers at an unregulated price, and pays a transmission/distribution charge to the traditional utility (now a "wires" or "pipe" company), which remains regulated as a natural monopoly—at least for the short term.

The "commodity" will not be the homogeneous product it is today. While the BTU content may be the same, its price will reflect whether it is firm or interruptible, or whether it is peak or off-peak. With electricity, "green BTUs" (electricity generated from favored renewable sources) may be distinguished from standard supplies for pricing purposes.

The unbundling of telecommunications in the last two decades has paved the way for similar policy debates and reforms in the natural-gas and electric industries in the United States. The wholesale open-access gas market (where producers or marketers sell gas to utilities or other entities for resale) became universalized in the period from 1985 to 1993. This wholesale open-access electric market was born with federal legislation in 1992 and is maturing rapidly today.

On the retail side, numerous states across the country are currently debating or implementing the opening phases of customer choice with gas and electricity. Enron Corporation expects approximately 10 percent of the national retail electric market to be open to competition and customer choice by 1998, with this percentage increasing until the entire market is open by 2006. Federal legislation could, of course, accelerate this timetable by several years. Gas markets will be opening up to retail competition at the same time.

Enron is actively trading in Europe, where the gas and electric market—which is about the size of the U.S. market—is moving into competition in such countries as England, Germany, and Norway. British Gas Energy has just announced that it plans to become a "U.S.-style integrated energy company" by capturing 10 percent of the retail electricity market in 1998 and sending customers one bill for gas and electricity.

The advent of customer choice makes energy management more important than ever for domestic and international businesses, large and small, and for households as well. There will be higher transaction costs because it will be necessary to negotiate for a commodity that was previously a default offering. But the reward will be significantly lower rates—as much as 30 to 40 percent below what consumers are paying today.

CONVERGENCE OF GAS AND ELECTRICITY

With open-access reform in the United States occurring simultaneously with gas and electricity at the retail level, companies are positioning themselves to market both energies to the same consumers on the same bill. The merger of Houston Industries, an electric utility, and NorAm, the parent of the gas distribution company in Houston, Texas, is one example of what's happening with other companies in California, Kansas, Maryland, and Wisconsin, as well as in Texas and other states.

This convergence of gas and electricity marketing includes firms specializing in customer-driven risk management products linked with firms that physically deliver the product. The integration of real-time information systems tracking supply and demand with hard-asset operations is creating the brand-new entities of our title—the new energy majors. The proposed megamergers between Enron and Portland General Corporation, as well as the one between Duke Power and PanEnergy, will create the first two such majors. Other mergers of this type can be expected in the next few years.

ECONOMIES OF SCALE AND SCOPE
IN THE NEW ENERGY COMPANY

Gas and electric mergers are a natural response to the increased economies of scale and economies of scope inherent in a restructured, consumer-driven industry. As an open-access market matures, the marketing pioneers respond to shrinking margins by improving internal operations. This has encouraged mergers to increase a firm's national presence, to realize greater cost economies, and to make alliances that will preferentially secure new supplies and markets. In recent years literally dozens of gas marketing companies have merged or gone out of business. Today, five megamarketers account for 70 percent of the U.S. natural-gas market, and the top 10 firms account for more than 90 percent of the market.

Independent electricity marketing is a comparatively young industry in the United States, dating from around 1994 when transmission access first made wholesale transactions possible. Nevertheless, economies of scale are already in clear evidence. In 1996, Enron Capital & Trade Resources, the nation's top electricity marketer, accounted for 26 percent of market share. The top three companies accounted for 45 percent of the market, and the top eight firms accounted for 82 percent of the market. The remaining 18 percent of the business was divided among 77 other firms. As the market matures, the distribution of market share at the top can be expected to flatten somewhat. It will probably end up looking like the U.S. gasoline market, where no major has more than a 10 percent market share.

Economies of scope, which encourage portfolios of different types of power generation, have spurred many natural-gas trading companies to add electricity as a product line. In only a few instances has a top electricity marketer not cut its teeth on gas. It's early still, but gas and electricity trading may well have a more complementary relationship than traditional oil and gas trading—another aspect of the gas-electricity convergence.

It will be interesting to see how far the industry will evolve through economies of scope. The synergies of selling gas and electricity directly to consumers may lead the new energy majors into alliances or mergers with telecommunications and security system companies serving the same homes and businesses. And, in fact, this is already occurring. In the future, energy, telecommunications, and security services may lead to other household ventures. Perhaps the energy services company of today will evolve into the household services company of tomorrow. This is fertile ground for the imagination—but effective implementation will be necessary for even the best ideas.

Another expansion of core competencies through economies of scope concerns the trading of U.S. Environmental Protection Agency pollution permit credits, which are issued to companies that don't exceed federal emission standards. Air-quality regulators have discovered that the most economical way to deal with businesses such as electric power plants, which are major emitters of sulfur dioxide, carbon dioxide, particulates, and nitrogen oxide, is to allow trading in pollution permit credits. In this way, firms with the lowest-cost means of pollution abatement can reduce their emissions and sell credits to firms that have higher abatement costs.

Enron is the nation's largest market maker with sulfur-dioxide permits. And it is poised to make similar markets—domestically or internationally—with nitrogen oxide and carbon dioxide permits as well.

RETAILING FOR THE FIRST TIME

Retail access to gas and electricity has transformed Enron and other business-to-business firms into business-to-customer entities. However, companies seeking a share of the $270 billion domestic retail gas and electric market will now have to find a way to differentiate their products and services in the eyes of the customer. Marketing brands and launching national advertising campaigns stressing price, reliability, and service will be a necessary first step. Given the invisibility of both methane and electrons, a company's most important marketing edge will be the public's goodwill. There will also be a distinct "first mover" advantage for companies already in the branding phase.

The new energy majors will be able to tap into a wealth of marketing expertise and practices to break into a market dominated by traditional retailers. The challenge for these new major-branded upstarts is reaching consumers in an increasingly decentralized marketplace. The old days of three television channels and a few national magazines are long gone. Today, with the proliferation of cable channels, specialized publications, and new mediums such as the Internet, the opportunities for national exposure are very different.

Major sporting events are proving to be one of the best vehicles for reaching a mass audience. One of the new energy companies has already acquired the naming rights to a sports stadium—Riverfront Stadium in Cincinnati, Ohio, has now become CINergy Field. Not too far down the road a college-football bowl game may be named after a gas and electricity provider.

The entrepreneurial calculus of the new energy major is very different from that of a traditional public utility company. While the latter traditionally added up costs and priced products to earn a reasonable return, a new major must start with the consumer and work backward to determine what is economically viable in a world where customers have choices. As one of the new breed of energy marketers put it, we need to "get into our customers' heads, understand their needs, develop solutions, and put together the capabilities required to deliver those solutions."

Where Will It All Lead?

The $50 billion in finalized and pending gas and electricity mergers over the last three years hint of much more to come. The market's evolutionary discovery process is still young, but here are some possible industry megatrends:

- Mergers and alliances between the new energy companies and interactive technology and information technology companies
- Competitive metering, billing, information, and conservation services formerly monopolized by the utility provider
- "Energy solutions" companies taking equity positions in energy-intensive industries for which they perform risk-management services
- Branding and aggressive advertising by new retail providers
- Distributed generation and computerized transmission choices, making the "wires industry" as workably competitive as the open-access interstate gas transmission industry has become today
- A new "Seven Sisters" of energy majors that will increasingly rival the activities of the original seven sisters—the oil majors; this may well lead to a new industrywide convergence

In this new world, the public utility industry will fade into memory. Competition and technological change is turning the gas and electric industry into yet another mass-marketing segment of the U.S. and global economy.

LESSONS LEARNED

While many of the winners and losers in the new energy industry have yet to be determined, it is clear that some firms are well ahead of others—and Wall Street knows who they are. There is a prototype model of revolutionary change at work in the gas and electricity business that offers lessons for other industries. We offer four:

- First, a company can help create its own competitive environment and its own future by leading industrywide change. This is what management theorist Gary Hamel calls "rule breaking" to "get to the future first." Of course, not all industries are ripe for such a revolution. But where regulation has restrained natural market outcomes that benefit consumers, major change is inevitable. Don't just ask Enron—ask Southwest Airlines, or MCI!
- A second lesson is to make sure your firm can create the new products the revamped market requires. Will customers be looking for price certainty where there was little or none before? If so, create a market for speculators as well as hedgers so you can offer fixed prices. On the other hand, will customers be shopping for different levels of price and performance and a menu of choices that reflect the associated trade-offs? If so, devise a way to offer it to them profitably.
- Lesson three is to stay alert to opportunities to expand your company's core competencies. We've already seen economies of scope bringing gas-trading concepts to the marketing of electricity. The trading of EPA pollution permit credits will be the third leg of this stool for some companies—and others could emerge. Keep in mind that for the trailblazing company there will be hits and misses, but the failures are simply part of the drive for success, given market uncertainty.
- Finally, successful "rule breakers" must have a clearly defined vision and a highly visible corporate image in order to attract the internal and external support needed to make revolutionary change possible—and to keep it thriving. Employees, customers, and public officials are all parties to a successful, sustainable industry restructuring, particularly where market structures are replacing highly regulated ones.

CREATING THE FUTURE

You want market share? Well, go create a market!

Recently recognized by *Fortune* magazine as the most innovative company in its *Fortune* 500 listing, the folks at Enron aren't waiting around for new markets to evolve. They know that in today's fast-moving world, getting there first means creating the market you want to capture. And that's just what they're doing.

Enron's future now lies in retailing the products and services they traditionally wholesaled. To reach their new customers, they need to be the driving force that opens up these markets to consumer choice. They know they need to create consumer awareness and reshape the way the consumers think about buying energy *well ahead* of the market's actually being there.

This is why Enron recently engaged WPP Group's Ogilvy & Mather to create a new consumer-oriented corporate image and ad campaign. Because traditional pipeline companies like Enron have never had to sell directly to the consumer, they've never had to worry much about name recognition. But that's changing fast in a deregulating industry with a $270 billion a year retail natural-gas and electricity market. Enron is eager to claim a big piece of that market, so they're preparing themselves *and* consumers for an era in which customers get to choose their energy suppliers the same way they choose their long-distance telephone companies.

Enron is also creating the infrastructure it will need to service this new market. They're gearing up for wireless metering, and building a billing center near Columbus, Ohio, with the capacity to produce statements for up to 30 million customers.

Enron is driving to create national brand recognition well in advance of this new market. And this campaign is all-consuming. As Beth Tilney, senior vice president for marketing and communications, says, "Support for our new brand must be behind everything we do: our Web page, our direct mail pieces, the way we answer the phone, the way we think and act as employees."

Enron could choose to think only of today and focus on maximizing profits. Instead, it has chosen to set the standard for a new industry by designing the rules of the game to be played in the next millennium. In the end, this will benefit consumers, Enron shareholders, and Enron employees.

Bring on the brave new world!

28

REINVENTING PHILIPS DOWN UNDER: CUSTOMERS SEEK SYSTEMS SOLUTIONS, NOT BLACK BOXES

Justus Veeneklaas, Philips Australia

Philips Australia, the Australian operation of the $41 billion technology giant Philips Electronics N.V., is led by Justus Veeneklaas, who first joined Philips in 1967 at the company's headquarters in Eindhoven, Holland. He has since embarked on a challenging international career that has included Philips postings in Germany, New Zealand, Africa, Hong Kong, and the United Kingdom. He was named chairman and chief executive of Philips Australia in 1990.

Since he arrived, Veeneklaas has been driving a radical change in business strategy at Philips Australia, which employs more than two thousand people and generates sales of $790 million a year. That change involves a fundamental shift away from Philips' traditional role as a technology company that simply makes "black-box" electronic products to one that provides comprehensive technology solutions to solve customers' complex business problems. It is the fundamental shift from product-oriented to customer-driven thinking, and it's already producing impressive results.

FOR MORE THAN A century, Philips Electronics has built its reputation through its groundbreaking research and its ability to design and manufacture innovative and often amazingly complex products. These breakthrough products—from the world's first car radio in the 1930s to the subsequent inventions of audiocassettes, compact discs, energy-saving lighting, and the brand-new digital versatile disc—have helped create a Philips culture centered on research and engineering excellence. For many years, making the latest, greatest products—what those within Philips call "black boxes"—was the company's primary focus.

But times have changed in many of its markets, so that in some instances the power of technological innovation was vitiated. Customers increasingly demanded not simply products, but products that were integrated and linked to solutions—often total solutions including hardware, software, systems integration, installation, training, service, and, yes, great black-box wizardry.

So Philips Australia has started down the long road of changing many of the fundamental ways in which it has viewed its business over the past century. It is in the process of reinventing its organization and changing its corporate culture to become a truly *solutions*-driven company. The focus is no longer solely on making stand-alone electronic products— products that, given today's rapid advances in technology, have largely become commodity items with razor-thin profit margins. The strategy is now moving toward an emphasis on creating total systems that combine the products and services of Philips—and those of other companies, even competitors—into turnkey technology solutions that add value for customers and build profits for Philips.

To transform itself into a total solutions provider, Philips is:

- Forging strategic alliances with companies that provide products and services that complement Philips' own components
- Taking on and managing the significant risks and responsibilities that come with being the prime contractor and systems integrator on complex, multifaceted projects
- Creating new ways of tuning in to changing customer demands for total solutions providers and measuring how well the company meets those demands
- Driving a continuous and consistent message throughout the entire organization mandating multidisciplinary, cross-functional, and cross-divisional teaming
- Redesigning business processes and systems infrastructure to support a multidivisional approach to business

The results of this transformation are striking. Between 1992 and 1996, Philips Australia saw its percentage of revenues derived from "project" work—in which it serves customers as the total solution provider—grow from zero to 25 percent. It is the company's goal to sizably increase that figure in another five years. However, Philips is not attempting to transform itself entirely into a total solutions provider. We want to engineer a change that will produce a company that combines the creativity and innovation of a black-box culture with the comprehensive service orientation of a total solutions provider.

During this transformation, we have come to the realization that we can't do it all alone. To successfully manage complex projects, forming alliances and partnerships with other companies is a necessity. These companies may be niche contractors that supply a single hardware or software product to the project, or large companies that provide a significant portion of the overall solution. They may be companies that are customers of various Philips product groups, or even competitors of some of those groups.

For example, Philips Australia has forged strategic alliances and project partnerships with Siemens in medical technology applications, with Ericsson in full-service networks, and with Hughes in advanced traffic control and tolling systems. In the process, we have tapped into rich new veins of profitable business activity.

In Philips's medical division, the goal is now to seek contracts to provide advanced technology for entire hospitals—not, as in the past, to painstakingly sell individual diagnostic and therapeutic equipment department by department. Philips recently offered this approach to Sydney's new Children's Hospital, through a partnership with Siemens. The two companies are fierce competitors in most medical equipment markets around the world. But in Australia—born of the insight that one must think in nontraditional ways to gain ground in a swiftly changing world—they are joint venture partners. This enabled Philips, Siemens, and several other product and service providers to offer a complete range of integrated medical systems, something none of them could have possibly done on its own.

In Philips's traffic and engineering systems division, partnering has allowed it to change its value proposition. Instead of being a local manufacturer of road traffic controllers, we have now become a global designer and marketer of intelligent traffic and tolling systems that help improve urban transportation flows.

In another example of the importance of partnerships in taking on complex projects, Philips is currently managing more than a hundred subcontractors and other suppliers in its three-year, $550 million contract with Telstra, Australia's government-owned telephone company. The goal of this project is to deliver a state-of-the-art digital fiber-optic and coaxial cable network. Because the opportunities—and risks—are enormous in projects of this size and complexity, we are leveraging this experience by creating an "international competence center" in Australia. It will serve as the key clearinghouse for new ideas and the development of best practices for Philips' digital broadband business worldwide.

Delivering value as a systems integrator requires a new attitude about risk. In assuming the role of total solutions provider, we're taking on risks and responsibilities far greater in scope than ever before. As prime contractor on technology projects, we are ultimately responsible for the cross-functionality between hardware and software systems. We are also responsible for the performance of our subcontractors in delivering their specified components on time and to required quality standards.

That's why every subcontractor's components are subjected to Philips' own exacting reviews of technical specifications, quality control, logistics performance, and other functional measures before they go to the customer.

Before we take on any major assignment, we conduct our own rigorous analysis to identify all the potential technical, financial, and resource risks associated with the project in order to determine whether it is commercially and strategically viable for Philips and our partners.

The size and extended time frames of these projects—coupled with the complexity of managing an extensive network of subcontractors and other providers—play against certainty. To minimize risk and eliminate some of the inevitable uncertainties, we have formalized a project status and reporting mechanism that both encourages a sense of shared responsibility among the project's partners and fosters open, honest, and frequent communication with customers.

Reports are distributed to key customer contacts and to our major partners on the project, examining issues relating to every aspect of the job—right down to the quality of various components, the timeliness of their delivery, and the turnaround times for repair of faulty items. The reports paint a clear picture of the overall progress—and more importantly, the possible risks—of the entire project. This discipline forces all parties to focus on plans for immediate corrective actions that will mitigate, if not eliminate, future project risks.

In our new role as total solutions provider, Philips has also found it critically important to stay in touch with changing customer demands on a regular basis, and to measure how well the company is performing against these demands. An extensive customer "listening" program is in place to discover:

- What decision criteria customers use to select a total solutions provider
- What their perceptions are of Philips in the marketplace
- What criteria they use to evaluate delivery performance

This is essential to making the transition from a focus on products to a focus on customer service. There's a "hard," qualitative, specifications-laden aspect to measuring outcomes for a black-box producer. It is driven by precision. However, listening to customers, with all their diverse and often ambiguous requirements, is altogether different.

Our concerted listening effort is producing valuable insights about what our customers really want and how well we are performing against these requirements. This information allows us to target our improvement actions toward those areas that will truly make an impact on our customers.

Another way the company's culture is moving toward a focus on the customer is through periodic "Customer Days"—a full day in which *every* staff member is asked to focus on ways to satisfy customer needs. During Customer Days, multidisciplinary teams across the entire company attempt to create innovative ways to serve customers better—whether they be traditional external Philips customers or their own internal customers within the organization.

The best ideas are tackled immediately. Each improvement idea is allocated to a team of three or four people, who take ownership of that idea and link it to priorities set out in their division's business plan. These team members are then empowered to make a direct and very personal contribution to ensuring that the ideas are implemented. In the future, we also plan to link some part of our bonus and reward system to individuals' abilities to create and implement new and innovative ideas.

In making our transformation to a total solutions provider, Philips has not only had to reach out to communicate with our customers, we have also had to look inward, to communicate the change in strategy throughout our own organization. My management team and I have seized every opportunity—staff presentations, internal training courses, change-management seminars, and even Christmas party speeches—to hammer home the message that teamwork across divisions is necessary to deliver the type of integrated solutions that customers are increasingly demanding.

There were no flashy videos or glossy printed brochures explaining the objectives of the change process. Instead, senior executives conducted a series of face-to-face meetings in which they personally spent considerable time with each and every manager, division by division. In return, these managers were obliged to articulate in writing the strategic direction of their group or division. In every case, the primary goal was to get managers to focus on how their area could best contribute to large, complex projects.

In managing large projects there has to be cooperation and shared responsibilities across many business units. To promote cross-divisional teamwork, we instituted a series of management conferences, bringing together the company's top eighty-five managers. They are given the opportunity to discuss case studies of successful Philips projects, and to develop best-practice ideas that they can apply in their own business units.

We are also investing heavily in training to give our employees the skills they need to carry out the new business strategy. Over the past few years, we have doubled our investment in management training programs aimed at promoting teamwork, lateral thinking, and the acceptance of rapid change. Philips's new training programs emphasize project management in multidisciplinary teams. The objective is to encourage people from diverse professional backgrounds to analyze problems and create complete solutions—to break out of the tunnel vision mentality that stand-alone business units tend to perpetuate, and instead to take advantage of the best ideas across the entire organization.

Nurturing new thinking and a broader peripheral vision often requires a fresh perspective. Philips is recruiting aggressively at the graduate student level and placing these young people in a pragmatic, eighteen-month training program that exposes them to all aspects of our business, from individual product lines to support functions. They emerge as versatile managers-of-the-future, with knowledge across many business areas and a network of relationships throughout the entire company. Their experience is fostering the multidisciplinary, cross-functional perspective that is the key to Philips' future success as a total solutions provider.

Thinking and working laterally across the organization requires not only changes in corporate culture but changes in processes as well. An organization's core processes, running the breadth of the modern corporation, are the new building blocks of competence. Our fundamental shift from products to services mandated a comprehensive rethinking of Philips' core processes.

We are reshaping our processes with the overarching objective of integration across the business. Not surprisingly, this process redesign requires modernization of the information technology (IT) infrastructure. Playing the role of a total solutions provider requires integrated IT systems that allow divisions to share information and to work together in a seamless fashion. Cooperating on sophisticated technology projects often involves forming what amounts to a "virtual company," consisting of four or five Philips business units.

To encourage cross-divisional integration, we have instituted two initiatives at a process level that underpin the concept of a virtual company:

Peer-Level Involvement and Reviews of Business Plans

Business units no longer prepare their business plans in isolation. Before board approval of these plans, there is a mandatory review and discussion of potential business-development synergies. This approach enables us to raise the visibility of individual business plans across the entire organization and to identify joint opportunities. It also leverages the benefits of shared learning by drawing on the diverse market and product experiences of the various business units.

Integrating Accountability for Selling and Delivering a Project

Although several divisions may work together on a project, that project has only one single point of accountability. The appointed "project owner" is responsible for seeing a project through from inception to negotiation, design, delivery, and postimplementation review. This role gives the project owner free reign to draw on whatever resources are necessary across the organization to ensure the success of the project, thereby fostering a culture of cross-divisional teamwork.

These business units can only work together effectively if they follow similar business processes and work methods, and if they're networked together by compatible IT systems. Putting these processes and systems in place, and getting them right, underlies all of our broader efforts to create a culture that emphasizes teamwork, and a business strategy that offers total solutions to complex customer problems.

Success will continue to come through making those great black-box products for which Philips is so justly famous. But this success will increasingly depend on the ability of our various divisions and business units to work together—sharing information and creating ideas that address the big-picture problems that customers want solved. And we are well on the way to building the proper balance in our business—preserving the culture of technological creativity that produces world-class electronic products, while developing the broader skills and mind-set that will enable Philips to become a leading manager and integrator of complex technology solutions well into the twenty-first century.

29
STRATEGIC ROOTS OF INNOVATION

Glen L. Urban,
MIT Sloan School of Management

Not every business school professor gets to test his ideas in real life. Glen Urban, Dean of the MIT Sloan School of Management since 1993, is one of the rare exceptions, and he has a proven track record on both fronts. Urban is a top gun in the field of academic marketing management with numerous papers—two of which have won prestigious prizes—and five textbooks to his credit. Two of his books deal with innovation and new product management. And it is in these areas that the freewheeling Urban—who is also an avid sailor and sculptor, sporting hand-painted ties and longish hair—is putting his marketing-centered ideas into practice.

Indeed, in the world Urban envisions, top managers will serve more as artists than as controllers or cost managers. The capacity to manage intellect and imagination and transform them into products will be the critical executive skill of the next century.

Clearly, this is how Urban approaches his own job. And by most measures, it is producing results, since applications to MIT Sloan School have more than doubled and in 1995 U.S. News & World Report rated the school as the number one graduate business school in the country. In the 1996 ranking, Sloan placed second.

Ten years ago, comparisons between running a business school and running a business were pretty tenuous. Today, there are many more parallels and similarities: The competition is as tough, the stakes as high, and the demand for change as intense inside the walls of academe as they are out in the global marketplace. For the top B-school players, the old clubhouse atmosphere is long gone, replaced by an intense rivalry—for the best students, faculty, and endowment-fund backers. And this is continuously exacerbated by the annual ratings published by Business Week *and* U.S News & World Report.

*Practicing managers can glean some useful insights from the predica-
ments and responses of business schools jostling for the lead in a tight field.*

THE KIND OF BUSINESS a B-school seems to resemble the most is a
capital-markets trading unit, or a Paris couturier, a repertory theater, or
perhaps an America's Cup boat. In short, any enterprise that lives or dies
by the quality of its ideas, its ability to anticipate trends, and its skill at
crafting strategies against real needs and executing them brilliantly.

Most people think of innovation as being embodied in new product
ideas. A popular diagram in old management textbooks illustrated a fun-
nel-shaped process, with ideas sprinkled in the top of the funnel, and
new products and services emerging from the bottom. In a simpler
world, this may have reflected reality. But not today. Real innovation
starts with a strategic outlook—the product of many minds and diverse
inputs—then proceeds to a consideration of technology, and then moves
on to product or service design. Contrary to popular notions, brainstorming over a wide array of alternatives is not the sole source of successful ideas. Ideas are cheap and often plentiful, while good top-down
strategic insights are very rare. Because the strategic insight must relate
to existing core competencies (themselves a product of history), in practice the innovative CEO does not look at that many alternatives.

In short, innovation is not the consequence of a moment of brilliance.
Rather, it is the fruit of an integrative approach—the melding of strategy,
marketing, R&D, production, and finance. Consequently, most successful corporations are becoming repositories and coordinators of intellect.

The same can be said of MIT Sloan. The capacity to manage human
intellect and imagination, to find and explore innovative options through
technology, and to transform those processes into marketable products
and services is the core of the school's success.

LEVERAGING INTELLECTUAL CAPITAL

One of the abiding truths of the marketplace is that true strategic insights are very difficult to come by. And any management that thinks its
strategy is unique is probably naive. Every company can look over its
shoulder at some very smart competitors who are equally able to read
the vectors of change. This is what propels most market segments toward strategic convergence, and toward a conventional wisdom of where
trends and opportunities are headed. This is also the case with B-

schools. The top half dozen graduate-level institutions don't differ that much, either in capabilities or broad strategic postures. After all, they target and serve the same population.

For MIT Sloan, one of our best mapping tools is the ongoing dialogue among alumni, faculty, students, and recruiters. This is how strategies and designs are tested against reality; how innovation flows from consensus building. A CEO can only influence and offer up some seminal ideas—in the end, it's up to others to make them grow. In this way, a B-school is the same as any other service business. Innovation is the result of a participatory process coupled with a relentless determination to make things happen (planning, control, follow-through, prototyping, revision).

Since the CEO does not have the authority to dominate the innovation agenda, he or she needs a style different from the older model of military organizations. Today's CEO must be able to swim in the flow of ideas that stream from the various dialogue participants, and have an ability to leverage intellectual capital. Today, and especially in the years ahead, when it is likely that leading companies will spend up to a quarter of their sales on research and innovation, the ability to harness creativity is critical. In this environment, a CEO must make his or her mark gently, in indirect ways, all the while giving others much of the credit for ideas.

UNDERSTANDING TECHNOLOGY

Another requirement for innovation is that the CEO and management team must have a strong grasp of technology. The old model of the CEO as a delegator and well-rounded generalist is less and less relevant to contemporary circumstances. There have been too many media exposés of corporations wasting millions on information systems that were highly dysfunctional. In part, this staggering waste has been brought on by CEOs and others in top management abdicating their responsibility to understand the "black box." Whether acting out of fear or insecurity, the opportunity losses they've brought about by failing to be on the leading edge have run into many billions of dollars.

Technology, linked to MIT's long-standing reputation as a technology leader, is at the heart of MIT Sloan's innovative repositioning. A major investment in a sophisticated technology infrastructure that facilitates both "distance learning" and "lifelong learning" has allowed MIT Sloan to move to the head of the class.

TRANSFORMATION AND MARKET REPOSITIONING

In five short years, the Sloan School has dramatically improved its position among the top ten B-schools. This transformation centered on five key initiatives:

- The first was Sloan's decision to expand its scale, a prerequisite for B-school survival and innovation. The smallest of the major institutions, we lacked the organizational mass and stature needed to attract top-ranked faculty and students. Thanks, in part, to an aggressive marketing program—plus better branding with a name change from the Alfred P. Sloan School to the MIT Sloan School—the number of applicants has more than doubled in the last three years; the student acceptance rate of offers made by MIT has grown to an impressive 83 percent. At the same time, the school's physical plant was expanded, allowing it to increase its class size by 50 percent.
- The second initiative was to leverage MIT's high standing in engineering, science, and technology into a unique multidisciplinary curriculum, with some programs jointly sponsored by the engineering and business schools. These include global technology management for middle managers, a manufacturing management program with industry internships, and an information management initiative on large-scale systems. This program is arguably one of the most innovative MBAs in the country; the result of extensive market research and our ability to deliver against those needs. Moreover, MIT Sloan's state-of-the-art remote-learning technology—using combinations of video, computers, telephones, the Internet, and other capabilities—will allow students anywhere in the world to participate in the learning experience.

  This type of niche strategy has the added benefit of being difficult for other institutions to duplicate, since most of MIT Sloan's B-school rivals have very competitive relations with their sibling engineering schools.
- The third innovation was to address nongraduate executive education, a potentially high-profit arena where MIT Sloan faced many challenges competing with business schools who had an impressive infrastructure of hotels and conference centers to handle their customers. In this area, we saw ourselves faced with two choices: create me-too programs and facilities—or innovate our way out of the dilemma with a unique value proposition for future growth.

The first great wave of the information society was shaping up as we analyzed the results of our market research. This showed that while a lot of executives needed to enhance their knowledge of business processes, the problems of time constraints and other by-products of corporate downsizing made going back to school difficult if not impossible. From these conflicting factors, innovation was born.

MIT Sloan bet that it could leapfrog its competitors by investing heavily in a distance-learning infrastructure, calculating correctly that management could and should be taught in new ways. MIT's reputation for technical and communications prowess lent credibility to Sloan's promotion of this new capability in its marketing initiatives.

- MIT Sloan's fourth innovation came from looking beyond the traditional view of graduate-level institutions, which held that learning occurred only when students were actively enrolled in a degree program.

We opted to make lifelong learning an integral part of the curriculum. Today's MIT Sloan students will make a down payment of $1,000 on the future stream of educational products they will be able to access electronically. This is a lifelong service that will be available to them over the course of the next five, ten, and twenty years as they advance through their careers.

In our view, it is impossible to train people for a successful life-long business career in a one-time, two-year stint. The Sloan Knowledge Network will give students access to courses, specialized data, and/or faculty consultations when they need it—a significant improvement over a parchment diploma and a handshake!

The lifelong learning paradigm is predicated on the notion that the graduate business schools' long-standing role of churning out middle managers has become obsolete. Within the coming decade the shrinking demographics of the total population for business education may force about a third of all B-schools out of business. As for the survivors, the gap between the top and the middle tier will become wider, because the leaders will have changed their paradigms. These institutions will become the breeding ground for supermanagers who will know it all—change, globalization, environmental responsibility, sustainable development, technology—and they'll know it with rigor and depth. The schools that don't change will get stranded in the past and wither.

- MIT Sloan's fifth major initiative was to go global. We saw our opportunity in China and Southeast Asia. In the next century, the majority of successful managers will require a working knowledge of China and other emerging markets in the Far East. MIT Sloan made a deal with Fudan University in Shanghai to train their faculty and develop a joint curriculum for a global MBA. We also made similar arrangements with business schools in Taiwan, Malaysia, Singapore, and India. MIT Sloan developed the critical mass needed to create a virtual worldwide business school network. This $10 million program flows directly from our skills in remote learning and institution development.

To fuel its repositioning, MIT Sloan has tried to identify those niches where it could differentiate itself and quickly establish a leadership position backed up with good brand equity. More importantly, MIT Sloan has woven innovation into the fabric of the institution, allowing it to permeate and encompass all activities. We believe that the role model to follow is an organization building an infrastructure that allows for constant and consistent innovation.

30

PERFORMING RAPID INNOVATION MAGIC: TEN SECRETS OF A MODERN MERLIN

David M. Kelley, IDEO Product Development

IDEO Product Development is a little big company. That is, it's small as measured by number of employees but big in influence. David M. Kelley, chief executive officer and founder, presides over the largest and most award-winning industrial design firm in the United States, a talent-rich band of three hundred employees. From its California headquarters, IDEO has been surfing a wave of design and engineering feats for almost two decades—achievements that range from the first Apple computer mouse to the twenty-five-foot mechanical whale that stars in the Free Willy *movies.*

IDEO's designers, engineers, and human factors experts form instant creative teams that are the secret weapons of a host of leading-edge companies—Apple, Hewlett-Packard, and NEC, among others.

IDEO operates like a hectic-paced, modern-day Merlin. The demand for the little company's magic touch exceeds its capacity to take on new projects. Since its founding in 1978, IDEO has built a unique company culture that bases employee prestige and status on winning the most exciting opportunities to innovate. What IDEO has learned—how to routinely make leaps of innovation instead of just improvements—should be studied by every company seeking an innovation advantage.

IDEO's satellite offices—many located around its Palo Alto headquarters, but also in San Francisco, Chicago, Boston, London, and Tokyo—are a delightful jumble of prototypes of products the firm has developed, endless models of work in progress, and thousands of wacky toys that the engineers disassemble in their constant search for inspiration.

Because of IDEO's track record, Kelley and his firm have repeatedly been retained as a consultant to large companies, such as Samsung and Steelcase, that are intent on transferring the IDEO passion for high-speed innovation to their own organizations.

EVEN INNOVATIVE COMPANIES CAN get the blahs. Most CEOs recognize the signs, but they aren't sure what to do to jump-start innovation. Maybe the number of annual patent filings is decreasing, or new company products are boring customers. Perhaps a rival's product beat them to market. Nowadays everyone needs more innovation horsepower: the creative capability to outpace the market, to get products on the market with more speed, to offer cutting-edge technological expertise, to demonstrate a clear perception of what delights customers, and to develop superior processes.

Because of IDEO's international reputation for high-speed creativity, CEOs often ask our advice about how their organizations can create, nurture, strengthen, or regain a culture of innovation. It's flattering for our tiny company to have large leading-edge firms seeking to learn from us. Such firms are usually surprised to discover that our culture of discontinuous innovation, dedicated to leaps of creativity, is largely based on techniques we learned, one or two at a time, from our large corporate clients. Here's a list of ten secrets that any organization, large or small, can effectively incorporate, once it decides that innovation is an essential source of competitive advantage.

TEN SECRETS FOR INSTILLING THE INNOVATION ATTITUDE

Fostering an environment where innovation can flourish starts by recognizing that a big change in attitude is in order. First, CEOs need to issue this prime directive: High-speed, market-focused, discontinuous innovation means competitive advantage. Even if your organization has good reason to be proud of its innovation record, this announcement signals the need for improvement.

But beware of seeing innovation as primarily a communications problem. Merely announcing that your organization has made innovation a key strategy won't produce an instant product-development renaissance.

Instead, top management has to start treating the innovation initiative as a critical experiment in which every level must participate. To give everyone a stake in the experiment, tell your managers, "We're going to try a new arrangement of the offices of the senior people. We're going to put you all together in an open collaborative space that will replace all our big offices and conference rooms. But this is an experiment. In twelve months I'm going to ask you to vote on which office design you prefer. If you don't think a collaborative space works, we'll go back to our former system." Authentic experiments like this—ones offering the fear of risk, the thrill of possible reward, and the discomfort of shaking up the status quo—capture managers' attention.

No. 1: Encourage Creative Conflict—Innovation Happens on Opinionated, Multidisciplinary Teams with Strong Leadership

Team innovation is an experiment that causes headaches in many companies. Successful, multidisciplinary innovation teams thrive on the exchange of strongly held opinions, although some people experience these sessions as uncomfortably conflict ridden. Many companies tried using multidisciplinary teams for product development when the idea first became popular. Most abandoned the team approach when the teams' sessions provoked dissension that was difficult to manage. However, suppressing conflict is one of the cultural behaviors that inhibits innovation.

When multidisciplinary teams are doing their jobs, constructive, creative debate rages between strategic marketing, design, engineering, manufacturing, and sales people. By definition, this is a messy, opinionated process. Each function must be a vigorous advocate for its viewpoint. Good conflict occurs when people have opposing opinions about what will make a product better.

It's surprising how many companies don't assign manufacturing managers to innovation teams. In fact, manufacturing managers aren't even invited to initial meetings called by the marketing manager to consider new product ideas. If they are, they can usually be counted on to start a row by calling attention to the problems involved in manufacturing a product intended to make customers say, "Wow!" That's when designers jump into the argument, championing advanced machining technology as a solution. Next, the engineers suggest the use of exotic materials. This starts another row. These approaches do create contention. But it's just this kind of creative conflict that produces a hierarchy of ideas for a prototype.

In order for productive ideas to emerge, this conflict should play out under the direction of a strong, fair leader who encourages open and forceful differences. The leader should encourage contention, not just tolerate it. The essence of being an effective leader in this context is the ability to provide a rigorous, candid environment where all issues are aired, all voices heard, and commitment to the best solution is garnered. Hidden agendas are put on the table. Naysayers are converted to enthusiasts. And the participants walk away from the meeting convinced that the right solution has been recognized, regardless of their own position when they walked in the door.

In effect, these teams are experiments in task learning. Task learning occurs when multidisciplinary team members absorb valuable new skills, such as conflict management, that contribute to the success of their projects. The team's experience has a healthy effect on company culture because once team members experience successful techniques in action, they tend to emulate the best behaviors and spread them to the rest of the company.

No. 2: Big Ideas Come from Small Teams

Big organizations command resources, but small groups generate camaraderie and electricity. Innovation teams within large corporations are inspired to meet stretch goals when they learn to think and act like agile, high-energy elites.

These powerhouse teams need their own identity. Although IDEO's entire staff totals only three hundred people, in the San Francisco area alone we maintain six offices with strikingly different appearances. Most locations design their own work space—a typical site is home to just thirty people, and has a nickname and its own decor.

However, there's more to these separate campuses than just slogans on employee T-shirts. Each of these facilities concentrates on distinctive skills. More importantly, each wishes to be viewed as the place to find the most highly respected team members, and they subtly compete with each other to be the best place to work in the company. They want to be known as the location that wins the toughest assignments and the clients that are avidly seeking state-of-the-art technology.

No. 3: Learning Happens Away from the Desk

Lightning rarely strikes managers behind a desk. In fact, at IDEO it's taken for granted that the most important work occurs wherever employees are learning the most. Employees with inquiring minds visit experts, see new technology in operation, observe fascinating products in use. That's how managers find the knowledge needed for the big ideas and genuine epiphanies of discontinuous innovation. In contrast, many hierarchical organizations assume that their employees are only productive when they're in the office.

At IDEO, the payoff for sanctioning learning away from the desk occurs when employees present their latest discoveries each week at a fun-filled show-and-tell session. Presenters gain status by being the first to acquire and demonstrate practical knowledge, such as a new technology for molding prototypes out of superglue. However, at these weekly idea bazaars, toys, gadgets, new processes, and exotic materials also compete for attention. A tiny motor from a Japanese toy might find its place in a prototype computer. The world's lightest solid, only four times heavier than air, is passed around—a material marvel in search of an application. The net result of these sessions is fast-paced technology transfer.

No. 4: Understand the Product's User

Successful innovation depends on cultivating the ability to empathize with the user of the product or service. You can't ignore the human side of new-product introductions. The IDEO rule encapsulating this notion is: "Remember your mom." In other words, could your mother readily use this product? If not, what changes would make it a product she could enjoy using? Learning this kind of humility is often a saving grace for brilliant young design engineers, and it can spell the difference between success and failure for a multidisciplinary team exploring new product opportunities.

IDEO engineers relearn humility all the time. For example, as the firm that designed the first Apple Computer mouse, the designers expected to have quick success inventing an easy-to-use mouse for preschool children. But little kids kept trying to "drive" the prototype mouse as if it were a toy car. A totally different approach was a big hit— a giant track ball that children could roll with the palm of their hand.

No. 5: Live in the Future

IDEO constructs mock-ups of the future so that our engineers and clients can experience what it will be like to live and work in the next century. We learned this technique from Xerox in the late seventies. Displays of future tech wowed visitors at the Xerox Palo Alto Research Center. The demonstrations were especially inspiring to young technology tourists like Steve Jobs, later a founder of Apple Computer, historically one of IDEO's significant clients.

The secret is to physically mimic revolutionary conceptual breakthroughs affecting the home and office environments. This technique is about the only way to understand the secondary and tertiary needs of people in these environments. For example, IDEO envisions an office of the future with interactive television channels connecting managers with their vendors, suppliers, factories, product-development teams, distributors, warehouse, customers, focus groups, and multinational subsidiaries—all broadcasting twenty-four hours a day. Such offices will require new furniture, new products for recording meetings and storing information, and new software for converting meeting content into an instant intranet newsletter.

No. 6: Destigmatize Failure

Companies must learn to tolerate failure and beware of infatuation with success. Organizations that don't tolerate some mistakes, breakdowns, or detours take too long to plan and replan where they're going. In contrast, we do our pioneering largely by enlightened trial and error. Allowing people to fail at first—indeed, expecting them to learn a great deal from falling or stumbling forward—is part of the IDEO culture.

Experienced engineers know that the most valuable learning starts to occur when their elegantly designed apparatus fails. The faster a project flops, the quicker it gets better. A favorite way of making this point at IDEO is to recall the person who bragged that he went skiing for a week and never fell down. He must not have been testing his limits. Teams have to push limits; their leaders have to encourage wild ideas. Some of the wild ideas will be outlandish, but they enlarge the boundaries of what's thinkable.

Remember too that success can be bad for you. Some leading companies get complacent and forget the obsessive, chronically dissatisfied management style that made them so successful. Companies with a 70 percent market share soon start feeling invincible and begin to believe that their customers will buy anything they make.

Don't just try to reproduce past successes. Real innovation isn't a rabbit you can pull out of the same hat over and over. Breakthrough opportunity is usually well disguised, so don't flatter yourself that you've mastered the art of recognizing it just because you've seen it once.

No. 7: Join Prototyping to Brainstorming for Fast-Track Innovation Results

The twin flying horses that pull IDEO are continuous prototyping and creative brainstorming. Brainstorming mines the intellectual raw materials; prototyping shapes them into something that can be communicated, demonstrated, tested, and improved. The two techniques work best when conducted in rapid-fire sequence . . . brainstorming stimulates prototyping stimulates brainstorming stimulates prototyping, et cetera.

IDEO has a favorite slogan that explains why these techniques develop synergy when used in tandem: "Enlightened trial and error outperforms the planning of flawless intellects!" Translated into action, this means don't wait to perfect either product or strategy. Don't hang around at the starting gate. First brainstorm—in a group, or by asking individuals to come up with creative suggestions, or both. Then quickly prototype the best ideas. Critique the prototypes. Make fixes fast. Try again. Get feedback from end users to make a prototype significantly better at each iteration. Sometimes the next step is more brainstorming. Sometimes it's more prototyping.

IDEO's motto is "Fast, fearless prototyping." Don't be embarrassed to play with crude prototypes in Round 1. This will bring you more quickly to Round 2. How crude? At IDEO, the initial prototype for the first Apple mouse was a butter dish with some parts glued inside to hold the rolling ball.

Some R&D organizations are specification-driven, others are prototype-driven. Prototyping organizations get to the finish line faster. A case in point is a major office equipment firm that invested several years of effort in designing and detailing the specifications for a truly revolutionary copying machine. During the two-year design phase, nobody noticed an obvious flaw—the specs required a twenty-five-pound replacement cartridge. Prototyping would have revealed at the outset that changing such a heavy, dirty cartridge was a formidable and unappealing chore that threatened the entire product concept.

To accelerate the learning of newly formed multidisciplinary teams, IDEO often employs the strawman approach to prototyping. That is, when we're trying to help a client invent one of the world's greatest kitchen appliances, we don't try to present a flawless first mock-up. In the initial team meeting, marketing, manufacturing, sales, engineering, and design can't wait to explain what's wrong with the mock-up. In doing so, they articulate what they think the perfect kitchen appliance would be like. By expressing their ideas and debating alternatives, the group defines the project's hierarchy of needs.

Prototyping Lessons

1. Each product prototype should demonstrate something specific that can't be shown with a sketch—weight, sound, feel, movement, and a host of other physical characteristics of a product.
2. Encourage rapid learning, not elegance. Don't allow team members to waste time criticizing a prototype for easily fixable flaws, such as a bad paint job.
3. Prototyping increases the payoff from multidisciplinary teams. For example, by teaming manufacturing specialists with designers during the early prototyping stages, the resulting products are likely to be less expensive to make.
4. Prototypes should evoke emotional responses, such as, "It's too damn [pick one] . . . big, small, heavy, expensive to make, tricky to assemble, similar to the competition, or boring."

No. 8: Memorize the Project Leader's Mantra

Leaders of innovation projects—whether focused on new products, unique services, or process change—should memorize this mantra that has guided hundreds of successful innovators:

- *Understand* . . . by immersing the team in the project. Learn the history of a product. Rip up competitors' offerings. Visit the market. Research all the applicable science.
- *Observe* . . . the users. If you are designing a vacuum cleaner, watch people vacuum.
- *Visualize* . . . by making lots of prototypes. Encourage criticism. Rapid turnaround and lots of learning are what counts.
- *Evaluate* . . . evaluate, and reevaluate. Evaluate and visualize over and over again until the final design emerges.
- *Implement* . . . after ensuring that manufacturing has approved the final prototype as feasible and practical.

No. 9: Teams Need Leaders and Mentors, Not Legions of Bosses

Hierarchy stultifies innovation. At IDEO there are no bosses. Rather, we have project leaders who take their direction primarily from the customer or the marketplace. Not all companies can institute flat, project-based structures like IDEO's, in which most employees don't have titles.

But all organizations that want to be innovative can find ways to empha-size collegial, team-based values over hierarchical values. To do this:

- Pick project leaders and team members based on their skills and ability to mentor, and reward them based on the recommendation of their team peers.
- Encourage peer competition and peer review. Adopt annual per-formance peer reviews. At IDEO each individual selects three peo-ple familiar with his or her work to render judgment.
- Foster a nonhierarchical communications system. You shouldn't have to check with a project leader before you pose a tough ques-tion to individual team members.

No. 10: Fresh Ideas Occur Faster in a Fun Workplace

Look around your office. Is there anything frivolous, frolicking, or fun-loving in sight? IDEO employees work surrounded by bikes, toys, and other visual inspiration. In contrast, some companies won't even allow employees to hang posters—and their work spaces resemble airport conference rooms. Not exactly brainstorm country.

To identify their area distinctively, one group of IDEO engineers (nicknamed the "Spunks") bought a surplus airplane wing from a junk shop. After polishing it to a brilliant shine, the wing became the land-mark sculpture for their open, collaborative space. Next, they built phone booths for private conversations during breaks in late-night work sessions. They weren't just decorating, they were creating a clubhouse—a place where people have fun learning from each other.

The physical layout of the work environment should support team communication. Private offices isolate leaders from their teams and team members from peers. An IDEO solution is to put the furniture on wheels so that team members can quickly regroup their work areas to fit the communication needs of their current project.

Will these ten secrets transform a big bureaucracy into a hotbed of creativity? Perhaps. Big companies that form talented teams often pro-duce winning products—witness IBM's laptop computer. Large complex organizations that meet certain criteria are actually more innovative than smaller companies. Research shows that the most innovative companies have:

- A wide variety of specialized occupational types
- A large number of different horizontal units

- Employees who are academic high achievers
- Decentralized decision making
- Superior technical competency—that is, many technically trained people with a variety of skills

As we said earlier, IDEO learned many of these secrets from observing the best practices of big companies in many different industries. Since our founding in 1978, we have essentially conducted thousands of innovation experiments. Each industry—computers, medical, packaged goods, entertainment—has innovation process skills it performs supremely well. Surprisingly, most companies aren't mindful of what is uniquely effective about their processes. Over the years, we have adopted many of our clients' clever techniques. Now, as evangelists for high-speed, discontinuous innovation—creativity that results in products that delight customers—we are happy to share this accumulated wisdom.

FINDING AND FIXING WHAT'S WRONG WITH YOUR INNOVATION PROCESS

Does your organization view innovation as a key competitive weapon?

Remedy: Institute multidisciplinary team experiments. Require structured brainstorming and quick prototyping.

Do ideas have to travel a long road up a hierarchy?

Remedy: Look for opportunities to streamline both structure and lines of communication. Don't tolerate complaints from managers who don't like having people "go over their head" with an idea or a problem.

Do your project teams get results?

Remedy 1: Make it an honor to be picked for a project team, invited to a brainstorming session, or asked to develop a prototype.
Remedy 2: Support your local brainstormers. Put resources into prototyping.

Does it matter a great deal who is the "author" of a new idea?

Remedy: Be willing to look both outside and inside the company for insights. Encourage hiring from outside your industry. Invite people with special knowledge of innovation processes in other industries to conduct teaching sessions.

Are your brainstorming sessions boring? Unproductive? Humorless? Cranky?

Remedy: Ban negativism and "killer" phrases like "The market's not ready for that," or "That would cost too much to make," or "We don't have the capability to implement that." Learn to build on initial ideas. Learn to appreciate other peoples' ideas as much as your own. Don't stifle humor. Budget plenty of time for exploring new ideas.

Is your office space unconducive to creativity?

Remedy: Let people control their work environment. Redesign office space to encourage communication. Buy furniture that can be moved to bring people together. If you have decentralized your R&D people, make sure they all have one special place to get together in an environment where they can learn from each other.

PART VI
Customer Relationship

In MARKETING THESE DAYS there is a bright side of the street and a dark one. Current and projected advertising outlays in the United States are at an all-time high, yet many of the old and sacred precepts of marketing are not working in today's environment. Result: Brand-name products are facing a kind of identity crisis. Although the power of great brands like Coca-Cola and Nike has never been stronger—or more aggressively exploited—brands as a whole ain't what they used to be. This has come about because of changing consumer attitudes, fragmented channels of distribution, power shifts away from manufacturers into the hands of retailers, the staggering costs of new brand generation and expenses of establishing a mature brand's extensions.

Brands achieved the pinnacle of their importance after World War II, a time of vast unsatisfied appetites for goods in the United States and Europe, and a time that saw the dominance of TV as a medium. Thanks to channel power, marketers who barraged passive and accepting consumers with unique selling propositions enjoyed unassailable brand-name success. They could and did ignore other aspects of the value chain and other media and distribution channels.

Life is no longer so sweet and simple. Today, purveyors of brand-name products and services need to find ways to deliver sharply articulated value to increasingly satiated and discerning consumers, and to target a much wider array of market segments and channels of promotion. This transition is eloquently described in chapter thirty-one by Young & Rubicam CEO Peter Georgescu, who appropriately quotes the rock hit "It's the End of the World as We Know It."

But if the marketers' new paradigm is more elusive and paradoxical, it is nonetheless rich with promise despite the turbulence. Brands that weather the new discontinuities, convergences, category shifts, and channel diversities will emerge with greatly strengthened equity value. That is why brand strategizing has moved from the periphery to the center of CEO preoccupations; the issues are too important and too interrelated with the rest of the company—from R&D to customer service—to be the province of mere specialists anymore. There is also increasing recognition of the power of corporate branding, which can support many life cycles of product brands.

The spotlight on brands, whose value nowadays is frequently recognized in financial statements, has given employment to thousands of researchers in the field of brand value measurement and analysis. Increasingly, they are looking at the multidimensionality of a brand's constituents and adopting new terminology to express these concepts. Georgescu speaks about "relationships," noting that "in the past, companies and their agencies had little recognition of the importance of the relationship between a brand and a customer," and, "relationships transcend actual products and have a sense of kinship, affinity, or identification." Relationships are the antidote to the great scourge of today's marketing, which Georgescu identifies as significant manufacturing overcapacity in most product segments.

Companies must forge customer relationships of both depth and duration. Hence, the key role played by corporate values and culture in animating and standing behind a brand. Strong and consistent values lead to long and fruitful customer relationships. Such a formula is familiar to packaged goods marketers, but it now demands—as one might expect in an economy more and more dominated by services—new interfaces between things and images, artifacts and their icons. A product is no longer perceived as an object waiting on the shelves of a store, but as something both tangible and intangible that has a role to play in a consumer's life.

This shift in perspective has brought forth the popular notion of "living the brand." For companies, "living the brand" means having a greater understandings of consumers' wants and needs. But it also means addressing a wide range of actions that have little formal connection with conventional marketing—for example, company recruiting practices, performance measures, environmental postures, and styles of doing business. Apart from its importance in customer relationships, "living the brand" has an internal richness. It inspires and motivates the staff and speaks directly to suppliers and partners. As a result, corporations need to incorporate a wide range of brand values into their decisions, both strategic and tactical.

Coca-Cola, IBM, McDonald's, MTV, and Nike all have highly evolved brand values that are responsive to market needs. These companies communicate and perform consistently in ways that support and nurture those values. Their dedication and passion about customers is echoed in chapter thirty-two, where CoBank's CEO Douglas Sims explains the dynamics of his company's service ethic in the wholesale banking sector. According to Sims, customers basically prefer long-term relationships to transient ones. He writes that they "tend to find it rewarding and advantageous to be loyal to a business. In fact, the level of repeat buying in many sectors indicates that there are powerful incentives to customer loyalty that overcome the cacophony of marketing offers and discounts."

Another important development is the large number of industries in which marketing has become more prevalent. The entertainment industry, for example, no longer thinks in terms of letting the intellectual product speak for itself. The same is true in financial services, another category that is spending big. In many industries there seems to be a Darwinian struggle for brand supremacy, fueled by the fear that weaker brands are vulnerable to the ravages of commodification and discounting.

Top brands create a bond with consumers, in part because they provide certainty and consistency in a complex and kaleidoscopic world. They have what's known in show biz as "marquee value"—beacons that lure dazed and indecisive customers. They succeed in part because of the power of the intangibles they project. Many of the older hallmarks of a brand—a name, symbol, or design that points to significant differentiations—fail to capture the emotional dimensions of "living the brand," where and how it fits into an individual's life, and the context in which an individual makes the purchase.

For instance, many generations of U.S. consumers have bought automobiles with a minimum of information and a maximum of hype and intimidation in dealer showrooms. Only recently have the automobile manufacturers begun to reach out to potential customers—women especially, who are easily turned off by dealers—with full disclosure of product information via 800-info numbers and Internet sites, as well as alternative outlets to dealer showrooms. Automakers who don't express the thought that it's important to them for consumers to make informed and optimal decisions can have no "relationships."

Customer relationships have the advantage of adaptability. Consider the OshKosh B'Gosh story in chapter thirty-three. The company had been making long-wearing striped denim work overalls since 1890, bought principally by midwestern farmers. Still, it was able to adapt its core values of quality and durability for a highly successful assault on the children's clothing market. However, a serious test of these core values came in the eighties, when, according to CEO Douglas Hyde, "It was a point of pride that we continued to maintain quality standards, even when surging demand might have tempted us to cut corners and ship as much product as possible. In the end, this proved to be the key differentiator between OshKosh B'Gosh and our competitors. Most of the other major children's wear lines were not particularly well made. The prevailing industry philosophy seemed to be: 'They're going to grow out of it quickly, anyway.' At OshKosh B'Gosh, however, we never wavered from our 'when in doubt, put in another stitch' philosophy."

By living the values that stemmed from its historical roots, OshKosh became dominant in its category. Similar lateral moves of brands that reflect the powerful core values of the company have been made by Harley-Davidson, Caterpillar Tractor, and Virgin Atlantic Airways.

It's clear that CEOs and other managers are on the threshold of a new era. "Living the brand," with focus on a company's core value and customer service, will present a host of new challenges. But just how successfully these challenges will be met is open to question. For one thing, the rate of new brand creation has been poor. Then too there has been a lot of cost cutting, reengineering, and downsizing of corporate marketing units. Alternatively, there have been strenuous moves to cut costs in the distribution chain, in manufacturing, or by consolidating advertising agencies—all in order to squeeze out cash.

One good sign: More companies are investing some of that cash in marketing research. "I predict a quantum leap in corporate long-term investments that increase our knowledge of the complex dynamics of brands," says Y&R's Georgescu. "There is no other way to proceed in an environment where goods and services can no longer be sold into a climate of preexisting demand, but instead must demonstrate relevance and intimacy with demanding customers."

31

CREATIVE MARKETING IS THE CORE STRATEGY FOR THE NEW MILLENNIUM

Peter Georgescu, Young & Rubicam

Peter Georgescu was eight at the time the Iron Curtain came down on his native Romania. This momentous event separated him and his thirteen-year-old brother from his parents, who were visiting the United States, as his father was an executive with Standard Oil. The communists tried to blackmail the elder Georgescu, threatening the safety of his sons unless he spied for them. But he staunchly refused.

For seven years Peter's father and mother shook heaven and earth to get him and his brother released. Finally, President Dwight D. Eisenhower interceded in their case, and in 1954 the Georgescu boys were welcomed to the United States and hailed as anticommunist heroes on the front page of every newspaper, plus appearances on the Today *and* Ed Sullivan *shows.*

Peter Georgescu then advanced through the American meritocracy: Phillips Exeter, Princeton, an MBA at Stanford, and a trainee job at the privately held Young & Rubicam. Since becoming its president in 1994, he has turned the Y&R advertising unit, one of the largest in the world, into a hot shop boasting many big account wins. He has also become one of Madison Avenue's most prominent critics of the standard 15 percent commission revenue structure, and an advocate of pay-for-performance.

The lanky, soft-spoken Georgescu has strong views on issues rarely taken up by his professional peers. He writes memos for general circulation about the evils of domestic violence, expresses unequivocal intolerance of race or sex discrimination, and gives individuality more breathing

space at Y&R than in the past. He is also the United States' unofficial am-
bassador to Romania.

A DECADE AGO, THE rock group R.E.M. had a hit called "It's the End of the World as We Know It (And I Feel Fine)." It's a wonderful apocalyptic song that applies to the present condition of thousands of companies and their leaders. Many of them feel fine, thanks in part to a huge global surge in corporate profits and equity prices. But the environment they have known and enjoyed is at the point of dissolution, and a new paradigm is taking over.

The world of business has been altered by a confluence of two forces, which gather momentum as the twentieth century draws to a close:

- The decade-old obsession with cutting costs has reached the point of diminishing returns. Raw material supplies, systems, or people costs cannot be squeezed further without serious sacrifice of quality. The incremental benefits gained by pushing suppliers on prices, from outsourcing, from reengineering, or from downsizing are simply no longer there—in part because of the very diligence and energy with which excess fat was hunted down and cut out. Thus most of the productivity gains from shrinking supply costs are already in the bag.
- Since the end of World War II, consumer demand in developed countries has been powered by a strong tide of unsatisfied needs for goods and services. Increments in these nations' standards of living created a consistent and dependable excess of demand. Consequently, most providers of consumer goods and services had a relatively easy time generating revenues and didn't worry overmuch about growth and how to achieve it.

   However, sometime in the eighties, industry by industry, this condition of excess demand fizzled out. Today, there are few global industries not experiencing significant excess production capacity. For example, in autos, 30 percent of potential is lying fallow. And this excess of supply, stemming from an abundance of capital, technology, and workers, will continue to exacerbate the ferocity of competition. Today, consumers are clearly in charge. In this new world, the gap between winners and losers will widen.

If these scenarios are compelling, they beg the question of what new responses from companies are necessary to crank up sales: What must we do differently to keep shareholders happy in this increasingly demanding climate? If we were to consult the old gurus of supply-side cost shrinkage, there would likely be a great deal of throat-clearing, followed by halting pronouncements and generalizations. It turns out that boosting unit sales is much harder than reengineering jobs away. That's because growth seeking is not a simple process-driven endeavor; it is neither mechanical nor programmable. On the contrary, it demands a long-term commitment to creativity in all facets of the business—marketing in particular.

Many of today's CEOs and their lieutenants grew up in the now-vanished world where marketing was a little like throwing fish to seals. In their hunger for goods and services, consumers purchased whatever products were known to them and easily available. However, faced with a surfeit of choices, today's consumers are eminently interested in brand distinctiveness. Yet that is harder than ever to achieve. The speed and pervasiveness of new technologies, for example, attack points of difference in products that would have survived in less hypercompetitive times. And when formulas for success emerge in one company, rivals pounce on those features and replicate them with great energy and speed. Then too the distinction and insulation from competition that used to come from patents is nowhere near as ironclad as in the past.

Only a major push on creativity can overcome these forces and produce powerful and motivating product differentiation. Creativity? Haven't we heard that one before? Isn't creative marketing what generations of ad men on Madison Avenue have been paid to accomplish? And a lot of that older advertising was pretty good for its time and place. But that world was predominantly transaction-driven. Manufacturers slapped a trademark on a package or service and from time to time ran ads that reminded the public of their existence. In a way, those ads reflected a limited idea of the power of marketing.

In the past, companies and their advertising agencies had little recognition of the importance of the relationship between a brand and a customer. Indeed, the real understanding of the dynamic of brands is less than a decade old. A clear distinction must be made between brand names, which are as old as the hills, and the new concept of brands evolving today. The brand, as I see it, is expressive of a relationship between the product or service and the customer—a sense of kinship, affinity, or identification.

A brand is a set of differentiating promises that link products to customers. The brand contract offers two promises: (1) consistency of quality, and (2) an ingredient, or quality, that symbolizes something special, a clearly superior benefit. The specialness may arise from functional superiority or from some emotional gratification that the product or service engenders.

On the customer side of the relationship, the customer (1) is usually prepared to feel some loyalty, and (2) is willing to pay a higher price than that charged by the lowest-priced producer.

So you see, the relationship between a brand and a customer transcends actual products. Where these relationships have strong foundations, they may well embrace several generations of different products. In short, products may come and go, but a brand need never die when properly managed. Everything that marketers do should be directed toward strengthening the brand contract on a daily basis. That is the target for all the weapons at our disposal—public relations, database marketing, advertising, design, new media, old media.

Now let's go into a bit more depth on the workings of brands. There are two main determinants of a brand's strength: (1) that it has a pronounced and powerful differentiation, and (2) that it has a deep relevance to the user. Today's more exigent environment makes brand management a strategic imperative—particularly since consumers are much better educated than in the past, more sophisticated, and more fickle.

Whether they realize it or not, whether they want to be or not, everyone is in the brand business. The only exception, possibly, is the lowest-cost producer on a global basis, who may use price as a weapon to gain market share. All others, however, will have to realize that brands— brand creation, maintenance, enrichment, and the like—are critical to the bottom line. The marketers who create differentiating and creative solutions for their brands will experience golden years in the new millennium. Those who merely push vaguely at product awareness will find themselves falling behind.

Although the two macroeconomic trends I've singled out suggest a pretty severe pressure on corporate profits, they also signify the probability of a renaissance of marketing. Precisely because growth is so intractable and elusive, marketing will assume the strategic center in many corporations. Their renaissance will also have a considerable impact on the economics of advertising agencies. Heretofore, advertisers looked at agencies as a cost. Although in theory everyone conceded that a great ad might be worth many hundreds of millions, it was compensated through exactly the same structure as a bad ad—usually a percentage of media purchases. In effect, agencies got paid for showing up for work, since promotions of variable quality and impact all earned the same rewards.

Not too surprisingly, agency billings were sucked into the great corporate supply squeeze that we described earlier. Clients relentlessly chipped and chopped and sometimes hacked away at agency commissions. Agencies responded by providing poorer service and by underinvesting in the creativity and research that bring forth new value. However, a handful of agencies—Young & Rubicam among them—are trying to break free of this model by advocating a radically different compensation structure based on results. The agency puts itself on the line, accepting the risk and penalties of failure, but sharing the rewards of success. In this bold new framework, advertising becomes an investment in a future outcome rather than a cost.

Pay-for-performance is a healthy response to supply-squeeze economics. Many agencies have been running scared over the last decade as clients have increasingly treated their work as a commodity. This is a shortsighted approach and a self-fulfilling prophecy. The only defense is marketing solutions of irrefutable quality and value, ideas that yield a discernible competitive edge. But such solutions don't grow on trees. They require deep, long-term investments in resources; and they require unrelenting commitment and faith in the creative process—of a greater order than we've seen in the last decade.

Advertisers and agencies have underinvested in real marketing know-how and have been too drawn to marketing voodoo. There is still a lot to be discovered about the brand-customer relationship. This is why Young & Rubicam has invested $20 million plus over the last four years in research on consumer perceptions of brands. This huge base of knowledge has improved our grasp on how brands and consumer relationships are created, maintained, and measured. After all, it's only with accurate measurement that the pay-for-performance approach is going to appeal to marketers.

Other agencies and their clients are starting down this same road. So I predict a quantum leap in corporate long-term investments that increase our knowledge of the complex dynamics of brands. There is no other way to proceed in an environment where goods and services can no longer be sold in a climate of preexisting demand, but instead must demonstrate relevance and intimacy with demanding customers.

There is one last implication of the two macroeconomic trends I've described. The hyperaggression and mean-spirited aspects of the supply-side squeeze (both between rival institutions and within these companies and organizations) is not sustainable. Nor is it good for society as a whole. Pressed to deliver short-term, lean-and-mean performance, and to produce more with fewer resources, organizations and individuals have reverted to primal drives and behavior. But now that the supply squeeze has hit the wall, the attendant mean-spiritedness must evolve into something more constructive—its internal contradictions must be resolved.

Creativity cannot be produced with a pistol to the head. The quality of an organization's products is a reflection of how it treats its employees. If we want to give extraordinary service to customers, workers have to be treated with respect and dignity, professionalism and freedom. They must be encouraged to become the very best they're capable of. In an environment where brands will drive strategy, not the reverse, such corporate values must become more ubiquitous than they are today—otherwise the creativity just won't be there.

So I'd like to sum up with some questions CEOs need to ask themselves to see how they measure up today—and for the millennium to come:

- What have I done in the last (week, month, quarter, year) to put my brands in a stronger position than they were before?
- What have I done to add to my organization's knowledge and insight into the relationship between our brands and our customers?
- Are some of these brand-customer relationships flagging because they lack distinctiveness?
- What have I done to further my intelligence about competitors' brands?
- Is our corporate culture conducive to creative thinking?

32

CREATING COMPETITIVE ADVANTAGE THROUGH CUSTOMER LOYALTY

Douglas Sims, CoBank

The mid-eighties found much of the U.S. Farm Credit System in desperate straits. The tremendous surge in the price of farmland followed by a disastrous decline had left many of the banks that made farmland and crop loans nearly bankrupt. However, one healthy corner of the Farm Credit System was occupied by thirteen banks for cooperatives. As part of the restructuring of the Farm Credit System in 1989, eleven of those thirteen banks, with $10 billion in combined assets, were merged to create CoBank–National Bank for Cooperatives.

Today, CoBank is a federally chartered global wholesale bank with $20 billion in assets, specializing in lending to cooperatives, selected rural enterprises, and financing agricultural exports. Its customers range from small local agricultural cooperatives and rural utilities to cellular telephone companies and such household brands as Ocean Spray. CoBank provides 80 percent of the bank debt used by U.S. agricultural cooperatives each year. As a cooperative itself, CoBank, by law, requires its customers to put up some equity. But the two thousand current customers are by no means captive. Nearly all have relationships with some of CoBank's commercial rivals.

Perhaps it's not surprising, then, that a hallmark of CoBank's business style centers on cultivating customer loyalty. Yet the full extent of CoBank's devotion and attention to the cause of developing customer loyalty is both impressive and instructional. In such a cyclical industry, CoBank has learned to take the long view in building client relationships. CoBank staff are fond of noting that many customers have been with the bank for a full quarter century, through good times and bad.

The level of customer loyalty is truly unprecedented, with less than 1 percent customer turnover on CoBank's base business. Pollster Gallup reports CoBank's customer satisfaction measures among the highest seen by the survey firm. And, in fact, CoBank remained unshaken even through a recent cost-cutting effort that closed offices, cut staff, and consolidated services—pruning CoBank's cost of servicing customers by 30 percent. Indeed, CoBank's experience illustrates how investing in customer loyalty produces rich dividends.

WE ALL WANT OUR customers to be loyal. The large budgets of most marketing organizations are clear evidence that most businesses want much more customer loyalty than they actually have. Ironically, businesses spend large amounts of money wooing and winning other companies' customers simply to replace the customers they've already lost. Instead, what if that money were spent on improving products and customer service in ways that would enhance their ability to hold on to their customers? Most organizations could achieve much higher levels of growth and profitability if they could reduce the turnover of their current customer base.

Yet the unfortunate fact is that all too often customers find few reasons to remain loyal to a particular vendor of a product or service. In too many cases, the competition is primarily based on price. The products offered are largely undifferentiated, and the service the customer receives does not overcome this lack. Businesses want the reward of customer loyalty without providing the products or services that earn it.

Loyal customers are valuable to businesses for several powerful reasons, especially in:

- *Avoiding costs.* There are few more expensive endeavors in business than acquiring a new customer. It takes time and effort, and the cost of acquiring them often exceeds their contribution to the bottom line for a significant period of time. For example, in the consumer credit business, it can take as long as two years to defray the expense of acquiring a new credit card customer.
- *Creating repeatable processes.* Repeating customers tend to enter into a pattern of relationship that permits long-term planning. This allows businesses to design and build cost-effective processes that can meet their needs again and again.
- *Focusing efforts.* A relatively steady pool of customers helps businesses reduce the number of diverse requirements they're forced

to handle. Focusing reduces market confusion and makes it easier for companies to make intelligent decisions about how best to anticipate and meet customers' needs.

Customers tend to find it rewarding and advantageous to be loyal to a business. In fact, the level of repeat buying in many sectors indicates that there are powerful incentives to customer loyalty that overcome the cacophony of marketing offers and discounts.

In the agricultural lending arena, there are any number of banks poised to swoop in when times are good, round up some business, and collect the fees. But agriculture is nothing if not cyclical, and these fairweather friends are usually nowhere to be found when times are hard. They were just looking for business transactions, not business relationships—a fact that is not lost on borrowers.

In 1994, CoBank was named administrative agent for a $650 million syndication for Farmland Industries, Inc. While CoBank was certainly not the largest of the eight banks in the syndication, Farmland executives commented at the closing dinner that they'd selected CoBank for the lead role because of its loyal service through many good years and bad.

QUALITIES THAT ENGENDER CUSTOMER LOYALTY

What fosters that sense of loyalty in customers? There are usually four elements involved:

- *Intrinsic value.* The first and most obvious reason for loyalty is value. The customer derives greater tangible value from the selected product or service than the competition can offer for the same price. Often, the company has a technical advantage or specific expertise.

  One example of intrinsic value is the business CoBank conducts with numerous rural telephone companies. Many of these small telephone companies have recently been evaluating the purchase of rural exchanges that are being sold off by communications giants US West and GTE. Take a small western phone company. Although it may have little experience with acquisitions, its management can clearly see that adding an additional five thousand phone lines in Montana would have a sizable impact on its business.

  What CoBank brings to the table is a knowledge of that company's business, its management, and its financial capabilities. This, added to its experience with such purchases across the country, gives it a unique perspective for assessing valuations for these small exchanges. In short, CoBank offers a knowledge base and expertise that newcomers to the market can't match, and our customers recognize that.

CoBank offers intrinsic value to its agricultural customers by providing large open lines of credit, a necessity when dealing in the volatile agricultural commodity markets. For instance, in early 1996, volatility in the grain markets led to CoBank's having a $1.5 billion run-up in loan volume in only five days. That's a scenario that even much larger commercial banks would have a hard time managing, but we recognize it as part of our responsibility to our customers.

- *Transaction costs.* When all offerings are perceived to be similar and there is little or no variation in price, customers often find it makes little sense to waste time searching for alternatives. Many routine commodity purchases are made on this basis.

Since money is a basic commodity, CoBank faces this transactional inertia. As a result, we have sought to differentiate ourselves, not with promotions or advertising, but with superior knowledge of the industry. CoBank also works to provide a level of service not readily matched by competitors, thereby reducing any impetus for customers to shop around or go through the effort of building a new banking relationship.

- *Sunk costs.* Frequently customers find that, while they might be willing to switch brands or vendors, they're constrained by sunk costs or deferred benefits available only through the current provider. Many frequent-flyer programs are based on this logic. Once a company is selected and points accumulated, the cost of switching in terms of lost inducements leads frequent flyers to remain with the same airline.

A similar phenomenon is evident in the software industry. As companies compete to offer Internet access software, many firms are giving the software away for free. They do this in the belief that if the customer can be induced to use a given application, the time spent in learning that software will be a sunk cost that the customer will be reluctant to replicate unless the value of the alternative is dramatically superior. In CoBank's case, the capital investment that customers make in the bank can be viewed as a sunk cost.

- *Social or emotional commitment.* Vendors tend to appeal to their customers' emotional side to encourage loyalty. In consumer marketing one of the key objectives is to use emotion and imagery to connect the product with other values that the consumer finds appealing. In business-to-business marketing, this role is played out by creating solid relationships. The investments that businesses make in entertaining are largely efforts to build closer personal and social relationships with valued customers.

At CoBank, we understand the value of relationships and we work to build them at several levels within each client company. Equally important, however, are the relationships CoBank helps foster between customers. We frequently sponsor conferences for client CFOs and CEOs. Remembering that cooperatives are social and political as well as business organizations, one CoBank executive notes, "Very often the interaction among these executives is as important as the interaction between the bank and the individual customer."

There are many products and companies that have one or more of these attributes, and yet they still don't experience particularly high levels of customer loyalty. In fact, most organizations struggle with constant customer turnover, spending far too much money simply replenishing a customer base that they've allowed to slip away. In general, these organizations do many of the right things to encourage repeat business. All airlines have frequent-flyer programs, and almost all business-to-business marketers emphasize relationships. So why do they still fail to hold on to their customers?

Businesses that achieve high levels of customer loyalty in the face of many competing alternatives tend to have corporate cultures that really do put the customer first. Companies whose customers are particularly loyal tend to behave loyally to their customers. Such organizations clearly understand why customers are loyal to them and tend to stress whatever it takes to generate that loyalty. These organizations instinctively understand how to serve their customers better, meeting their customers' needs earlier and more often than their less culturally aware competitors.

THE CRITICAL DETAILS

How do these organizations achieve high customer loyalty? It's not really that mysterious. It's about diligent attention to the critical details: Organizations with high customer loyalty tend to do a few basic things well. There are a number of practical steps that organizations can take to increase the level of customer satisfaction and loyalty:

- *Value customer relations.* To create customer loyalty, assign your best people to customer relationships. Top management must be committed to investing a significant amount of time calling on and interacting with individual customers or groups. At CoBank, the top four officers of the company personally call on over two hundred key customers in a given year. Customer relations account for nearly half of the work hours of those four executives.

- *Invest in aggressive customer sensing.* Organizations with high customer loyalty make significant investments in understanding their customers' evolving needs through satisfaction surveys, focus groups, call centers, and other mechanisms. This enables them to factor the customer's voice into their decision making.

  CoBank holds ten stockholder meetings a year, seeking feedback at them all. In addition to rolling cross-sectional surveys of customer satisfaction, we conduct annual satisfaction surveys of our largest customers.

  Before we embarked on our cost-cutting journey, we first surveyed all our customers about what they expected from their relationship with CoBank. Discovering that what customers valued most was quick service, not physical proximity to their banker, we were then able to close offices and consolidate a number of functions. These moves provided a 30 percent savings in costs with no drop in customer satisfaction.

- *Encourage broad-based relationships with customers.* A business's knowledge of and contact with a customer should never come from a single account manager's relationship with a single client employee. Such narrow contact leaves a business vulnerable to misinformation and inaccurate evaluations. Also, this kind of client relationship is fragile, and provides an opening for the competition when that contact changes.

  Ideally, customers should have a number of relationships with a business. This way they'll feel more connected to the company as a whole than to individual employees. In addition to the account manager contact, CoBank seeks to develop relationships between the CEOs, the CFOs, the corporate communications staffs, and more. In part this is because a single account manager cannot deliver all the services a customer requires. Not only do these multiple relationships provide better and more complete information, they more securely connect the client to CoBank.

- *Breed an attitude of ownership.* Let customers realize that their well-being is interdependent with yours. At CoBank, we work to emphasize to our customers that their success is our success, and that CoBank's success is a tribute to our customers.

- *Respond to customer desires.* Put the approach that the customer is always right to work for you. If a customer wants a certain product, that's the product to create. If a customer needs a product delivered in a certain manner, develop that capability.

A few years ago, a charter change allowed us to expand our business of lending to rural utilities. Although we faced entrenched players, CoBank successfully won new business by being flexible and responsive to customer needs.

When some of our customers ventured into new areas, such as cellular telecommunications and cable businesses, CoBank readily worked with them in whatever way they required. For example, while some competitors balk at sharing a credit with another lender, or altering the terms of their standard lending format, CoBank will willingly share a credit, negotiate loan terms, and tailor its services to each customer's needs. It's not surprising that this is one of the fastest growing areas of the bank's business.

- *Go the extra mile for customers.* Sometimes going the extra mile means providing a product because customers have asked for it, not because it's the most desirable market. CoBank provides nearly $3 billion a year in financing for agricultural exports. Most of this financing is provided under export loan-guarantee programs with CoBank, accounting for half of all federal loan guarantees issued by the Department of Agriculture.

  These loans have narrow spreads and require intensive documentation. And while we are an efficient competitor in this international market, it is not a particularly profitable business. However, agricultural companies, which are highly sensitive to global markets, want their bank to be in those global markets day in and day out—so CoBank is there.

- *Seek to broaden the relationship.* Once a significant relationship has been established with a customer, seek to broaden it with products and services aimed at leveraging those strong links. Invariably this will lead to greater product and service alliances with other organizations that have different capabilities.

  CoBank views such alliances as building capacity. They make it possible for us to bring other lenders to the table, to bring appropriate experts on board to answer inquiries about equity financing, or to respond to any other customer inquiry with the needed resources. CoBank wants to be the gateway to the services its customers require. We want to help resolve problems for customers even when we aren't the entity supplying the required expertise.

- *Don't just understand what customers want, understand what they're worth.* Valuing your customers is not about losing money.

The best account managers have a clear-eyed understanding of how valuable a given customer is to them and what level of service can be justified. That also involves assessing not only today's relationship, but future potential when making decisions about investing in a specific customer.

CUSTOMER LOYALTY PAYS OFF

Creating loyalty among customers is key to long-term economic success. It allows organizations to focus on developing and winning new customers that add value to the enterprise, rather than merely replacing lost customers and justifying service failures. A stable customer base allows companies to grow according to their own strategic development plans instead of simply reacting to the changing requirements of an ever-changing customer base.

Investing in customer loyalty pays off. For example, CoBank has financed Ocean Spray since the bank began backing cooperatives in the 1930s. Today, Ocean Spray has annual sales of $1.5 billion. In 1997, CoBank received the Supplier of the Year Award from Ocean Spray, as well as the Lifetime Achievement Award for its years of service, which Ocean Spray has presented only one other time.

CoBank's relationship with Mexico has a more recent history but is no less valued by the borrower. CoBank stood firm during the Mexican peso-devaluation crisis of the mid-eighties, when many other U.S. banks withdrew support. As a result, CoBank was recently sought out by a major Mexican bank for an alliance arrangement in which Mexican farmers and agribusiness owners who want to purchase U.S. agricultural products outside of the government guaranteed-loan program will be referred to us. This alliance offers exactly the kind of opportunity that customer loyalty creates.

33

NEW PRODUCTS THAT REMAIN TRUE TO CORE VALUES

Douglas Hyde,
OshKosh B'Gosh, Inc.

OshKosh B'Gosh is the leading seller of children's branded clothing in the United States and has clocked a tenfold sales increase in the last decade and a half. Which is all quite amazing when you consider that for the first eighty-five years of its existence, the company was in a totally different business and mind-set. As recently as the late seventies, OshKosh B'Gosh, which takes its name from its Wisconsin hometown of Oshkosh, and a vaudeville routine that added the "B'Gosh," was a prominent manufacturer of denim work clothes sold mainly in the Upper Midwest. The brand projected durability and quality craftsmanship, reflecting the company's values, which were steeped in the midwestern work ethic. This chapter tells the story of how these values were transported and adapted to an entirely different, and dangerous, market—high-end children's fashions.

Douglas Hyde was the pilot of this diversification, which hewed closely to the company's core values of durability, quality, heritage, and family values. Doug Hyde is the third-generation family member to run the company. He learned the business from the bottom up, starting as a summer order filler while a high school student in the late sixties. At first the elder generation of Hyde family members didn't share his enthusiasm for this corporate redirection, but in the end he prevailed.

OSHKOSH B'GOSH DIDN'T STRIKE many observers as a particularly adept change agent during most of the seventies. Our family-run and -controlled company was still relying on the same line of basic work wear for men, mainly the striped denim overalls that had accounted for the bulk of our sales since the 1890s. A small line of children's wear had not yet captured our management's consciousness.

However, in the mid-sixties, when a Wisconsin-based regional mail-order catalog included a few of OshKosh B'Gosh's kids' items, they sold out. This is when we began putting out our own small catalog of children's clothes to local independent retailers. Still, our corporate image, inside and outside the company, remained that of a maker of men's work clothes.

Earnings boomed with a seventies fad among teens and college students of wearing overalls and painter pants, but it also kept our company focused on adult wear. However, sales to traditional adult work-wear outlets were beginning to slump, and when the fad died out, OshKosh B'Gosh's traditional line of work clothes seemed impossible to turn around.

This is when I led the charge into the largely untested children's-wear market, always keeping a close watch on the company's core values of quality and durability. What had started as a gamble quickly showed that it had all the makings of a sure thing. Buyers for East Coast department stores, including Macy's and Bloomingdale's, began demanding more children's overalls. We contracted for and built production factories as quickly as we could, but the demand was so high through much of the eighties that we couldn't always completely fill orders for many major accounts.

During the eighties, we introduced knit tops that complemented our line of children's overalls. They were an instant success, and by the mid-nineties, knit tops were generating even more sales than overalls. Pursuing a "head-to-toe" strategy, OshKosh B'Gosh expanded the line to include children's hats, shoes, and other accessories, almost all of which proved to be big sellers. By 1983 children's wear accounted for half of our sales, and by 1997 it was up to 95 percent of sales.

It was a point of pride that we continued to maintain quality standards even when surging demand might have tempted us to cut corners and ship as much product as possible. In the end, this proved to be the key differentiator between OshKosh B'Gosh and our competitors. Most of the other major children's-wear lines were not particularly well made. The prevailing industry philosophy seemed to be: "They're going to grow out of it quickly, anyway." At OshKosh B'Gosh, however, we never wavered from our "when in doubt, put in another stitch" philosophy.

A 1996 EquiTrends consumer survey ranked both children's-wear brands and brands at large in terms of perceptions of overall quality. OshKosh B'Gosh ranked in the top ten in world-class quality.

BRANDS PERCEIVED BY CONSUMERS AS BEING WORLD-CLASS IN OVERALL QUALITY

- Craftsman tools
- Kodak photographic film
- Hallmark greeting cards
- Mercedes-Benz automobiles
- Levi's jeans
- Fisher-Price toys
- Hershey's milk-chocolate bars
- Lexus automobiles
- OshKosh B'Gosh children's wear
- Lego toys

The dramatic reorganization of OshKosh B'Gosh's customer focus succeeded in large part because our children's wear had the appeal of a quality product and a heritage of craftsmanship. Our target customer shifted from an adult working man or farmer looking for work clothes to a middle- to upper-middle-class mother of small children looking for quality. Trend-setting consumers favored our products for their reverse snob appeal—the products had their roots in the sturdy work wear favored by generations of midwestern farmers. Thus our company's core values enabled us to leap over both the gender and generation gap.

When the company and the product image are one and the same, it is paramount that the CEO be the brand manager. At OshKosh B'Gosh, I was personally involved in all new product introductions—and, indeed, in all aspects of product marketing and imaging—to make certain that our products continued to fit our corporate image.

In a company like ours, the CEO must be closely involved in advertising decisions from the development process on. I don't simply sign off on the finished product, which is the case at many companies. I am also actively involved in producing the annual report, and even in what many might consider the "boilerplate" descriptions of OshKosh B'Gosh in press releases—because I know it's crucial to make certain that the company's core values are being projected and protected.

While CEOs are the brand's representatives to the outside world, they should be the brand manager inside the company as well. They make certain that the corporate culture and brand image are maintained at all levels. At OshKosh B'Gosh, new hires are indoctrinated in our company philosophy and vision the minute they walk in the door. To reinforce this training, I regularly debrief new hires to discover their preexisting impressions of the company and to ensure that they "get with the program."

CEOs are increasingly acting as global brand managers in successful knowledge-based companies, where product sales and manufacturing are in constant flux around the world. Whether the company is selling children's wear or semiconductors, it's up to the CEO to maintain and expand a consistent and coherent image for his or her company. This is as true for OshKosh B'Gosh as it is for Nike or The Gap, which are marketers more than anything else, having shifted production to lower-cost offshore markets.

CEO brand managers also run some of the world's most successful technology companies. Microsoft founder Bill Gates personifies his software company's relentless push for market dominance and technological advance. No major product ships without Gates's approval that it meets Microsoft's standards and fits the company's brand image. And at Intel, CEO Andrew Grove has made the "Intel Inside" label synonymous with the highest-quality, cutting-edge technology in the semiconductor industry. That brand management, in turn, has helped make Intel the most profitable company in the world.

It's not always a given that a company will stumble when the CEO fails to act as global brand manager, but it certainly raises the odds against success. Apple Computer, for example, has suffered numerous setbacks in recent years for a variety of reasons. But the fact that the once-thriving company has not had a CEO consistently driving the company brand in world markets has clearly played a major role in Apple's inability to reverse its sliding market share for much of the nineties.

A predominant corporate brand doesn't always confer an unqualified advantage. OshKosh B'Gosh's identification with children's wear has had its downside too. For instance, a line for older children didn't sell well because it turned out that this age group didn't want to be associated with clothing for "babies."

Attempts to expand into fashion-oriented adult wear have met with mixed results as well. Adding a line of maternity clothes failed to catch on with consumers, mainly because of poor execution. A line of men's sportswear had limited success in the United States, but it did much better in Japan and portions of Latin America.

Another factor is that our phenomenal success in the eighties may have kept us from seeing developing industry trends that would have a

CRITICAL SUCCESS FACTORS IN BUILDING AN
ENDURING BRAND IDENTITY

- *Identify core values of the corporation.* What are the basic principles that the company applies to its operations and planning that differentiate it from competitors? What is the "soul" of the company as expressed in a few guiding principles that help it achieve peak performance?
- *Instill core values at all levels of operations.* As with most living things, values grow from the bottom up, not the top down. Values may be articulated at the top, but all layers of the company need to buy into them.
- *Have the CEO take ownership of the core values and brand* as they are being instilled throughout the organization. The value system and brand image have to be constantly reinforced and refreshed from the top to ensure that they don't wither farther down the vine.
- *Make sure new products are true to company values and the brand.* The temptation to capitalize on a brand image can lead to new products that are only tangentially related to the brand and end up diluting its market impact.
- *Support risk taking to extend the brand.* Don't confuse aggressive corporate brand management and consistency with conservatism. If a new product enhances the brand, it should be pursued, even if it initially seems a radical departure from the existing product line.

negative impact in the nineties. For instance, commanding premium prices for our quality product may have kept us from responding quickly enough to a clothing industry trend toward lowering production costs by shifting manufacturing overseas. When competitors began producing significantly higher quality goods offshore at lower prices than we could match, it depressed earnings for a few years. Nevertheless, by then the OshKosh B'Gosh brand had become so firmly associated with quality that it remained preeminent.

Today, OshKosh B'Gosh has bounced back financially. We've put our focus where it adds the most value—by recognizing that we're a marketer, not a manufacturer, of children's wear. But we're also keeping a close watch on our core values of quality, sturdiness, and durability. Additional core values contributing to the OshKosh B'Gosh's success are:

- *Value.* OshKosh B'Gosh products have always been known as long-wearing clothing. Their value for the money and long-term durability were necessities in the adult work-wear market. However, in children's wear as well, mothers appreciated this value, since small children are notoriously hard on their clothes. It also gave us another way of differentiating ourselves from the competition.
- *Style.* OshKosh B'Gosh recognized that style, which wasn't much of a factor in our adult-wear line, was a key driver of success in branded children's wear. We embraced a fashion-forward style that leapfrogged our competition and set a new standard in children's wear and accessories.
- *Customer service.* We have always treated customer service as an extension of our commitment to value and quality. At OshKosh B'Gosh we have always believed that "the customer is always right," and we implement this philosophy in all customer service issues, including any and all complaints from customers.
- *Satisfaction.* My family and I have always had a strong focus on instilling pride in our employees based on the quality of our products, on caring for our employees, and on demonstrating our commitment to the customers. My third-generation management epitomizes our long-term commitment to stand behind OshKosh B'Gosh and all our products.

ACKNOWLEDGMENTS

This work would not have been possible without the perseverance and dedication of the following team:

- John Thackray, for his editorial excellence, intuitive sense of what makes for a strong story, and keen insights into the evolving role of tomorrow's global CEO
- Deborah Cohen, for her strategic guidance, intuitive market sense, project management abilities, and editorial insights
- Ana Cardenas, for her organizational and administrative follow-through
- Barbara Shor, for her copyediting genius
- Marion Lunt, for her extensive design talent
- Our many other contributors, including Roger Lipsey, Doug Kramer, Michelle Siren, Iris Rosenberg, Dallas Murphy, Laton McCartney, and Laura Walbert
- Our many subject matter experts at Price Waterhouse, including Peter Davis, Len Lindegren, Andy Embury, Gerry Miles, Michael Chayes, Paula Chronister, Celeste Coruzzi, Tom Murnane, and Sandra Kresch
- Our editor, Fred Hills, and publisher, Simon & Schuster
- And lastly, the leadership of Price Waterhouse for supporting us in undertaking such an ambitious endeavor.

INDEX